SUICIDAL BEHAVIOUR, BEREAVEMENT AND DEATH EDUCATION IN CHINESE ADOLESCENTS

Suicidal Behaviour, Bereavement and Death Education in Chinese Adolescents

Hong Kong Studies

Edited by

John W. L. Tse
City University of Hong Kong

Christopher Bagley
University of Southampton and Royal Free and University College School of Medicine, London

Routledge
Taylor & Francis Group
LONDON AND NEW YORK

First published 2002 by Ashgate Publishing

Reissued 2018 by Routledge
2 Park Square, Milton Park, Abingdon, Oxon OX14 4RN
711 Third Avenue, New York, NY 10017, USA

Routledge is an imprint of the Taylor & Francis Group, an informa business

Publisher's Note
The publisher has gone to great lengths to ensure the quality of this reprint but points out that some imperfections in the original copies may be apparent.

A Library of Congress record exists under LC control number: 2001053713

ISBN 13: 978-1-138-73094-6 (hbk)
ISBN 13: 978-1-315-18923-9 (ebk)

Contents

List of Figures

List of Tables

Foreword

This interesting book makes a valuable contribution in several ways. It combines an academic perspective with a series of practical applications for improving the quality of life of children and adolescents, not only in Chinese cultures but also in communities everywhere. The book also offers valuable insights into the field of cross-cultural psychology, as well as important lessons for educators in all parts of the world who are concerned with suicide prevention.

Sound statistical studies are balanced by valuable qualitative work, and the chapter by Catherine Tsang offers a particularly successful application of the use of grounded theory.

I commend this book to educators, clinical specialists and social workers not only in Chinese cultures, but also to all of those who work with multicultural populations in Europe and North America.

Gajendra K. Verma
Sarah Fielden Professor of Education
University of Manchester

The Contributors

Dr John W.L. Tse is an Associate Professor in the Department of Applied Social Studies at the City University of Hong Kong. He has degrees in education from Canada, and a doctorate from the University of Nottingham, England.

Dr Christopher Bagley is Professor of Social Work Studies at the University of Southampton. He previously held a chair of child welfare at the University of Calgary, and was Reader and then Visiting Professor in the Department of Applied Social Studies, City University of Hong Kong. He is also a Research Fellow in the Academic Department of Psychiatry, Royal Free Hospital, London.

Banny Bing-Yee Cheng, MSW, is Centre Director of The Comfort Care Concern Group, Hong Kong.

Joyce Lai-Chong Ma, PhD, is Professor and Chair of the Department of Social Work at the University of Hong Kong.

Mak Hoi-Wah, MSW, is Assistant Professor in the Department of Applied Social Studies, City University of Hong Kong.

Catherine Tsang Yuk-Chun is Senior Social Worker at the Bradbury Hospice in Sha Tin, Hong Kong. Her chapter in the present volume is based on her MSc dissertation at the University of Southampton.

Anthony Muk-Leung Yau, MPhil, is an instructor in the Department of Applied Social Studies, City University of Hong Kong.

1 Suicidal Behaviour in Chinese Youth: Search for Causes and Risk Factors

JOHN W.L. TSE AND CHRISTOPHER BAGLEY

Summary

Dimensions of distress are generally similar in studies of Chinese adolescents, in comparison with Western studies, and it is appropriate to use translated measures of mental health. However, additional measures may be necessary to capture aspects of a Chinese cultural identity. Impaired self-esteem, depression, suicidal ideas and behaviour were in a number of studies, interlinked in populations of Chinese adolescents. The once stable suicide rate in Chinese youth in Hong Kong showed a marked rise in the early 1990s, and although this rate has now stabilised, suicide remains a major cause of death in Hong Kong youth. Suicide in females relative to rates found in males, are particularly high. This could be linked to a preferred method of self-harm – jumping from high buildings – which is almost inevitably fatal. Identified risk factors are a sense of anomie or normlessness in a material and rapidly changing culture; a decline in family cohesion and strengths; sexual and relationship problems, including sexual abuse, and negative stereotypes surrounding an emerging gay identity; continued educational pressures and a high rate of school drop-out; and continuing levels of poverty and income inequality. At the same time, there have been increasing rates of substance abuse, and increasing rates of juvenile crime, increases which may share causes with pressures which lead some adolescents to consider or attempt suicide. Case studies of adolescent suicide are presented to illustrate these pressures. Schools could play a major role in suicide prevention, but large classes, the traditional role of the teacher, and a dearth of school counsellors have largely prevented this.

Introduction: Issues in Cross-Cultural Psychology

The research which we discuss, and the empirical work which we have undertaken and present in subsequent chapters frequently uses Western psychological instruments and concepts in the analysis of the psychological problems of youth in Hong Kong and other parts of China. In the past three decades the discipline of cross-cultural psychology has emerged with some salience, arguing that American models of measurement and psychological process may often be inappropriate in considering psychological issues in other cultures (Bond and Smith, 1993).

The psychologist Michael Bond who has observed Chinese culture for many years has carefully delineated the unique features of Chinese culture, as well as the many ways in which psychological processes are similar for individuals in both eastern and Western cultures (Bond, 1986 and 1991). At the same time Bond and his colleagues (Yang and Bond, 1990; Yik and Bond, 1993) have identified unique psychological and normative features of Chinese cultures.

While many Chinese people hold values, which are quite similar to those of Western peoples, there are some additional, apparently unique Chinese values. In a study of values held by nationals in 21 countries Bond and Pang (1990) identified a value dimension called 'social integration *versus* cultural inwardness' marked at one extreme by tolerance of others, patience, search for harmony, and trust in others; and at the other extreme, by a sense of cultural superiority, a desire for chastity in women and a control of their activity, with the frequent observation of rites and social rituals. Respondents in The Netherlands and Western Germany emerged as the most tolerant or socially integrated, with those in Pakistan, India and Bangladesh falling at the other extreme – as culturally and ritually inward. Britain fell towards the pole of tolerance, while Chinese respondents fell towards the pole of ritual integration and traditional values, although the differences between British and Chinese respondents were not extreme – both British and Chinese groups converged towards the middle of this value axis.

The second relevant value dimension differentiating cultures posed 'reputation and status seeking *versus* a sense of righteousness and morality'. British respondents had the *highest* score on this value dimension, being excessively concerned with being seen as a respectable and successful person. But Chinese respondents had a directly opposed set of values, having high scores on the value dimension representing concern with social and moral purity, together with a subjective sense of righteousness in relation to firmly adolescent suicidal behaviour. In fact, the rapid increase of risk factors may well indicate that there will be more adolescent suicide in the future (Tse, 2000):

- *Increasing divorce rate*: The stability and harmony within the family is crucial for the development of children, and divorce and separation means conflict and disintegration of the family, which would have significant negative impact on the children. In Hong Kong, the divorce rate has increased from 3,734 divorce case applications in 1983 to 12,732 in 1999. Within this period of 16 years, divorce rate has jumped 241 per cent.

- *Extreme poverty*: In Hong Kong, there is no official definition of poverty line, hence those individuals and families receiving Comprehensive Social Security Allowance (CSSA) may serve as important indicator of poverty. The CSSA cases increased from 56,090 in 1984 to 228,016 cases in February 2001. The increase in the last 17 years was 307 per cent.

- *Prevalence of depression*: In Hong Kong for example, researchers have carried out a community study on depression and randomly selected 3,786 students from primary 5 to form 2 (age ranges from 11 to 13). The results indicated that 19 per cent of the students had some depressive symptoms, with females tending to report more symptoms than males (Cheung and Lam, 1992). In a retrospective study of adolescents, researchers found that 20 per cent of the 10 to 14 years old group who died of completed suicide had serious depression, while in the 15 to 19 years old group, the prevalence of depression amongst suicides was estimated to be 37 per cent (Ho, Hung, Lee, Chung and Chung, 1995). Taking these research findings together, it is not difficult to see that the prevalence of depression has serious implications for the adolescent population in Hong Kong.

- *Increasing drug abuse*: According to the Central Registry of Drug Abuse, in 1988, 1,211 adolescents were known to have used illegal drugs. In 2000, the number increased to over 4,000 adolescents, which represents an escalation of 220 per cent (and, of course, these figures are likely to represent the tip of an iceberg). These figures were reported by frontline social workers in non-government organisations who met the abusers in the course of their work. Therefore, one has to be cautious in interpreting these figures, as they are likely to be seriously under-reported.

- *Juvenile delinquency on the rise*: In 1985, 3,321 juvenile delinquents between the age of 7 to 20 years old were prosecuted. The number inflated to 12,694 in 2000, which represents an increase of 282 per cent in the last 15 years or so.

- *Many school dropouts*: In Hong Kong, compulsory education was implemented in 1978 and the Director of Education has the authority to force students younger than 15 years old who have not yet completed form 3 to receive formal education. In 1990/91, 719 primary pupils and 3,025 form 3 or lower students dropped out of school or were absent for more than 14 days without a valid reason. The figures were 329 primary pupils and 1,468 for form 3 or lower students in 1995/96. At present, at least 3,000 children and adolescents drop out of school every year. Even though not going to school is a crime, the rate of school dropouts although falling, continues to be a matter of serious concern for social workers.

- *Severe child abuse*: In Hong Kong, according to the figures provided by Against Child Abuse, in 1990, 11 children were known to have been sexually abused and in 1998, 242 known case of sexual abuse were reported. While this large increase is likely due to a change in public attitudes, it does indicate the size of the problem which current statistics are likely to underestimate.

In 1999, the suicide prevention counselling centre, Hong Kong Samaritan Befrienders received 752 calls from children and adolescents (12.74 per cent of all calls received): 20.5 per cent of the calls from young people were principally concerned with anxiety and despair over failure to perform to the academic standards expected by teachers and parents; 14.9 per cent of all calls were focused on family disputes; and 24 per cent were concerned mainly with problems surrounding love affairs, and sexuality (including cases of children who had been sexually abused in the home). Such compelling evidence indicates that many children and adolescents are under chronic pressure and are severely distressed. Many vulnerable youngsters may contemplate seriously hurting or killing themselves.

As Ruzicka (1998) points out, the loss of youthful lives is not only tragic, but also economically wasteful. It is crucial to explore ways of preventing or relieving children and adolescents of their stress and depression, which may escalate and manifest into different forms of suicidal behaviour.

Epidemiological and Clinical Studies of Stress, Depression and Suicidal Behaviour

Epidemiological research with large samples of Hong Kong children and adolescents suggests that between five and ten per cent (varying according to the measuring instruments employed) are at risk from serious mental health problems and would benefit from counselling and support (Salini and Hoosain, 1985; Luk et al., 1988; Shek, 1988 and 1990; Wong, 1990; Cheung, 1996; Jing and Zuo, 2000; Su et al., 2000). Based on these various studies and using the most conservative estimate, there were in 2000 at least 50,000 children and adolescents in Hong Kong with serious psychological problems involving depression or suicidality at any point in time. Less than a tenth of this number obtained any kind of counselling or social work support because of the chronic under funding of youth social services in Hong Kong (Tse et al., 1994).

For example, a random survey by Ma (1992) of 1,107 high-school students in the district of Sha Tin, Hong Kong found that 245 (22 per cent) considered that one or more of their peers had considered suicide. Reasons given for their peers' 'suicidal tendencies' were: stress from school-work and poor examination results, 55 per cent; stress resulting from a broken relationship with a boy- or girl-friend, 48 per cent; poor relationships or conflict with peers and/or siblings, 44 per cent; persecution by or in debt to triad societies, 11 per cent. Those students experiencing more than one source of stress were those whom peers said were at greatest risk of suicidal behaviour. A total of 28 per cent of the 1,107 students in this survey said that they themselves had seriously contemplated suicide, currently or in the past: the reasons given for their own suicidal thoughts and feelings were broadly similar to those attributed to their suicidal peers. The importance of this study is that it indicates that many students communicate their suicidal feelings, as well as the underlying reasons, to their peers. It is atypical, however, for teachers to learn of these stressors.

The Confucian tradition, which still has strong influence on the values of education and family life in Chinese cultures, lays considerable stress on industrious scholarship and obedience to the wishes of elders, teachers and parents. Children are expected not only to study hard, but to succeed as well. Lack of academic success is usually attributed not to lack of intellectual capacity, but to lack of application and the failure to attend to the wishes of parents and teachers. Children who are failing in school are often labelled as 'lazy' or 'inattentive' – not concentrating hard enough for learning to occur. The parents of a child who is not doing well at school will often send the child to a private tutor, who will prescribe yet more homework. All of the child's spare time may be filled by scholastic tasks. In Hong Kong, in a survey of 1,967 primary 3 to primary 6 pupils indicated that 19.7 per cent had private tutor, 26.1 per cent participated in tutorial class, whilst the majority (77.9 per cent) spent half an hour to 3 hours per evening doing homework (Cheung and Chan, 1990). In another survey of some 400 primary 2 pupils (ages 6 to 7) it was found that on average they spent 4 hours and 19 minutes per evening doing homework and revision (Committee in Home-School Co-operation, 1994). When the amount of homework is compared with four other major cities in the world, Hong Kong primary 5 pupils ranked above all others in the amount of time spent (Chen and Stevenson, 1989). Taipei ranked second; the third city was Beijing, followed by Chicago. The city with least homework load was Sinto, Japan (only 52 minutes). These surveys clearly demonstrate that Hong Kong school children have to face extraordinary pressures from homework.

When excessive homework, chronic pressure from examination combined with the unrealistically high expectations from parents and teachers, the consequence may be very disturbing. A 10-year-old boy wrote an essay entitled 'The hardship and happiness of studying' not long before he leapt to his death from his 19th floor bedroom (SCMP, 1991/9/14).

> *The advantages of studying are to enhance knowledge, intelligence and living interest. Studying the health education lesson can increase general knowledge; studying science lesson can increase knowledge of nature. In music lesson (I) can sing; while in physical education lesson (I) can jog. How cheerful it is! Nevertheless, there is hardship in studying as well. Every day, there are many homeworks. They are not only in large quantity, but also difficult to do. Each recess is only engaging for 10 minutes.*
>
> *If getting one day more holiday (I) will be given 10 odd homeworks. Especially in long vacation, the homeworks will be more. At least, there are more than 20 odd homeworks. (I) can get no rest in any day. Dictations, quizzes and examinations will be more.*
>
> *Though after 12 o'clock in every night, I still have to revise my homeworks. I can't go to bed until one o'clock odd. At 6.50 hours, in the next morning, I have to get up. (I) am so hard.*
>
> *I do wish no more studying.*

In Hong Kong, children usually enrol in kindergarten at 4 years old and begin the arduous process of mastering the several thousand characters in the Chinese language (each word is represented by a separate pictograph). These 4-year-old children may bring home from school each day homework involving the copying of Chinese characters, as well as other work. These pressures increase with each school year. For instance, Au (1995) investigated the relationship between academic failure and self-concept among 239 junior form students. Results indicated that when compared with average students, academically low achievers tend to display learned hopelessness and that form 3 students had more negative self-concept than junior form students. It is likely that some senior form students who have negative learning experiences – and more years of academic failure – realise that regardless of how hard they work, they are unable to influence the outcome. These students are more likely to under-estimate their own ability, and over-estimate their mistakes. It seems that academic failure has a cumulative effect.

A school-based survey of the fears and worries of 11-year old children in Hong Kong (Chan, 1993) found that the main worry (in 53 per cent) was that they would fail their annual examinations and would have to repeat the school year. Other major worries were the burdens of homework; pressure from parents; inability to understand teaching in English; and rejection by peer groups.

A random survey of 600 Hong Kong students aged 11 to 20 (Ng, 1993) found that 19.5 per cent had at some time in their lives had serious thoughts about suicide, including contemplating how they might kill themselves; and a further 11 per cent had actually engaged in an act of deliberate self-harm or suicidal gesture. One possible cause of the marked rise in serious suicide attempts amongst young people in Hong Kong is the fact that personal crises which in an earlier decade would have resulted in suicidal gestures or attempts (involving wrist-slashing or overdosing) now involve jumping from high buildings. The motivations of those killing themselves may be the same as those identified in Chung's (1987) study of youthful suicide attempts; but the outcomes are now invariably fatal when the method used is jumping from a high building. Each student suicide (until 1993) received considerable publicity in the Chinese- and English-language media, and there may have been an imitative element in such suicides – a phenomenon previously observed in Europe and North America (Gould et al., 1988; Schmidtke and Hafner, 1988). However, a campaign by the present writers requesting that Hong Kong media be more restrained in the reporting of adolescent suicides was successful, and this may have contributed in part to a relative decline in the rate of adolescent suicide in Hong Kong (Yip, 1998).

What emerges from the the survey of 986 Chinese adolescents by Stewart et al. (1999) is that suicidal ideas remain a prominent feature in the lives of Hong Kong youth facing stress. The subjects were mid-adolescents obtained by stratified, random sampling of secondary schools. Suicidal ideation was measured by four items from the Chinese Beck Depression Inventory: 'I have thoughts about killing myself/I have thoughts about killing myself but I would not do it/I would like to kill myself/I would like to kill myself if I had the chance.' Questions on stress related to family situation and relationships; peer problems; school pressures; health problems; Triad (youth gang) pressures; and migration history. Results indicated some suicidal ideas in at least a quarter of respondents: 22 per cent of males and 39 per cent of females had suicidal thoughts but no intent; 4 per cent of males and 7 per cent of females had the intent to kill themselves; and 2 per cent of males and 5 per cent of females had serious, immediate intent. Significant correlates of suicidal ideation for both sexes were perception of parents as uncaring, not understanding and restrictive, and generally negative relationships with parents; negative pressures within school; personal health problems; youth gang pressures; and current depressed mood. For females only, sibling conflict and broken homes were significant; for males only, examination pressures were significant predictors of suicidality.

It is clear from the survey by Stewart et al. (1999) that many of the variables that predict suicidal ideas also predict depression, and in many cases youth who are seriously depressed also consider suicide. This implies that studies of general mental health in adolescents are also relevant in considering strategies for suicide prevention. Shek (1997), for example, studied 429 randomly sampled high school students and their parents, and reported that adolescent hopelessness bore significant relationships to levels of family dysfunction independently reported by both father and mother. The correlations with hopelessness (average 0.22) were amongst the highest obtained among an array of measures. Shek argues, however, that the measure of family functioning, translated from an American instrument may not have been the best for measuring such links, and more appropriate, indigenous measures should be developed which encompassed traditional Chinese family values such as propriety, filial piety and forbearance.

Various forms of behavioural epidemics linked to suicidal ideation have been described, particularly wrist-slashing in some schools, apparently related to worry about examination failure in vulnerable adolescents (Yip et al., 1998). Suicide has also been attributed to the burden of academic pressures: for example, the coroner's inquest on a 10-year-old boy who jumped from a high building was told that the boy left a suicide note apologizing for the fact that despite extra tuition and extra homework he was still failing, bringing disgrace to his family (Beck, 1992).

As Marzuk et al. (1992) have shown in North America, the availability of multiple residence in tall buildings is associated with a significant increase in jumping from such buildings as a form of suicide. The suicide rate in Hong Kong youth may be increasing for several reasons – the increase in stressors identified by educational experts (Ming Pao, 1991; Ma, 1992; Sui and Watkins, 1997; Hui, 2000); imitation and behavioural trends (the Werther effect); and the availability of a frequently fatal method – jumping from high buildings (Yip, 1998). Unfortunately, the idea of adolescent suicide now seems to be embedded in aspects of Hong Kong's popular culture, even though some newspaper now refrain from popularising dramatic cases of suicide. For example, in 1997 a film 'Made in Hong Kong' received showing not only in Hong Kong but also to a wider international audience. The film features two of most common forms of self-harm in Hong Kong youth, wrist cutting and jumping. The publicity material for the film states: 'A schoolgirl commits suicide leaving two bloodstained letters behind. Moon (Sam Lee) a kid from a housing estate, finds them and from then on things start to go wrong for him.'

An additional factor which may underlie high suicide rates in Hong Kong, is the survival of a traditional Chinese value, which holds that suicide is justified or indeed required when a person has committed a shameful act, which brings disgrace on his or her family. Suicide is a method of atoning for this shame, after which the dead person can be held once again in honour and esteem. In Ma's (1992) survey of high school students in Sha Tin, 42 per cent declared that suicide was acceptable or indeed honourable behaviour in the face of stress or shame; 38 per cent said that suicide was a dishonourable or stupid solution to current problems; and 20 per cent were unsure about whether suicide was an acceptable solution to life's problems or not.

Suicide Prevention: Educational Pressures and School Resource Problems

Of one thing we can be certain from the extensive case histories available – the adolescents involved were often confused about whether they wanted to die or not, and often communicated their doubts, fears and intentions to fellow students. Consider the following case of a double suicide involving a boy of

14 and a girl of 12 (*South China Morning Post* (SCMP, 1992)):

> *The two were in the same school class, and were known to be sweethearts. School friends of Wing-sze and Wai-yip testified at a coroner's inquest that Wing-sze (the girl) had two weeks earlier slashed her wrist in school following an accusation from schoolmates that she was no longer a virgin, and had disgraced her family. Wai-yip was said to be struggling with schoolwork, and was extremely worried about the results of an examination he had recently taken. Close friends of the pair restrained Wing-sze from injuring herself further at the time of the attempt, but did not report the event to teachers or parents. The couple seemed to be in a state of shock after the implications of their romance became clear (neither of the families were aware of the relationship). On the day the students died, four schoolmates spent more than an hour frantically trying to dissuade them from jumping. The students followed the couple after Wai-yip said he wanted to jump off the building. A schoolmate told the coroner that Wai-yip asked him which was the highest building in the area. 'I replied Wo Ping House and Wai-yip then said he would jump down from there'. Wing-sze was sitting on a nearby bench, crying, and then said 'If you do so I will surely accompany you'. When the two students left the school grounds, four schoolmates followed them, as they went up to the 21st floor. Wai-yip climbed up on the railing; his friends persuaded him, momentarily, against jumping. But Wai-yip threatened to jump immediately if a teacher was called, and another of his school friends was sent for. He arrived with two other friends, and a group of about seven young teenagers watched as the two found a stool, which was high enough to enable Wing-sze to climb onto the parapet. The coroner was told that Wing-sze was especially nervous about an upcoming school examination. She came from a family split by divorce, and saw her father very infrequently. Wai-yip also came from a broken family. Both students were said to have very low self-esteem, and had invested much in the relationship with one another. Both students feared they would be expelled from school because of their romance, and would disgrace their parents further. Press reports following the young couple's death treated them with the status of heroes of a Chinese folk tale, like a pair of doves united forever in love and death.*

It is our contention that incidents such as these are by no means inevitable. It is possible to identify children and adolescents who are more likely to engage in suicidal behaviour and provide timely intervention.

In the early 1990s the government promised to improve the ratio of school social workers to students from one per 3,000 to one per 2,500. In the late 1990s, only special schools, practical schools and band 5 schools (for students with poor academic performance) had one social worker per school. In mainstream schools the school-social worker ratio was one for three schools. Following strong demands from professionals and politicians for a better ratio, the 'one social worker per school policy' was formally adopted in year 2000. Nonetheless, this does not mean recruitment of more social workers. It is simply a re-deployment of social workers from Children and Youth Centres into the school setting. The 'one social worker per school policy' implies that in the school setting the social worker/student ratio has improved to around 1:1000. But, given the closure of Children and Youth Centres the overall social worker/youth ratio has not been enhanced.

At the same time, teacher morale appears to be low (Cheung, 1993). One of the reasons has been the inability to cope with large classes. The present class size remains at 42 students per class in secondary school and 38 pupils per class in primary school. The stringent education budget, which has direct impact on social worker- and teacher-student ratio, may have indirect influence on adolescent suicidal behaviour. For instance, in 1991, high-school teachers referred 10,780 students to school social workers for investigation and support: of these referrals 31 per cent of these referrals involved adolescents experiencing emotional or family crisis, including 82 who had made a serious suicide attempt. Social workers were only able to accept referrals of the most seriously disturbed adolescents (for example, young people who had actually attempted suicide) and 3,840 cases had to be turned away, despite significant behavioural, emotional or family problems (Ren, 1992). It is likely that a number of these young people whose referrals could not be accepted moved on to serious suicidal crises of the kind described by Chan (1991).

Suicidal Problems: A Case for Continuing Concern

Suicidal ideas and behaviours have continued to be of concern for Chinese researchers, counsellors and psychiatrists in the decade of the 1990s (Lo, 1993; Hau, 1993; Sam, 1993; Chan, 1995; Zeng and Le Tendre, 1998; Samaritan Befrienders, 1998; Ho and Hung, 1998; Stewart et al., 1999; Leung and Zsang, 2000).

Zeng and Le Tendre (1998) identify academic pressure as a significant correlation of suicidal behaviours in students in Hong Kong, Japan, South Korea and Taiwan 'which share a common emphasis on educational advancement and make extensive use of exam systems'. In a Hong Kong study Yip (1998) identified several syndromes associated with youth in an examination oriented culture including 'feelings of loss and confusion, over-involvement of details of the examination, worry and anxiety, spontaneous comparison with other examination candidates, over-sensitive to others' comments, over-calculation of result, withdrawal and repression'. Ack and Watkins (1997), Tong and Lau (1998) and Hui (2000) have also identified excessive academic pressures as sources of stress and poorer self-esteem in Hong Kong adolescents. Sam's (1993) study of completed suicide in Hong Kong adolescents identified academic stressors as antecedent causes in 22 per cent of the 18 males studied.

Ideally, a strong family culture stressing traditional values of filial piety, propriety and forbearance should buffer adolescents who are highly stressed because of examinations and other stresses external to the family. However, when fathers are absent, alcoholic or actually abuse their child, the psychological burden on the child may be heavy indeed. Although sexual abuse of children is probably less prevalent in Chinese cultures than in the West, when a father abuses his child it represents a particularly profound violation of the principle of filial piety, with commensurate psychological distress (Luo, 1998). In Hong Kong, about half of the population live in low rent public housing and given a very stringent space allocation formula of 5.5 square metres per head, living conditions are poor. It is common to find families crammed into a crowded space, with little or no personal privacy. In such conditions a whole family of five or six people, may sleep in a bunker bed. Such sleeping arrangements can, according to social work reports, be conducive to child sexual abuse. Fathers expect filial piety; but the obedience granted to fathers also implies a standard of conduct amongst fathers, and when men fall below this standard the violation of trust (as in the case of sexual abuse) is profound.

Tang (1996) found that child physical abuse is a rather common phenomenon in Hong Kong. Results indicated that in a sample of older adolescents in the past 12 months, 62.5 per cent had been verbally abused, 13.2 per cent had experienced minor physical abuse while 8.5 per cent had experienced 'severe' physical abuse (which included being kicked or punched, or hit with by an object). The complexity of various kinds of abuse may be an important indicator of adolescent suicidal behaviour and it can be a significant predictor of completed and attempted suicide in the teenage population (Tse, 2000).

Another dimension of sexuality may be significant in youthful suicidal behaviours in Hong Kong. Western research (reviewed by Bagley and Tremblay, 2000) indicates clearly that up to a half of all serious suicide attempts in youth are linked to persecution or self-doubt surrounding an emerging homosexual or lesbian identity. The situation is further complicated by the fact that sex education is not systematically taught in schools and that adolescents (in Hong Kong as elsewhere) often find it difficult to discuss sexual matters, or obtain reassuring information about personal sexuality. Traditionally, sexual matters in Chinese cultures have been treated as taboo subjects. In a survey of over 1,200 adolescents, the Hong Kong Federation of Youth Groups found that out of 39 topics, adolescents identified five sex-related items in the top ten 'hard to discuss' list (*Apple Daily*, 2000). Adolescents reported difficulty in disclosing or discussing: sexual abuse (45.3 per cent); sexual fantasies (42.9 per cent); unhappy sexual experiences (34.6 per cent); promiscuity (33.6 per cent) and sexual orientation (33.5 per cent). The reasons for difficulties in discussing these matters were: 1) not sure whether the listener would keep the secret (45.1 per cent); and 2) worry about being laughed at (36.3%). These findings indicate how adolescents might develop these fears and worries into feelings of self-doubt and suicidality.

We can discover no clinical or epidemiological studies of the stress which living in an apparently homophobic culture imposes on youth in Hong Kong. Nevertheless, the internet resources reviewed by Tremblay (2000) identifies an important web site for gay youth in Hong Kong, which received more than 50 'hits' a day in 2000 including interchanges on a message board (HKGY, 2000). Suicidal behaviour among adolescents is featured in Hong Kong newspapers, but in negative ways. For example, two lesbians (aged 13 and 14) committed suicide (Sing Pao, 2000); another two lesbians aged 13 and 15 year olds were found overdosed (*Apple Daily*, 1999b); a 13-year-old gay youth attempted suicide (*Apple Daily*, 1999a); and two lesbian adolescents slashed their wrists (*Oriental Daily*, 2000). At present, there is no anti-discrimination legislation to protect homosexual people from persecution. Given the prejudice homosexuals face in a homophobic culture, these individuals may be subject to extreme stress. The role of stress surrounding gay issues in suicidality in Hong Kong youth is an important topic for future research.

Several researchers comment on the high female to male ratio in completed youth suicides in Hong Kong. This method of suicide reflects the fact that in a crowded region, many dwellings are situated in high-rise apartment blocks. Once jumping from height is seen as *modus non vivendi*, it may assume some cultural and imitative significance. In Europe, North America and Australia female adolescents have a much higher rate of suicidal gestures through overdoses; but in some Hong Kong females who would otherwise make non-lethal attempts at suicide may jump instead, with certain death likely. Thus, in

Sam's (1993) study of completed suicides in Hong Kong, 77 per cent of deaths of adolescent females resulted from jumping from a high building.

While epidemiological studies on suicidal attempts and gestures are methodologically difficult (many incidents may not be reported to or recorded by hospitals), Pan and Lieh-Mak (1987) estimated that in those aged 10 to 19 the rates were 20 and 60 per 100,000 in males and females respectively. These estimated rates are far lower than those obtained from various school-based surveys. Fong (1993) asked 316 Form 1 and 2 students (equivalent to junior high) in Hong Kong about prior self-harm, and found that 28 per cent had thought at some time that 'life was not worth living', with 16 per cent currently having this idea. Twelve students (3.8 per cent) had engaged in deliberate self-harm of some kind – a much higher rate than that obtained from hospital data, probably reflecting the fact that these were not in the main suicide attempts, but acts of sub-lethal self-harm. Nevertheless, such acts must be accounted as an important 'cry for help'. Ho, Lee and Ho (1994) in a survey of 225 adolescents found that 5.8 per cent reported some kind of deliberate self-harm in their lifetime. In a more detailed study of 563 Hong Kong adolescents Chan et al. (1993) found that 10.7 per cent reported prior self-injury (including wrist slashing), with a rate of serious suicide attempts of about one per cent.

A clinical study of Hong Kong youth who engaged in self-cutting by Yip et al. (1998) identified several overlapping antecedents of such behaviour; stress involving unpleasant past experiences including separations and life disruption because of migration from other parts of China; family disruption because of divorce; school failure and isolation from classmates and teachers; poor ego functioning, reflected in negative self-image; and introjection or internalisation of chronic self-denigration and self-harm. The hardship faced by new immigrants from Mainland China is a rather unique phenomenon in Hong Kong. Most new immigrants, who come from poor families living in a socialist country, may have to overcome 'culture shock' and find it particularly difficult to adjust in a super competitive, survival-of-the-fittest, capitalistic society that is modern Hong Kong. Some newly arrived children and adolescents are over anxious and worry excessively about academic failure, housing and financial difficulties. When such chronic distress and severe stress prevail, sometimes even very young children would contemplate suicide. New immigrants may be considered as a high-risk suicide group. For instance, an 8-year-old boy, who had emigrated from China three years earlier, leapt to his death apparently 'due to pressure from examination' (*Tin Tin Daily*, 2000). As most pupils start learning English in China from primary one onwards, some may find it hard to catch up with their English in Hong Kong. It is common to find 13- or 14-year-old students from China studying at primary level. When a pupil has to repeat a year, it means not only a loss of face but also additional financial burden on an already very poor family. These tend to increase the likelihood of suicidal behaviour.

In her suicide note, an 18 year old who migrated from China five years before, wrote: 'I am very tired. In the past five years, I hated Hong Kong, this disgusting place. I still remember the past 13 years of life in China ...' (*Apple Daily*, 1999c). In her award-winning essay entitled 'The days I spent in Hong Kong', she revealed her ambivalence and anguish in settling in Hong Kong and yet refused to disobey her parental wishes. She stated: 'How could I throw away the country I lived for 10 years? How could I leave my dear friends with whom we met for many years? ... The tiny tin shed was extremely narrow, even with two persons standing you find it crowded. Is it a living space for humans? I remember my home, it was big and cosy, with clean and tidy furniture ... I studied in a provincial-class key secondary school, and now I am demoted to a village primary school with only 50 or 60 students. I found that was completely unacceptable! ... I did my first homework assignment, which was at primary 2 level. It was difficult to describe my feelings. It was simply an insult!' (*Apple Daily*, 1999c). She was ostracized and discriminated against by her classmates, and she complained: 'My classmates look down on me and love to call me 'Mainland girl,' they know that I don't speak Cantonese, and they often laughed at me. Is coming from China a crime?' (*Apple Daily*, 1999c).

No one knows the extent or severity of extra-marital affairs in Hong Kong. But the relatively deprived living conditions in Mainland China means that keeping a concubine there for many Hong Kong men is both affordable and available. But at times of economic recessions and a high unemployment rate, it is difficult to make ends meet for the head of two families. When infidelity and financial difficulty, combined with the traditional thinking that 'Parents have a right to take children's lives' (*Hong Kong Standard*, 1998), the result may be a very disturbing homicide-suicide formula. Such incidents or attempts have been regularly reported in the news. After a mother threw her sons aged 6 and 10 from the window of her flat, she jumped to her death. It was reported that her husband kept a concubine in China and failed to provide financial assistance to his family in Hong Kong (*Tin Tin Daily*, 1998a). In an attempt to stop the husband from keeping a concubine, a mother tried to throw her 9-year-old daughter off the 30th floor window (Sing Pao, 1999). A concubine forced her daughters to drink detergent when she was abandoned by her 'husband' (*Tin Tin Daily*, 1998b).

The plight of the new immigrants, those adolescents who are still struggling with their sexual identity, and those who have experienced excessive academic pressures and those who are physically and/or sexually abused, must not be left unanswered. In terms of suicide prevention strategies, individual intervention must of course occur before the act of fatal self-harm, and the identification of students with suicidal feelings is important. The identification and treatment of those who have engaged in actual self-harm is crucial.

Conclusions

Suicidal thoughts, suicidal actions both sub-lethal and lethal in intent, and completed suicide in youth are an important social, educational and mental health problem for Hong Kong youth. Though rates of completed suicide have stopped climbing in the late 1990s, they still remain unacceptably high, and no clear prevention strategies are in place.

A variety of antecedent stressors are implied in this youthful suicidal behaviour: stress and guilt concerning relationship and sexuality issues; family disruption and breakdown; and educational pressures of various kinds. School counsellors and teachers can only refer or deal with the most distressed youth, and many suicidal young people may be missed. Indeed, there is some evidence that the distress of some young people is known only to peers. This has implications for prevention strategies, which will be addressed in subsequent chapters.

References

Ack, S. and Watkins, D. (1997). Coping with stress in Hong Kong: an investigation of the influence of gender, age and the self-concept. *Psychologia*, 40, 59–66.

Apple Daily (1999a). A lack of warmth in family – two lesbians found over-dosed. *Apple Daily*, August 7, p. A12.

Apple Daily (1999b). 13-years old gay over-dosed feared mother does not understand. *Apple Daily*, September 25, p. A12.

Apple Daily (1999c). 'Classmates despise me ... Is this a place human lives?' Hong Kong people's discrimination forced new immigrant girl to die. *Apple Daily*, September 25, p. A02.

Apple Daily (2000). Adolescents most afraid top ten topics. *Apple Daily*, December 18, p. A6.

Au, R. (1995). Academic failure and learned hopelessness in Hong Kong academically low achievers. *Bulletin of the Hong Kong Psychological Society*, 34/35, 83–100.

Bagley, C., Mallick, K., Verma, G., Bolitho, F., Bertrand, L., Madrid, S. and Tse, J. (1999). Adjustment, stress and family life in adolescents in Canada, Britain, Hong Kong, India, Pakistan and The Philippines. *International Journal of Adolescence and Youth*, 7, 263–78.

Bagley, C. and Tremblay, P. (2000). Suicidal behaviours in gay, lesbian and bisexual youth: an account of causes, and estimates of prevalence. *Crisis: Journal of Crisis Intervention and Suicide Prevention*, in press.

Beck, C. (1992). Sentenced to a regime of non-stop study. *South China Morning Post*, 20 September, p. 31.

Bond, M. (1986). *The Psychology of Chinese People.* New York: Oxford University Press.

Bond, M. (1991). *Beyond the Chinese Face: Insights from Psychology.* Hong Kong: Oxford University Press.

Bond, M. and Pang, K.-K. (1990). Trusting the Tao: Chinese values and the restructuring of psychology. In U. Gielen (ed.), *Chinese Morality: Values, Reasonings, and Education.* New York: Academic Press.

Bond, M. and Smith, B. (1993). *Social Psychology Across Cultures: Analysis and Perspective.* London: Harvester Wheatsheaf.

Chan, D. (1995). Reasons for living among Chinese adolescents in Hong Kong. *Suicide and Life-Threatening Behavior*, 25(3), 347–57.

Chan, D., Wong, S. and Sui, K. (1993). *The Values of Secondary School Students and Self-Destructive Tendencies in Hong Kong* (in Chinese). Hong Kong: Breakthrough Research Group.

Chan, D.W. (1991). Adolescent suicide: the need for prevention and postvention. *Hong Kong Journal of Mental Health*, 20, 2–4.

Chan, T. (1993). Repeating class is children's biggest fear. *Hong Kong Standard*, 14, January, p. 3.

Chen, C.S. and Stevenson, H.W. (1989). Homework: a cross-cultural examination. *Child Development* 60, 551–61.

Chen, X. and Li, B.-S. (2000). Depressed mood in Chinese children: development significance. *International Journal of Behavioural Development*, 24, 472–9.

Cheung, C.-K., Lee, J.-J. and Chan, C.-M. (1994). Explicating filial piety in relation to family cohesion. *Journal of Social Behaviour and Personality*, 9, 565–80.

Cheung, D. (1993). Poor deal turns away teachers. *South China Morning Post*, 26, January, p. 3.

Cheung, S.-K. (1996). Reliability and factor structure of the Chinese version of the Depression Self-Rating Scale. *Educational and Psychological Measurement*, 56, 142–54.

Cheung, S.-K. and Bagley, C. (1998). Validating an American scale in Hong Kong: the Center for Epidemiological Studies Depression Scale. *Journal of Psychology*, 132, 169–86.

Cheung, S.-K. and Chan, W.W. (1990). *Hong Kong Primary School Pupils' Homework Pressure: A Research Study.* Hong Kong: Boys' and Girls' Clubs Association of Hong Kong (in Chinese).

Cheung, S.-K. and Lam, C.W. (1992). *Hong Kong Adolescents' Help Seeking Behaviour*. Hong Kong: Boys' and Girls' Clubs Association of Hong Kong (in Chinese).

Cheung, T. and Lau, S. (1985). Self-esteem: its relationship to the family and school social environments among Chinese adolescents. *Youth and Society*, 16, 438–56.

Chiang, C.-W. (2000). *Suicide Figures in Hong Kong 2000.* Hong Kong: Samaritan Befrienders.

Choy, L. (1993). Government study too hard on families. *South China Morning Post*, February 4, p. 3.

Chung, S. (1987). Attempted suicide in children and adolescents in Hong Kong. *Social Psychiatry*, 22, 102–6.

Committee on Home-School Co-operation. (1994). *Survey on Parents' View on Homework and Schoolbags.* Hong Kong: Author.

Fong, S. (1993). A study on suicide ideation and attempted suicide in 316 secondary school students. *Hong Kong Journal of Mental Health*, 22, 43–9.

Furlong, S. (1992). Government proposes to increase size of classes. *South China Morning Post*, January 11, p. 9.

Gould, M., Shaffer, D. and Kleinman, M. (1988). The impact of suicide in television movies: replication and commentary. *Suicide and Life-Threatening Behavior*, 1, 90–99.

Hau, K. (1993). Suicide in Hong Kong 1971–1990: age trend, sex ratio and method of suicide. *Social Psychiatry and Psychiatric Epidemiology*, 28, 23–7.

Headley, L. (1983). Suicide in Hong Kong. In L. Headley and N. Farberow (eds), *Suicide in Asia and the Near East* (pp. 97–100). Berkeley, C.A: University of California Press.

HKGY (2000). Web Site http://hkgy.homestead.com/index~ns4.html.

HKYRC (2000). *A Study on the Alcohol Drinking Habits Among Youth in Hong Kong.* Hong Kong: Youth Research Centre.

Ho, K., Lee, M. and Ho, W. (1994). *A Study of Adolescent Suicidal Pathways.* Hong Kong: Hong Kong Playground Association.

Ho, T. and Hung, S. (1998). The prevention of youth suicide: research and services. *Hong Kong Medical Journal*, 4, 159–202.

Hong Kong Coroner (1989–1999). *Annual Reports.* Hong Kong: Government Printer.

Hong Kong Council of Social Service (1982). *Estimating the Size of the Potential Clientele of School Social Work Service.* Hong Kong: HKCSS.

Hui, E. (2000). Personal concerns and their causes: perceptions of the Hong Kong Chinese adolescent students. *Journal of Adolescence*, 23, 189–203.

Jing, Q. and Zuo, Q. (2000). Mental health problems of Chinese school children. In N. Singh, J. Leungand A. Singh (eds), *International Perspectives on Child and Adolescent Mental Health.* Amsterdam: Elsevier.

Kwan, A.Y.H. (1988). Suicide among the elderly: Hong Kong. *Journal of Applied Gerontology*, 7, 248–59.

Landrine, H. (1992). Clinical implications of cultural differences: the referential versus the indexical self. *Clinical Psychology Review*, 12: 401–15.

Leung, J.-P. and Zhang, L.-W. (2000). Predictors of life satisfaction in Chinese adolescents: self-concepts and relationships with significant others. In N. Sing, J.-P. LeungandA. Singh (eds), *International Perspectives on Child and Adolescent Mental Health.* Amsterdam: Elsevier.

Leung, K. and Lau, S. (1989). Effects of self-concept and perceived disapproval of delinquent behavior in school children. *Journal of Youth and Adolescence*, 18, 345–59.

Lo, A. C. (1992). Assessing High Risk Suicidal Students in Hong Kong. Paper presented at *Managing Suicidal Students Seminar, Association of Psychology and Educational Counsellors of Asia*, Hong Kong.

Luk, S., Leung, P., Lee, P. and Lieh-Mak, F. (1988). Teachers' referral of children with mental health problems: a study of primary schools in Hong Kong. *Psychology in the Schools*, 25, 121–9.

Luo, T. (1998). Sexual abuse trauma among Chinese survivors. *Child Abuse and Neglect*, 22, 1013–26.

Ma, S. (1992). *Secondary School Life in Sha Tin* (in Chinese). Hong Kong: Sha Tin District Board.

Markus, H. and Kitayama, S. (1991). Culture and the self: implications for cognition, emotion and motivation. *Psychological Review*, 98, 224–43.

Marzuk, P., Leon, A., Tardiff, K., Morgan, E., Stajic, M. and Mann, J. (1992). The effect of access to lethal methods of injury on suicide rates. *Archives of General Psychiatry*, 49, 451–6.

Ming Pao (1991). Why adolescents kill themselves. *Ming Pao Daily News*, April 1, p. 3 (in Chinese).

Ng, S. (1993). *The Problem of Teenage Suicide.* Hong Kong: Breakthrough Publishers (in Chinese).

Oriental Daily (2000). Two distressed lesbians slashed arms intended to die. *Oriental Daily*, September 25.

Pan, P. C. and Lieh-Mak, F. (1989). A comparison between male and female para-suicides in Hong Kong. *Social Psychiatry and Psychiatric Epidemiology*, 24(5), 253–7.

Ren, R. (1992). 4,000 students denied crisis counselling. *Hong Kong Standard*, August 3, p. 1.

Ruzicka, L. (1998). Suicide in countries and areas of the ESCAP region. *Asia-Pacific Population Journal*, 13, 55–74.

Salini, F. and Hoosain, R. (1985). Hyperactivity among Hong Kong Chinese Children. *International Journal of Intercultural Relations*, 9, 77–185.

Sam, C. (1993). Suicide among children and adolescents in Hong Kong. *Journal of the Hong Kong College of Psychiatrists*, 3, 19–27.

Samaritan Befrienders (1998–2000). *Annual Reports*. Hong Kong: The Samaritan Befrienders.

Schmidtke, A. and Hafner, H. (1998). The Werther effect after television films: new evidence for an old hypothesis. *Psychological Medicine*, 18, 655–76.

Shek, D. (1988). Mental health of secondary school students in Hong Kong: an epidemiological study using the General Health Questionnaire. *International Journal of Adolescent Medicine and Health*, 3, 191–215.

Shek, D. (1990). Depressive symptoms in a sample of Chinese adolescents: an empirical study using the Chinese version of the Beck Depression Inventory. *International Journal of Adolescent Medicine and Health*, 5, 10–16.

Shek, D. (1997). The relation of family functioning to adolescent psychological well being, school adjustment, and problem behavior. *Journal of Genetic Psychology*, 158, 467–479.

Shek, D. (1998). Adolescent positive mental health and psychological symptoms: a longitudinal study in a Chinese context. *Psychologia*, 41, 217–25.

Sing Pao (1999). Mainland-Hong Kong driver kept concubine wife attempted to throw daughter downstairs. *Sing Pao*, October 2, p. B01.

Sing Pao (2000). Two distressed runaway girls were helpless. *Sing Pao*, August 16, p. A9.

Siu, A. and Watkins, D. (1997). Coping with stress in Hong Kong: an investigation of the influence of gender, age, and the self-concept. *Psychologia*, 40, 59–66.

So, L. (1993). *A Review of the Adolescent Suicides in 1992*. Hong Kong: Advisory Committee on School Guidance and Support Services, Education Department of the Government of Hong Kong.

South China Morning Post (1991). Jury urges schools to review punishment to stem suicides. *South China Morning Post*, September 14, p.1.

South China Morning Post (1992). Pair jump to death after virginity taunt *and* Test fears led to talk of suicide. *South China Morning Post*, April 14, p. 3; and 21 November, p. 3.

Stewart, S., Lam, T., Betson, C. and Chung, S. (1999). Suicide ideation and its relationship to depressed mood in a community sample of adolescents in Hong Kong. *Suicide and Life-Threatening Behaviour*, 29, 227–40.

Su, L.-S., Li, X., Wan, G., Tang, Z. and Luo, X. (2000). Child Behavior Checklist for Chinese children. In N. Singh, J.-P. Leung and A. Singh (eds), *International Perspectives on Child and Adolescent Mental Health* (pp. 249–64), Amsterdam: Elsevier.

Tang, C. (1996). Adolescent abuse in Hong Kong Chinese families. *Child Abuse and Neglect*, 20, 873–8.

Temblay, P. (2001). *Gay Youth Suicidality*. A continuously updated web site at: http://www.virtualcity.com/youthsuicide.

Tin Tin Daily (1998a). Concubine tragedy woman forced two daughters to drink detergent. *Tin Tin Daily*, November 10, p. A08.

Tin Tin Daily (1998b). Concubine tragedy caused the death of mother and sons. *Tin Tin Daily*, October 20, p. A01.

Tin Tin Daily. (2000). An 8 year-old could not handle exam pressure jumped to his death. *Tin Tin Daily*, June 12, p. A10.

Tong, C. and Lau, C. (1998). Self-concept and depression of secondary one students in Hong Kong. *Proceedings of the 1st International Conference on Child and Adolescent Mental Health*, Hong Kong, June.

Tse, John W.L. (2000). *Youth Suicide: Facts, Prevention and Crisis Management*. Hong Kong: Chinese University Press.

Tse, John W.L., Bagley, C. and Mak, Hoi-wah (1994). Prevention of teenage suicidal behaviour in Hong Kong: development of the Health Intervention Training-Mutual Aid Network (HIT-MAN). *School Psychology International*, 15, 99–114.

White Paper (1991). *Social Welfare in the 1990s and Beyond ... Draft White Paper of the Working Party on Social Welfare Policies and Services*. Hong Kong: Government Printer.

Wong, C. (1990). Psychiatric Morbidity in Hong Kong Children. Hong Kong: Centre of Asian Studies, University of Hong Kong.

Yang, K.-S. and Bond, M. (1990). Exploring implicit personality theories with indigenous or imported constructs: the Chinese case. *Journal of Personality and Social Psychology*, 56, 1086–95.

Yik, M. and Bond, M. (1993). Exploring the dimensions of Chinese person perception with indigenous and imported constructs: creating a culturally balanced scale. *International Journal of Psychology*, 28, 71–95.

Yip, K.-S. (1998). An exploratory study of stress and coping of adolescents in facing public examinations in Hong Kong. *Proceedings of the 1st International Conference of Child and Adolescent Mental Health*, Hong Kong, June.

Yip, K.-S., Ngan, M. and Lam, I. (1998). An exploratory study of self-cutting behaviours in secondary school students in Hong Kong. Proceedings of the *1st International Conference of Adolescent Mental Health*, Hong Kong: June.

Yu, C. (1999). A city in spiritual confusion. *China Graduate School of Theology Bulletin*, July, 1–2.

Zeng, K. and Le Tendre, G. (1998). Adolescent suicide and academic competition in East Asia. *Comparative Education Review*, 42, 513–28.

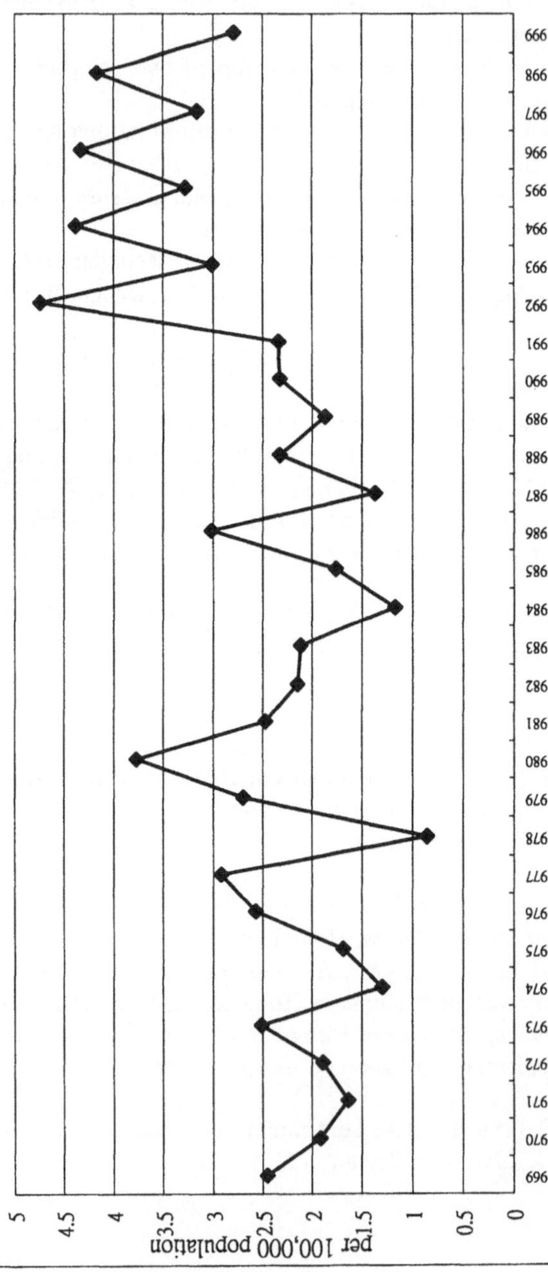

Figure 1.1 Annual average child and adolescent suicide rate (1969–1999)

2 Preventing Suicidal Behaviour in Chinese Youth: The Role of Peer Counselling

JOHN W.L. TSE, CHRISTOPHER BAGLEY AND MAK HOI-WAH

Summary

Elements of suicide prevention programmes for adolescents, described in previous studies, are reviewed. School-based programmes described by western researchers have had limited success. We propose that mobilising peers as allies in suicide prevention programmes for adolescents could be a significant way forward. To this end the Health Intervention Training Mutual Aid Network (HIT-MAN) has been developed in Hong Kong. The object of this programme is to encourage adolescents both to support, and in some cases refer, friends who have been thinking about suicide, or who manifest behaviours reflecting very low self-esteem and depression. Teachers can organise HIT-MAN groups, which can be part of extra-curricular activities. Methods of programme organisation, curriculum implications, and possibilities for evaluation are described.

Introduction

Although the problem of rising rates of suicidal behaviours in Chinese youth in Hong Kong has been well established (see previous chapter), no successful prevention strategies have been attempted. School counselling, as we argued in the previous chapter, is an underfunded service, and the role of the main telephone crisis counselling service, the Samaritan Befrienders, is uncertain. While strategies for the development of positive mental health in adolescents is implied in some research studies (Shek, 1998), ways of achieving this goal are not well developed.

Ideally, a suicide prevention strategy for Hong Kong youth should address what Chan (1995) calls 'the reasons for living', not the reasons for wanting to die. Chan, in standardising a Chinese version of the *Reasons for Living Inventory* in 279 Hong Kong students, identified a set of 'positive values and self-efficacy', as well as the achievement of a sense of optimism as key elements in the rejection of suicidal ideas. These elements include love of life, desire to live, having many things to do now and in the future, seeing life as beautiful and precious, caring about one's self and finding a purpose in life. Not wanting to hurt family, concerns about what friends and others would think about suicide were also listed as important values countering suicide, which was seen as a generally weak and selfish act. Fear of the suicidal act itself was salient only for females. Overall 'reasons for living' were quite similar to those established with American adolescent samples.

While fostering these positive values should be an important goal for suicide prevention programmes, there remains the question of how to reach those youth who are in fact highly suicidal, are alienated from family and friends, and who feel that life holds nothing more for them.

Elements of Suicide Prevention Programmes

Possible bases for suicide prevention programmes for adolescents have been outlined in the review of Hong Kong adolescent suicides by Ho and Hung (1998). Discussing North American and European clinical studies, they report that more than half of youth who killed themselves had some diagnosable mental illness. There is, however, a danger of tautological conclusions in such research; it may have been inferred that the act of suicide was itself the major sign of psychiatric illness, and previous actions and communications of the youth may be reinterpreted to fit a diagnosis, which represents some comfort to the bereaved. The inference that the suicide was almost inevitable because of the onset of serious psychiatric illness is more comforting than the idea that the self-killing resulted from reactions to intolerable, perhaps family-related stress.

Ho and Hung (1998) do point in their review to literature to the fact that family dysfunction can be an important antecedent of various kinds of suicidal behaviour; about a quarter of youth who kill themselves have had a first-degree relative who has done so in the past, and up to a quarter of suicide attempters have a parent who has engaged in deliberate self-harm at some time. Up to a half of adolescent attempters have a close relative with diagnosed mental illness. Low self-esteem is an established precursor of both attempted and completed suicide, a finding, which holds even when the effects of concurrent depression are controlled for. Youth suicide, argue Ho and Hung (1998) is a function of both stress factors in the interpersonal environment, and the individual's underlying mental state of vulnerability. In Hong Kong, they argue that high levels of family dysfunction and conflict are important stress factors in adolescent suicidal behaviours:

> *Based on the limited data available, we believe some of the specific features of youth suicide similarities [to findings from western research] and the escalating rate of divorce, diminishing support from the extended family network, increase in child abuse cases and youth substance abuse may mean that Hong Kong youngsters have to face an increased number of risk factors. Unless ameliorative changes are made, it is possible that youth suicides will continue to increase in the future.* (Ho and Hung, 1998, p. 198)

School-Based Suicide Prevention Programmes

Shaffer et al. (1988), after a review of programmes in the United States, concluded that most suicide prevention programmes of a formal or curriculum nature failed to focus on students specifically at risk from suicidal behaviour, spreading scarce resources too wide in address all students in brief but ineffective suicide prevention teaching modules. Rather than squandering scare resources on prevention programmes for students who will never be at risk from suicidal behaviour, there should be a focus on those at risk – a strategy requiring a primary focus on the *specific* problems of individual students (Bagley, 1992). This implies programmes of screening for suicidal ideation and behaviour concentrating scare resources on individuals as members (or potential members) of supportive peer groups.

For example, in suicide prevention programmes in British secondary schools we were able to show that the mental health of adolescents with poor self-esteem and high rates of suicidal ideation improved significantly (in comparison with matched controls) through a programme aimed at drawing on various resources including social workers, school counsellors and classroom teachers (Bagley, 1975; Bagley et al., 1979). The classroom element involved sociometric identification of popular and unpopular students in classroom settings. Those with diminished self-esteem and frequent suicidal ideas were often sociometrically isolated. Pairing a sociometric 'star' with an isolated student in some task-related activity usually resulted in the absorption of the isolated student within mainstream peer networks. Control subjects, on the other hand, remained isolated (Bagley et al., 1979).

American studies have described several types of suicide-prevention programmes in schools, but their full efficacy is unproved (Ho and Hung, 1998). The most effective type of intervention might be targeting individuals who have already made a suicidal gesture or attempt. But, in Hong Kong, the permission of each individual school must be sought for any programme, and co-operation is by no means guaranteed (Ho and Hung, 1998).

These authors conclude:

> *The school-based prevention programme in its present form has a limited impact and is unable to reach target students. Knowing that youths prefer to seek help among themselves and that they tend to know their peer's suicidal ideas and witness their peer's suicidal behaviours more often than do parents or teachers, it is logical to focus attention on mobilising peers as allies.* (Ho and Hung, 1998, p.200)

Development of the Health Intervention Training Mutual Aid Network (HIT-MAN)

Acknowledging that a peer-based approach might be particularly effective in reaching suicidal youth in Hong Kong schools, Tse, Bagley and Mak (1994) have pioneered the HIT-MAN approach. We describe below the elements of this programme, which has not been fully implemented or evaluated. Despite the nature of suicide and the urgent intervention which teenage suicide may call for, there are few school-based prevention programmes available in Hong Kong. In the past, much attention has been devoted to the study of suicide in the older population in Hong Kong (Headley, 1983) and in the provision of services for the elderly people (Kwan, 1988). There is, however, a general lack of school-based programmes in the area of teenage suicide prevention. Although Hong Kong is rich in material resources, the territory's social and educational services are seriously under funded. Class sizes are often larger than 40 and teachers as well as students are under great pressure. The role of teacher-counsellor is not well developed, and teachers have rarely had training in addressing the psychological problems of students (Lo, 1992).

In the remainder of this chapter we describe one possible approach to the suicide epidemic amongst Hong Kong adolescents – the development of an experimental programme of peer support linked to increases in teachers' awareness of factors which might contribute to student suicide.

Lack of Models of Effective School-based Suicide Prevention

The most common reasons given by educators for not talking about suicide and death are the mistaken fear that such teaching may actually encourage suicide attempts (Morrison, 1987); the lack of training which teachers have had for this role; and the competing demands of a curriculum which places strong emphasis on academic achievement and examination success. The common belief by teachers that talking about something may actually cause the event to occur (despite the overt message of the curriculum) is also encountered in the beliefs of many Hong Kong teachers that sex education programmes may initiate sexual activity. Given these circumstances, teachers may not be comfortable with coping with the dynamics of suicide prevention. Even in western countries where the increase in youth suicide began some two decades before a similar increase in Hong Kong, most suicide awareness instruction ranges from single-session presentations to three- or four-session modules (Clark, 1991).

Although systematic teaching about prevention programmes has been suggested as a potential method of helping teachers and social workers who deal with teenage suicide in other cultural settings (Garfinkel, 1989; Wass et al., 1990), no comprehensive programmes have been designed for use in Hong Kong. In the absence of a readily available and simple-to-use curriculum model, most teachers have been reluctant to offer suicide prevention education.

Students themselves can be of potential help in recognising such symptoms in their peers. Nevertheless, students may not grasp the implications of the cries for help from fellow students; or negative group pressures can actually make the situation worse, as in the case of Wing-sze and Wai-yip, mentioned in Chapter 1. Adeock et al. (1991) in an American study found that many students could not correctly identify common danger signs implying that a classmate might be contemplating suicide. However, since many adolescents who have not contemplated suicide themselves may well be observing suicidal feelings and behaviour among their peers, prevention programmes might do well to focus on all adolescents, since it has been established that organised and focused social support from school peers can have an important role in helping adolescents under stress (Bell, 1989; Hirsch and DuBois, 1992).

Considering the extent of the existing curriculum materials which teachers are required to cover, the present student/teacher ratio in Hong Kong, and the lack of school social workers and counselling/guidance teachers, it is difficult to implement suicide prevention programmes which require considerable professional resources. Piecemeal promotional pamphlets and sporadic staff development training on suicide intervention are insufficient for addressing the problem effectively (Lo, 1992). Schoolteachers and counsellors should be equipped with comprehensive knowledge and skills for assessing depression, the risk of suicide and appropriate referral of pupils who may be contemplating suicide (Bagley, 1992).

More innovative and positive approaches have to be implemented to combat the current suicide epidemic in Hong Kong schoolchildren. Nevertheless, even well prepared teachers may miss signs of severe stress and suicidal tendencies in their students, especially when class sizes are large. In our view, it is important to establish programmes of peer support for adolescents under stress, which can work in parallel with, and as an adjunct to, the counselling activities of teachers and social workers. To this end, we have developed the Health Intervention Training-Mutual Aid Network (HIT-MAN) for experimental adoption in Hong Kong secondary schools.

There is an important cultural factor aiding the adoption of systematic peer group support groups. To a much greater extent than in western cultures, Chinese students have a self-concept derived from interactions within group settings (Bond, 1986; Markus and Kitayama, 1991). A premium is placed on emphasising collective welfare and on showing a sympathetic concern for others. In Chinese culture the self is 'referential' rather than 'indexical' (Landrine, 1992). For these culturally specific reasons, the development of peer counselling should be particularly appropriate for adoption in Chinese cultural settings.

Helping the Coping Mechanisms of Students

As a means of identifying children and adolescents prone to suicidal behaviour, Blomquist (1974) proposed the creation of a 'friends network'. Every student in the school should have at least one friend upon whom to call for help. While social support systems exist informally amongst students, they have not been utilised in any formal manner in Hong Kong. Students experiencing excessive stress that can grow into a full-scale suicide crisis should be able to live and work among individuals who are sensitive to each other's distress, emotional needs and general coping behaviours. Thus, Johnson and Maile (1987) have argued that effective suicide prevention programmes for young people must almost invariably involve the use of some form of peer support or peer counselling.

Students should know where they can go for help. However, when students do not seek help directly, they must be identified and helped. It has been repeatedly observed that young people undergoing stress are more likely to communicate their feelings of pain and anxiety to other young people (Morrison, 1987; Bagley and King, 1991). The majority of adolescents talk about their problems with their friends, and only atypically with adults. The previously cited case of Wing-sze and Wai-yip clearly indicated that the young people involved (including those who knew that the couple intended to commit suicide) were afraid to approach teachers about the problem owing to uncertainty over their reaction. The traditional reaction of teachers has been to punish rather than help the children who are in trouble.

HIT-MAN

The Health Intervention Training-Mutual Aid Network (HIT-MAN) is an innovative programme developed by the present authors for experimental use in Hong Kong schools as a service for teachers and social workers facing the problems of suicidal youth, compounded by inadequate staffing and professional resources. HIT-MAN can be considered a suicide prevention programme, which helps students to identify problems of extreme stress, anxiety and suicidal feelings in their peers. Since most adolescents will turn to friends for help in time of crisis, it is logical to seek assistance from these friends from informal, but enduring and psychologically important groups long before problems become so acute that suicide is a serious option. An important assumption in this model is that children and adolescents have the ability to help others.

The objectives of HIT-MAN is to encourage youngsters both to support, and in some cases to refer, their friends who have been thinking about suicide or manifesting behaviours which indicate very poor self-esteem and signs of depression, to a trusted adult (who will also be part of the HIT-MAN training network).

In order to deal with teenage suicidal behaviour, Street and Franklin (1991) have urged that schools go beyond traditional models of teaching and intervention. HIT-MAN is a social network approach, which follows these guidelines with the primary purpose of promoting positive mental health through mutual support among students. The programme is a student-centred approach, intending to address students' needs with a minimum input from the existing teachers and other caring professionals. Through the initial formation of groups of buddies, students will be given opportunities to develop positive attitudes towards life and give each other much-needed friendly support. It is expected that the formation and continuation of such groups will be a voluntary activity for students. As students develop interest in the programme, other students can join or form groups on a voluntary basis.

In terms of suicide prevention, HIT-MAN is an early detection and intervention device. Designed not only as a programme for preventing suicide, it is also a way of helping students to address a wide range of social stressors by developing positive self-esteem based on group interactions in which sympathetic concern, praise and reward play significant roles. In contrast to programmes we have developed in England and Canada (Bagley, 1975, 1992), the HIT-MAN programme gives a direct role to students of helping each other within focused groups. In our judgement, this approach is more relevant than imported models, which may be culturally inappropriate for Chinese students.

Aims and Objectives

- To promote positive mental health among school-age children and adolescents.
- To build a low-cost early alarm system for detecting depression and suicidal behaviour.
- To facilitate interpersonal, social and leadership development.
- To create a network for mutual support among students.
- To provide additional linkage between students and teachers or other caring professionals.
- To generate a healthy team spirit within the classroom.
- To develop a trusting relationship among students and between students and teachers.

Procedures

HIT-MAN is treated as an extra-curricular activity; teachers are only required to meet each group once or twice a month – more frequently if an active crisis is reported by members. Membership of the groups is voluntary although some students whom teachers identify as having particular problems are encouraged to join. Teachers can set up one or two such teams in the class by selecting at-risk students.

Within each class, students can be divided into groups of six to eight students. Each member is taught to look for behaviours related to unhappiness, frustration, extreme difficulties, etc. Each member is assigned the role of being particularly concerned with one fellow student in the group. There is a leader in each group, and the leadership role is by rotation for a period of time, usually one month. Each group is encouraged to meet at least once a week. The group leader will report briefly to the teacher once a week – or as the condition of any group member may require. Individual members of the group have the right and the obligation to report directly to the teacher about the 'unhappy' behaviour of any particular student. Teachers are expected to meet each group at least once a month. Teachers may choose to meet with all groups on a Saturday morning (Hong Kong students have to attend school on Saturdays) for 30 to 45 minutes, or separately in other more convenient ways. Teachers give orientation, guidelines and instructional materials to group members. Students are educated in ways of identifying and reporting unhappy experiences and depressive behaviour in fellow students.

HIT-MAN works on the assumption that students probably know each other better than a teacher can ever know them. It is important to note that students are not being taught the skills of professional counselling. But they will be instructed in the techniques of being especially sensitive to the problems of their peers, and to know when to refer such problems to the teacher for further evaluation and referral as necessary.

Parallel Curriculum Content

The aim of the HIT-MAN programme is to help students to recognise and understand both their own feelings and those of others concerning suicide ideation and behaviours by the teaching of pragmatic skills such as stress management, communication, problem-solving and affect recognition. The primary objective of HIT-MAN is to enable at-risk students to develop positive attitudes, knowledge and skills concerning the problems of being a teenager in the busy and rapidly changing environment of urban Hong Kong.

Knowledge about reactions to stress, suicidal feelings and ways of communicating with others (peers and teachers) about these problems will be introduced as an element in existing education programmes.

The relevant curriculum content of these health education classes consists of the following themes: avoiding loneliness and isolation; communication skills; coping with depression; grief and loss; dating, kindness and courtesy in dealing with the opposite sex; decision making and problem-solving skills; disability and life skills; emotional development and personal well being; obligations of filial piety and parental control; how to deal with distress; improving self-concept; making friends; positive failure; positive success; relationship building; responding to suicide attempts; sex education; signs of depression; social skills training; stress management; value conflicts – traditional versus modern values.

Since the overall approach to curriculum development has to be student-centred, this curriculum may have to be adjusted so as to avoid the traditional stern didacticism, which has marked the teaching style of many Hong Kong teachers.

A national co-ordinating committee will be established as a means of providing overall training and support to the teachers on the HIT-MAN project, with the purposes of (a) nurturing linkages between teachers and students; (b) providing back-up support to the teachers; (c) monitoring the progress of the programme; (d) evaluating the programme and (e) designing and implementing changes whenever necessary.

Evaluation of the HIT-MAN programme

As with any innovative programme, HIT-MAN has an experimental basis. The use of control or comparison schools within an ecologically-based design is essential. However, it is problematic to know what indicators of success should be measured as suicide prevention programmes are notoriously difficult to evaluate (Bagley, 1968, 1973). At this stage, it is proposed to monitor levels of depression, self-esteem and suicidal ideation (using culturally appropriate measures) in a before-and-after design over the period of a school year. This initial evaluation will also address the following questions:

- Can the use of screening questionnaires completed by all students provide an effective basis for initiating HIT-MAN programmes within individual schools?
- Can the use of sociometry (identifying popular and isolated students) be a useful adjunct to HIT-MAN, for example in forming the most effective group structures?

- Will the introduction of HIT-MAN involve more work for teachers than we had originally anticipated?
- How will our approach work when teachers are unable to refer distressed students to a counsellor?
- Can HIT-MAN work without the introduction of more counsellors and social workers to counsel what is an anticipated rise in referrals? (The same problems beset the introduction of sexual abuse education programmes in British and Canadian schools – these programmes resulted in a flood of referrals to social work agencies, who were understaffed and unprepared for their new role as child abuse experts, see Bagley and King, 1991).
- What types of in-service training will be required for teachers involved in schools with the HIT-MAN programme? Can the programme work without such in-service training courses?
- Will the areas in which HIT-MAN is introduced experience an actual reduction in the amount of suicidality in comparison with control schools.

In the long term, innovations in the training of teachers are clearly necessary. All teachers must be given more training in order to help them see that it is their professional responsibility actively to prevent adolescent suicide through appropriate recognition and referral practices. One possible hindrance to HIT-MAN's implementation is the fact that teachers will not accept responsibility for supporting the role of students in giving peer support to classmates with emotional problems – either because they cannot accept the idea of greater autonomy for students and the partnership with student groups that HIT-MAN implies; or because hard-pressed and often exhausted teachers simply cannot find the initiative or energy to implement the curriculum changes which HIT-MAN involves.

All teachers should receive adequate training and professional support in the running of the HIT-MAN programme. They will be sensitised to appreciate the importance of developing not only students' academic skills, but also their positive mental health.

Will HIT-MAN have the result of increasing the locus of control of the students involved, students who have traditionally been locked into a set of authoritarian relationships between teachers and students? Will teachers themselves be able to adapt to these new roles and changes of attitude? It is important to point out that at the present time in Hong Kong there is much debate and argument amongst educators, teachers and school heads, as well as statements by politicians and newspaper editorials, on the need for increased resources and new priorities in education and social work.

Hopefully, HIT-MAN will ride successfully on the crest of this wave of changing professional and public opinion.

Conclusions

It is important to point out that the HIT-MAN support network should not just focus on students but should include teachers, counsellors, school heads, social workers, parents and other mental health professionals as consultants. The essence of such a programme is to increase awareness of and ways of coping with the problem of suicide among children and adolescents. HIT-MAN is an innovative way of dealing with student mental health problems in Hong Kong. The scope is comprehensive and will cover far more than suicidal behaviour. It is a low-cost innovation, which has the potential for counteracting problems of stress, anxiety, depression and suicidal ideas at an early stage.

References

Adeock, A., Nagy, S. and Simpson, J. (1991). Selected risk factors in adolescent suicide attempts. *Adolescence*, 26, 817–28.

Bagley, C. (1968). The evaluation of a suicide prevention scheme by an ecological method. *Social Science and Medicine*, 2, 1–14.

Bagley, C. (1973). Social policy and the prevention of suicidal behaviour. *British Journal of Social Work*, 3, 473–5.

Bagley, C. (1975). Suicidal behaviour and suicidal ideation in adolescents: a problem for counsellors in education. *British Journal of Guidance and Counselling*, 3, 190–208.

Bagley, C. (1992). Development of an adolescent stress scale for use by school counsellors: construct validity in terms of depression, self-esteem and suicidal ideation. *School Psychology International*, 13, 31–49.

Bagley, C. and King, K. (1991). *Child Sexual Abuse: The Search for Healing*. London: Routledge and Tavistock.

Bagley, C., Verma, G., Mallick, K. and Young, L. (1979). *Personality, Self-Esteem and Prejudice*. Aldershot: Gower.

Belle, D. (1989). *Children's Social Networks and Social Support*. New York: Wiley.

Blomquist, K. (1974). The school nurse's role in suicide prevention. *Journal of Psychiatric Nursing and Mental Health Services*, 12, 22–6.

Chan, D. (1995). Reasons for living among Chinese adolescents in Hong Kong. *Suicide and Life-Threatening Behavior*, 25, 347–57.

Clark, D. (1991). School-based prevention programmes. *Suicide Research Digest*, 5, 1–5.

Garfinkel, B. (1989). The components of school-based suicide prevention. *Residential Treatment for Children and Youth*, 7, 97–116.

Headley, L. (1983). Suicide in Hong Kong. In L. Headley and N. Farberow (eds), *Suicide in Asia and the Near East* (pp. 97–100). Berkeley, CA: University of California Press.

Hirsh, B. and DuBois, D. (1992). The relation of peer social support and psychological symptomatology during the transition to junior high school. *American Journal of Community Psychology*, 20, 333–47.

Ho, T. and Hung, S.F. (1998). The prevention of youth suicide: research and services. *Hong Kong Medical Journal*, 4, 195–202.

Johnson, S. and Maile, L. (1987). *Suicide and the Schools: A Handbook for Prevention, Intervention and Rehabilitation.* Springfield, IL: Charles C. Thomas.

Kwan, A.Y.H. (1988). Suicide among the elderly: Hong Kong. *Journal of Applied Gerontology*, 7, 248–59.

Landrine, H. (1992). Clinical implications of cultural differences: the referential versus the indexical self. *Clinical Psychology Review*, 12, 401–15.

Lo, A.C. (1992). Assessing high risk suicidal students in Hong Kong. Paper presented at *Managing Suicidal Students Seminar, Association of Psychology and Educational Counsellors of Asia*, Hong Kong.

Luk, S., Leung, P., Lee, P. and Leih-Mak. F. (1988). Teachers' referral of children with mental health problems: a study of primary schools in Hong Kong. *Psychology in the Schools*, 25, 121–9.

Markus, H. and Kitayama, S. (1991). Culture and the self, implications for cognition, emotion and motivation. *Psychological Review*, 98, 224–43.

Shaffer, D., Garland A. and Gould, M. (1988). Preventing teenage suicide: a critical review. *Journal of American Academy of Child and Adolescent Psychiatry*, 27, 675–87.

Shek, D. (1998). Adolescent positive mental health and psychological symptoms: a longitudinal study in a Chinese context. *Psychologia*, 41, 217–25.

Street, C. and Franklin, C. (1991). Psychological and family differences between middle class and low income dropouts: a discriminant analysis. *High School Journal*, 74, 211–19.

Tse, J.W.L., Bagley, C. and Mak, H.W. (1994). Prevention of teenage suicidal behaviour in Hong Kong. *School Psychology International*, 15, 99–114.

Wass, H., Miller, M. and Thornton, G. (1990). Death education and grief/suicide intervention in the public schools. *Death Studies*, 14, 253–68.

3 Self-Esteem in Chinese Adolescents in Hong Kong and Britain

CHRISTOPHER BAGLEY AND JOHN W.L. TSE

Summary

A comparison has been made of 364 Chinese adolescents in Hong Kong with no history of migration outside of China, with 363 Chinese adolescents who had migrated to Britain, and 381 British Europeans with no history of migration. Comparison levels of self-esteem (using the Coopersmith scale) and experience of and attitudes to school and teachers was made between the three samples. Self-esteem levels in both the British-Chinese and British-European groups were significantly better than those of the Hong Kong Chinese adolescents. An important covariate of higher levels of self-esteem was satisfaction with the school environment, and perceived levels of support from teachers. The longer that the British-Chinese youth had been in Britain, the better were their levels of self-esteem, and their satisfaction with their schools. It appears that the climate of education in Hong Kong, in which pupils are subjected to a more authoritarian model of education, is reflected to some degree in reduced self-esteem levels. These findings are consistent with those, which have identified educational pressures as one source of higher levels of suicidal ideation in secondary school students in Hong Kong.

Introduction

Self-esteem represents an individual's global evaluation of the perceived characteristics of self, and is usually stable and well formed by early adolescence (Mruk, 1999). Measured self-esteem at age 13 usually remains stable for the next two decades (Kling et al., 1999). Impaired self-esteem, or negative view of the self impairs an individual's ability to cope with stressful events, and a variety of events in childhood may themselves impair self-esteem (Coopersmith, 1967; Burns, 1982; Mruk, 1999). Adolescents with poor self-esteem are, in the face of stress, much more likely than others to become depressed and suicidal. Adolescents with low self-esteem may seek out the support of peers with an equally disillusioned view of self, and often these are deviant or disillusioned peer groups (Kaplan, 1980). Research in Hong Kong has replicated this model (Leung and Lau, 1989).

While Markus and Kitayami (1991) argue that the sources and salience of self-esteem may differ between cultures, the importance of self-esteem as a risk factor in the development of emotional disorder and mental illness is nevertheless stable between many different cultures (Bagley et al., 1999). Those results (elaborated in the next chapter) showed that the Rosenberg Self Esteem Inventory correlated 0.61 with a standardised measure of emotional disorder in 15- to 16-year-olds in Hong Kong classrooms. In the present study we present data on another well-validated self-esteem measure, the Coopersmith scale, completed by samples of Chinese adolescents in Hong Kong and Britain.

In an attempt to understand self-esteem across different cultures, Chan (2000) compared British-Chinese, British-European and Hong Kong Chinese children aged between 11 to 18 years. The findings showed that while no difference in self-esteem was observed between the British-Chinese and British-European groups, the former had significantly better self-esteem than Hong Kong Chinese children. Chan (2000) explained this difference in terms of the traditional Chinese authoritarian style of parenting, which is strict and demanding. As a consequence, the confidence of these children was likely to be impaired. At the same time, Hong Kong is a highly competitive society where parents spend relatively little time with their children. This kind of neglect, which is a rather common phenomenon, could negatively affect children's self-confidence. It is important to note that the British-Chinese participants were all of Chinese origin. They might have been born in the United Kingdom or at least settled for a lengthy period of time. This meant that the British educational system or other factors (such as the lack of academic competitiveness) might account for the difference. It would be interesting to examine the transition of the level of self-esteem among Chinese immigrants from Hong Kong through a longitudinal study. Such a study has yet to be carried out.

Research studies in Hong Kong have repeatedly come up with a consistent finding: academic pressure is the most important stressor among adolescents

(Hui, 2000; Ming Pao, 1998; Yau and Smetana, 1996). In a survey of over 2,100 form 1 to 3 students, Hui (2000) found that academic achievement was considered to be the most pressing concern. Perhaps even more striking is the fact that these students tended to attribute their difficulties to personal deficiencies. Yau and Smetana (1996) found that 16 per cent of the conflicts between parents and adolescents were due to schoolwork and academic achievement. Such a figure is higher than the result observed from European and American countries, which is generally about nine per cent. These figures reflect the relative importance Chinese parents place on academic achievement.

The Hong Kong Federation of Youth Groups carried out a survey on 537 students who were asked to rate the pressure to achieve at academic subjects (Ming Pao, 1998). When '0' refers to no pressure, and '10' refers to very high pressure, about 60 per cent rated academic achievement as 7 or above. Over 30 per cent said that when the academic results were unsatisfactory their parents would scold them, and that they felt hopeless and helpless. The pressure to achieve is so overwhelming that students, whose grades are failing, may find themselves under severe stress. Parents, who insist on setting lofty standards, and constantly criticising their children, further aggravate this process. It is against this background that students find schoolwork and study extremely discouraging and distasteful. (See Chapter 1 for more details.)

The Study Design

The main aim of this study was to see how well Chinese adolescents from Hong Kong had adapted to British culture in the waves of migration, which occurred in the years up to 1997 when Hong Kong, formerly a territory of Britain, became a special administrative region within the People's Republic of China. The study compared 364 adolescents in Hong Kong who had not migrated, 362 Chinese adolescents who had been resident for up to 15 years in Britain, and 381 adolescents of European descent in Britain: 89 per cent of the Chinese adolescents in Britain had origins in Hong Kong, but it has not been possible to separate out for analysis those with origins elsewhere (mainly Vietnam). Questionnaires in English were administered in British schools and in Chinese in the Hong Kong schools.

An initial idea explored was that the experience of migration would be traumatic for many of the Chinese adolescents now settled in Britain, since they would have to cope not only with the stress of adapting to a new set of cultural norms and practices, but also with the racism and social rejection which unfortunately exists in many sectors of British life today. This problem might be exacerbated by vulnerabilities reflecting patterns of settlement in the Chinese community, which are marked by social isolation due to patterns of economic activity (particularly, in the provision of Chinese restaurants). One restaurant will not be set up in an area served by another Chinese restaurant, for obvious economic reasons. Thus Modood and colleagues (1997) found a unique pattern of settlement of Chinese compared with other ethnic groups; 91 per cent lived in a local authority ward in which Chinese people made up less than two per cent of the population.

Thirty nine per cent of the 362 British Chinese adolescents in the present study reported that they had experienced racism 'often' or 'sometimes'. It is unclear from previous literature whether the experience of racism could diminish self-esteem, since there are many countervailing forces including ethnic pride, linked to firm cultural identity and strong family traditions, which certainly existed for the British Chinese (Verma et al., 1999).

Measuring Self-Esteem in Chinese, Chinese-British and European-British Adolescents

Self-esteem can be divided into several dimensions including those relating to characteristics in specific role performances (e.g., achievement in specific areas), factors such as complexity, consistency and salience, and the dimension of particular concern for clinicians, which involves a global or existential evaluation of the self (Campbell et al., 2000). The Coopersmith scale, for example is multidimensional, and includes two major sub-scales, one measuring this general evaluation of self, the other relating to self-evaluation in social and interpersonal relationships (Bagley and Evan-Wong, 1975; Bagley, 1989). It is the first, general evaluation scale, which we examine, in the present, clinically focussed study.

This 23-item scale contains items such as 'I wish I were someone else', 'I'm pretty happy', 'I have a low opinion of myself' and 'I can't be depended upon'. The invited responses on a 4-point scale range from 'Often' to 'Never'. Scoring of positively worded items is reversed so that the lower the score, the better the self-esteem – the theoretical range of scores is from 23 to 92.

The psychometric background to this scale is given in Bagley and Evan-Wong (1975) and Bagley (1989). In translating the Coopersmith scale for use with Chinese subjects, it is assumed that the instrument has some cross-cultural validity. There is evidence to support the idea that various measures of effect and self-evaluation do have some cross-cultural equivalence (Yang and Bond, 1990; Cheung and Bagley, 1998), although there may be additional and more complex constructs of personality, which are culturally specific (Markus and Kitayama, 1991; Yang and Bond, 1990: Mallick et al., 2000).

Results

Initial results were contrary to general hypothesis, in that self-esteem levels in both the European-British (mean 42.63, SD 8.9) and Chinese-British adolescents (mean 44.71, SD 9.4) were significantly better than those of their Hong Kong counterparts (mean 51.63, SD 10.1). Post-hoc analysis from analysis of variance ($f = 4.12, 2, 1107, p<.000$) was significant at the 1 per cent level, confirming that the Hong Kong Chinese youth (who had similar age and sex profiles to their UK counterparts) had significantly poorer self-esteem.

Specific analysis of the Chinese-British group indicated a statistically significant relationship with the time spent in Britain, and the level of self-esteem: the longer in Britain, the more likely it was that self-esteem levels were identical to those of the European-British group. The data presented in Table 3.1 illustrate this. These data indicate that the length of settlement in Britain is linked to level of self-esteem in the British-Chinese group (the correlation between self-esteem scale score and length of settlement is 0.20, $p <.001$) – the longer the period of settlement, the better the levels of self-esteem.

Were the initially lower levels of self-esteem those associated with problems of initial adjustment in British culture? If this were so, initial levels of self-esteem should be similar to or actually worse than those in the non-migrant Hong Kong Chinese youth. This is not the case however: the mean score for the 35 recently arrived youth at 47.56 indicating significantly better self-esteem than in the non-migrant Chinese youth (mean score 51.63, $n = 362$, $t = 4.55$, $p <.001$).

What factors then within the Hong Kong group might account for their lower self-esteem? This has been explored through questions relating to how Hong Kong teachers relate to students (Table 3.2). Results indicate some very clear and statistically significant differences in the cross-cultural comparisons. British Chinese respondents indicate that 'My teacher likes me' in 45 per cent of cases, compared with only 18 per cent in the Hong Kong Chinese students. No less than 69 per cent of Hong Kong students *disagree* with the statement

Table 3.1 Length of stay in Britain and responses of Chinese adolescents to selected items in the Coopersmith Self-Esteem Inventory

	Length of time in UK	Often/sometimes	Rarely/never	Total number
1 I often wish I were	< 5 years	49%	51%	35
someone else	5–10 years	38%	62%	42
	>10 years	28%	72%	276
2 I'm pretty happy	<5 years	62%	38%	34
	5–10 years	74%	26%	42
	>10 years	83%	17%	276

Note: All differences are significant at the 5% level or beyond according to Kruskal Wallis one way analysis of variance.

Table 3.2 Perceptions of teachers in contrasted cultural groups, by levels of self-esteem

	Group	SA+A	SD+D	Correlation with self-esteem
My teachers like me	UK Chinese	45%	42%	.16*
	UK Euro	36%	44%	.18*
	HK Chinese	18%	65%	.16*
I'm scared to ask my teacher questions	UK Chinese	24%	55%	.13*
	UK Euro	25%	56%	.16*
	HK Chinese	38%	54%	.15*
I'm scared if teacher asks me questions	UK Chinese	19%	53%	.13*
	UK Euro	21%	56%	.10*
	HK Chinese	32%	43%	.16*
Teachers tell me my class work is good	UK Chinese	80%	6%	.19*
	UK Europe	72%	10%	.17*
	HK Chinese	17%	69%	.13*
I've been told in class my work is poor	UK Chinese	5%	80%	.17*
	UK Euro	16%	71%	.15*
	HK Chinese	24%	44 %	.13*
Teacher tells me I am doing well	UK Chinese	73%	7%	.14*
	UK Euro	61%	16%	.16*
	HK Chinese	11%	32%	.15*

Note: 'SA+A' indicates 'Strongly agree or agree'; 'SD+D' indicates 'Strongly disagree/disagree'. A number of subjects responded 'Unknown' to the above questions – these proportions can be calculated from the above table by subtracting the responses indicated from 100. *Significance* of distributions within each group, for each question by chi-Squared, $p < .05$ or beyond. *Numbers*: UK Chinese, 362; UK European, 381; HK Chinese, 364. Significance of correlations: *$p < .03$ or beyond.

'Teachers tell me my class work is good' compared with 6 per cent of the British Chinese students. Lack of teacher encouragement is, in general associated with poorer self-esteem to a statistically significant degree, and this accounts in some measure for the self-esteem differences observed in adolescents respondents compared between Britain and Hong Kong.

Discussion

This study could not find evidence that adapting to life in Britain had been stressful for Chinese adolescents in terms of self-esteem, although the longer they were settled in Britain, the more favourable were their levels of self-esteem. However, recently arrived adolescents from Hong Kong had self-esteem levels, which were significantly higher than those of Chinese adolescents in Hong Kong who had not migrated. Adolescents in Hong Kong clearly relate to their teachers differently, and this may be a factor, which brings its own stresses, in terms of diminished self-esteem.

While there may be other sources of stress, which act to diminish self-esteem levels in Hong Kong adolescents (see Bagley et al., 1999 and the following chapter), there is clearly an association between teacher criticism of a pupil and his or her self-esteem level (the association applies equally to boys and girls). While the association is partial, there are no grounds for assuming that the association is not a causal one. It is well established in the self-esteem literature (Coopersmith, 1967 and 1975; Burns, 1982; Lawrence, 1996) that how a teacher relates to a pupil is one factor in elevating or depressing self-esteem. Put simply, excessive use of criticism, and lack of praise can over a long period of time depress an individual's self-confidence, and self-esteem. Not all pupils in a classroom are criticised or blamed to an equal extent, and probably secondary school teachers in Hong Kong are offering praise and blame for scholastic work rather than for good or bad behaviour such as class disruption, as would be the case in the British classroom.

The role of the Hong Kong teacher has been elaborated by Sham (1999): 'Hong Kong pupils treat their teachers as stern parents. They respond to them with silence, attention, fear and obedience' (p. 130). Sham cites Morris (1981): 'Questioning teachers or challenging teachers' judgements is considered unacceptable behaviour.' Another aspect of Hong Kong education is the much greater emphasis on examination taking and success, in comparison with British schools. Thus Fong's (1991) study reported that in their striving for examination successes, Hong Kong teachers 'are less concerned about their pupils as persons' – Hong Kong teachers seem to be autocratic and do not perceive that learning could be a pleasurable process. Sham (1999) observes: 'The Chinese teaching style is extremely formal, even from the earliest experience in kindergarten. Imagine entering a nursery age class – the 30–35 chairs and desks are arranged in uniform rows, nursery age children sit quietly or are holding a pencil trying to write their Chinese name, there are no toys or paint brushes' (p. 131).

Morris (1981) described the Hong Kong secondary school system '... a teaching and learning style which is characterised by being didactic, teacher-centred and theoretical. Rote learning, memorisation of passages, a strict adherence to the examination syllabus are the rule rather than the exception ... The pupil's role is that of a passive receiver of knowledge and diligence is perceived as the primary condition of success' (pp. 257–9). It is notable that there does not seem to exist in Chinese tradition the idea of innate abilities. The child who fails to succeed in educational achievement and examinations is sometimes thought to be lazy and lacking in moral character. The parents of the failing child may enrol him or her with a private tutor or class, so that in addition to a large amount of homework the child will also have to attend a tutor for part of the evening, and there will be little time for leisure or play.

What might counter the burdened life of the child in Hong Kong is a strong and supportive family system, which (as Coopersmith showed in his American work) should act as a buffer to the negative pressures surrounding educational achievement. However, when family life is dysfunctional or disrupted the Hong Kong child's ego may be under severe pressure, and as well as diminished self-esteem, depression and suicidal feelings may result, as will be seen in the next chapter.

References

Bagley, C. (1989). Development and validity of a short self-esteem measure for use with adults in community mental health surveys. *Psychological Reports*, 65, 13–14.

Bagley, C. and Evan-Wong, L. (1975). Neuroticism and extraversion in responses to Coopersmith's self-esteem inventory. *Psychological Reports*, 36, 253–4.

Bagley, C., Mallick, K., Bolitho, F., Bertrand, L., Madrid, S. and Tse, J. (1999). Adjustment, stress and family life in adolescents in Canada, Britain, Hong Kong, India, Pakistan and The Philippines. *International Journal of Adolescence and Youth*, 7, 263–78.

Burns, R. (1982). *Self-Concept Development and Education*. London: Chapman.
Campbell, J., Assanand, S. and DiPaula, A. (2000). Structural features of the self-concept and adjustment. In A. Tesser, R. Felson and J. Suls (eds), *Psychological Perspectives on Self and Identity* (pp. 67–87). Washington, DC: American Psychological Association.
Chan, Y.M. (2000). Self-esteem: a cross-cultural comparison of British-Chinese, White British and Hong Kong Chinese children. *Educational Psychology*, 20, 59–74.
Cheung, C.-K. and Bagley, C. (1998). Validating an American scale in Hong Kong: The Center for Epidemiological Studies Depression Scale. *Journal of Psychology*, 132, 169–86.
Coopersmith, S. (1967). *The Antecedents of Self-Esteem*. San Francisco: Freeman.
Coopersmith, S. (1975). Self-concept, race and education. In G. Verma and C. Bagley (eds), *Race and Education Across Cultures* (pp. 145–67). London: Heinemann.
Fong, Y. (1981). *Teachers' and Pupils' Perceptions of Effective Geography Teaching in Hong Kong Schools*. University of Hong Kong, MEd thesis.
Hui, E.K.P. (2000). Personal concerns and their causes: perceptions of Hong Kong Chinese adolescent students. *Journal of Adolescence*, 23, 189–203.
Kaplan, H. (1980). *Self-Attitudes and Deviant Behavior*. Santa Monica, CA: Goodyear.
Kling, K., Hyde, J., Showers, C. and Buswell, B. (1999). Gender differences in self-esteem: a meta-analysis. *Psychological Bulletin*, 125, 470–500.
Lawrence, D. (1996). *Enhancing Self-Esteem in the Classroom*. Eastbourne: Holt, Rinehart and Winston.
Leung, K. and Lau, S. (1989). Effects of self-concept and perceived disapproval of delinquent behavior in school-children. *Journal of Youth and Adolescence*, 18, 345–59.
Llewellyn, J. (1982). *A Perspective on Education in Hong Kong: Report of a Visiting Panel*. Hong Kong: Government Secretariat.
Mallick, K., Bagley, C. and Verma, G. (2000). Models of cross-cultural psychology: how British and Indian adolescents view themselves and their family life. *Indian Journal of Psychological Issues*, 8, 24–32.
Markus, H. and Kitayama, S. (1991). Culture and self: implications for cognition, emotion and motivation. *Psychological Bulletin*, 98, 224–53.
Ming Pao (1998/11/24). Younger pupils are experiencing academic pressure. *Ming Pao* (in Chinese).
Modood, T., Berthoud, R., Lakey, J., Nazroo, J., Smith, P., Virdee, E. and Beishon, S. (1997). *Ethnic Minorities in Britain*. London: Policy Studies Institute.
Morris, P. (1981). The adoption of the formal doctrine of an imported curriculum innovation. *Journal of Curriculum Studies*, 3, 257–9.
Mruk, C. (1999). *Self Esteem: Research, Theory and Practice*. London: Free Association Books.
Sham, S. (1999). Qualitative study of Chinese families in Britain. In G. Verma (ed.), *Chinese Adolescents in Britain and Hong Kong: Identity and Aspirations* (pp. 124–66). Aldershot: Ashgate.

Verma, G., Chan, Y.-M., Bagley, C., Sham, S., Darby, D., Woodrow, D. and Skinner, G. (1999). *Chinese Adolescents in Britain: Identity and Aspirations*. Aldershot: Ashgate.

Yang, K.-S. and Bond, M. (1990). Exploring implicit personality theories with indigenous or imported constructs: the Chinese case. *Journal of Personality and Social Psychology*, 59, 1087–95.

Yau, J. and Smetana, J. (1996). Adolescent-parent conflict among Chinese adolescents in Hong Kong. *Child Development*, 67, 1262–75.

4 Role of Family and Community Stress in Suicidal Ideas and Behaviour

CHRISTOPHER BAGLEY AND JOHN W.L. TSE

Summary

Findings from a comparative study of some 1,400 adolescents aged 15 to 16 in Canada, Britain and Hong Kong are presented. The Hong Kong Chinese males and females had about the same levels of suicidal ideation as their Canadian and British counterparts. However, both Chinese males and females have rather more responses indicating frequency of self-harm. Correlates of the suicidality scale (combining indicators of ideas and behaviours) in the Hong Kong sample indicate that perceived family discord is associated with suicidality in both males and females. For females, physical and sexual harassment in school, community and home was also linked to suicidality. These findings underscore the fact that a stable and supportive family climate is an important factor in suicide prevention, and its absence is a factor in suicidal risk.

Introduction

In the previous chapter we showed that Chinese adolescents in Hong Kong had significantly poorer self-esteem than did European-British students of similar age, and of Chinese-British students. These differences were attributed to the amount of educational pressure experienced by Hong Kong Chinese students, pressures which were often not alleviated by teacher understanding or support. In the present chapter we report findings from a separate study that has compared Canadian, British and Hong Kong students in a study relating self-esteem and suicidality to perceptions of family life. It would be worthwhile to examine the degree to which family discord and community stress affect adolescents' suicidal behaviour, since these factors are generally ignored in Chinese society.

On a theoretical basis, traumatic events such as physical and sexual abuse may be so overwhelming that adolescents are unable to apply coping strategies. As a consequence, vulnerable adolescents may be so upset and psychologically disorganised that they enter into a crisis state, which is characterised by discouragement, depression and despair (Brock, Sandoval and Lewis, 1996). Studies of physical abuse have indicated that a significant number of adolescents with suicidal behaviour have a history of being physically abused (Koss, 1993; Garnefski and Diekstra, 1997). Given the fact that corporal punishment is unlawful in Hong Kong, the chance of being physically abused in school is relatively low. But studies have revealed that physical punishment is widely practised as a method of discipline, which is applied by parents even to adolescents.

Lau, Liu, Cheung, Yu and Wong (1999), in a survey of over 3,300 secondary school students, found that 6.6 per cent had been beaten by family members (sometimes even for unknown reasons) in the past three months. Tang (1996) surveyed 136 university students between 17 and 18 years old. Results indicated that despite their age and status, 62.5 per cent had been verbally abused, 13.2 per cent suffered mild physical abuse while 8.5 per cent suffered severe physical abuse in the previous 12 months. In a research study on attitudes of Chinese parents, 90 per cent of those interviewed considered it appropriate to scold children for their mistakes and 50 per cent admitted that corporal punishment was being administered at home (Against Child Abuse, 1986). In a culture where filial piety is considered a virtue, it is understandable that parents may choose more extreme means of exerting their influence with an intention of making their children comply absolutely with their wishes.

In the West, research studies have repeatedly shown that people who have been sexually abused in childhood or even adulthood, and regardless of the gender of the victim, are more likely to exhibit suicidal behaviour (Dhaliwal, Gauzas, Antonowicz and Ross, 1996; Stepakoff, 1998). In a study of 19 Chinese females, who had been sexually abused, ages ranging from 6 to 24, Luo (1998) found that these victims were characterised by four distinct factors: traumatic sexualisation, betrayal, disempowerment, and stigmatisation with accompanying negative psychological impact. Traumatic sexualisation refers to psychological impacts such as confusion about sexual identity, and aversion to intimacy, while at the other extreme, some engaged in compulsive sexual behaviour, promiscuity and even prostitution. Betrayal-induced psychological impacts may include depression, grief, hostility and mistrust of men. Disempowerment refers to anxiety and fear and perception of self as a victim. Sexually abused females may also experience stigmatisation, including guilt and shame over loss of virginity, lowered self-esteem, self-imposed social isolation, and sense of difference from others. At present, no researchers have directly studied the impact of physical and sexual abuse on suicidal ideas and behaviours in Chinese adolescents.

It is generally agreed that social support, especially from family and close friends, can be considered as a buffer against severe stress and suicidal behaviour (Tse, 2000). However, in a cross-cultural comparison of students' stress in China, Japan and Korea, results show that even though Chinese students had more stressors and experiences the highest level of stress, they were the least active in coping with the stress (Kam, Won, Liu, Liu and Kitanishi, 1997). The role of social support in alleviating stress and depression may sometimes be rather complicated. In a study of 249 Chinese adolescents, social support was found to have a mitigating effect on depression only under high stress levels (Cheng, 1997). Such findings have important clinical implications for counsellors and social workers, who might mobilise social network to aid the individual in distress.

The traditional Chinese place great emphasis on the cohesion and harmony of the family. After a day of hard work, it is important for family members to gather together and enjoy supper. In the West, dinner tables are generally rectangular in shape, which literally gives special significance to the head of table who is the bread-winner. In the Chinese culture, dinner tables are circular which is more convenient for the head of the household to exercise 'control.' Very often, dinner time is the time for socialisation and conveying parental expectations. In the study of over 2,100 Chinese adolescents in Hong Kong and China, findings indicated that quarrels, worry over finances in the family, parental expectations of better academic performance, parental and sibling hassles were significantly related to adolescents' distress (Ngai and Cheung, 2000). With the decline of the extended family in Hong Kong, where the average family size is now only 2.7 persons, the role of family as a buffer against distress may be somewhat different and, therefore, should be further explored.

The rapid increase of divorce in Hong Kong, which represents widespread disintegration of families, is particularly worrying. In 1983, there were 3,734 divorce petitions to the court. In 1999 the number jumped to 12,732, representing an increase of 241 per cent in the last 16 years (Social Welfare Department, 2000). These figures indicate that increasingly more children and adolescents are raised by single parents. The rapid rise of divorce petition also reflects the instability of family in the local Hong Kong context.

These family breakdowns and disharmonies may be the tip of an iceberg. Many more children and adolescents could be experiencing distress and may be subjected to family discord and conflict. In a Hong Kong study, researchers found that a lack of parental understanding and peer acceptance were the two strongest variables in predicting depression among adolescents (Stewart, Betson, Lam, Chung, Ho and Chung, 1999). Findings from another research study revealed that the level of suicide ideation of teenage Chinese girls were affected by perceptions of low parental caring and high conflict with parents (Stewart, Lam, Betson and Chung, 1999). Family disagreements and frequent disputes indicate that the social environment is far from ideal for children and adolescents. Taking the above statistics and research findings together, it seems that many adolescents in Hong Kong are living in families which are not fully functioning in terms of child support and socialisation. This may, in turn, have negative psychological impacts. Those under stress may be at greater risk for experiencing the trauma of stressful events such as physical and sexual abuse and their sequels, suicidal ideas and behaviour.

Context of the Study, Measures and Subjects

The base line for this study was an epidemiological study of Canadian adolescents, which established normative values and correlations of a variety of stress factors, and adjustment in 2,100 school students aged 14 to 18 (Bagley et al., 1995). For the purposes of the comparative analysis with school students in Britain and China we have abstracted the data from the Canadian study on students aged 15 to 16, the age group focussed on in the comparative work. The following measures were compared between the three cultures.

The Ontario Child Health Scales

These are self-completion scales measuring adolescent adjustment, developed for the Ontario Child Health Study, and validated against psychiatric criteria (Sanford et al., 1992). These scales have been further validated in Britain (Place et al., 1999). The scale includes four sub-scales. Because of strong correlation between some of the sub-scales they have been combined into two scales: emotional disorder, depression and somatic disorders; and aggression, conduct disorder, and hyperactivity. Included in the first scale are the questions: 'I think about killing myself' and 'I deliberately try to hurt or kill myself' with the invited responses 'Never, Sometimes, Often'. These items relating to suicidality have been analysed separately.

The Rosenberg Self-Esteem Scale

This 10-item scale is the most widely used instrument in North America, and has demonstrated construct validity in Canada (Bagley et al., 1997). It also has construct validity in Britain (Bagley and Mallick, 2000), and the validity of the scale has also been established for a Chinese language translation (Leung and Lau, 1989). A high score on this scale measures positive self-regard.

Family Discord

This has been measured by the summary scale of the McMaster Family Assessment Device (FAD), a widely used instrument with established cross-cultural validity based on a well-established model of family functioning (Miller et al., 2000). The scale measures both negative and positive descriptions of family life (e.g., 'There are a lot of bad feelings in our family' and 'In our family we confide in one another'). Direction of scoring means that a high score on the FAD indicates negative perceptions of family life by the adolescents. Further validity data for the FAD has emerged in cross-cultural work (Bagley et al., 2001).

School Stress

This was measured by questions about events of theft or damage to the student's property, and physical and sexual harassment (Bagley et al., 1995). Questions about stress and pressure relating to school work, stress and examinations were not asked in the original Canadian study, and no data on this latter kind of stress exists for the Chinese sample.

Home and Community Stress

These questions were the same as those asked about school stress (theft and damage of property; physical and sexual assaults on person) except that these were events, which did *not* occur in school. Since the exact location was not specified, there is no certainty that these events occurred within the home, although it is known that physical and sexual abuse of children within their own families does occur, and can be particularly damaging in its psychological effects (Bagley and Mallick, 2000).

All of the questionnaires were administered in school classes, in a group setting, taking less than 40 minutes to complete. Questionnaires for Chinese students were translated into Chinese, and survived the reliability test of back-translation (translated back into English by a different translator with comparison of meanings with the original questionnaires). Schools in Alberta, Canada were drawn from a stratified, random sample of all schools. Schools in Britain were four state secondary schools in urban areas of the north and south of England. Schools in China were four public secondary schools in Sha Tin, Hong Kong.

Results

Table 4.1 presents the proportions in each culture, which 'sometimes' or 'frequently' report suicidal thoughts, and suicidal actions in the previous six months. At least 13 per cent of both females and males in each culture have had suicidal thoughts. Rates for self-harm are higher in females than in males, with some 13 per cent of females in each culture reporting such behaviour. However, the distribution of responses between the 'sometimes' and 'frequently' categories are different when Chinese males and females are compared with adolescents in other cultures. Chinese females are significantly more likely than all other respondents ($p < .05$, by chi-squared) to respond 'often' rather that 'sometimes' to questions about suicidal thoughts, and self-harm.

Table 4.2 shows that there are several statistically significant links between emotional and conduct disorders, better self-esteem, and suicidality with the measures of family discord, and stress in various contexts. Family discord has the highest correlations, and in every case for both males and females these correlations are significant at the one per cent level or beyond. While suicidality (combination of questions on suicidal ideas and action) is harder to predict, the correlation between the McMaster FAD and suicidality is 0.19 for males, and 0.21 for females in the Hong Kong sample.

School harassment has a negative impact on the self-esteem of females, and also accounts for some of their suicidal ideas and actions. Stress in the form of physical and sexual harassment in home and community is also linked to some degree to impaired self-esteem, and suicidality in females. The

Table 4.1 Comparison of 15–16-year-old adolescents in three cultures on suicide scale items

	Canadian males		British males		HK Chinese males	
'I think about killing myself'	Never:	82.5%	Never	84.8%	Never	79.3%
	Sometimes	14.5%	Sometimes	15.1%	Sometimes	12.9%
	Often	2.5%	Often	2.0%	Often	4.1%
Numbers	400		198		217	
	Canadian females		**British females**		**HK Chinese females**	
'I think about killing myself'	Never	76.1%	Never	74.0%	Never	82.9%
	Sometimes	19.2%	Sometimes	19.9%	Sometimes	7.3%
	Often	4.2%	Often	4.6%	Often	6.3%
Numbers	401		196		205	
	Canadian males		**British males**		**HK Chinese males**	
'I deliberately try to hurt or kill myself'	Never	91.7%	Never	92.4%	Never	87.1%
	Sometimes	6.0%	Sometimes	5.0%	Sometimes	7.4%
	Often	1.2%	Often	1.5%	Often	3.2%
Numbers	400		198		217	
	Canadian females		**British females**		**HK Chinese females**	
'I deliberately try to hurt or kill myself'	Never	86.3%	Never	86.3%	Never	82.9%
	Sometimes	11.0%	Sometimes	9.7%	Sometimes	7.3%
	Often	2.2%	Often	2.5%	Often	6.3%
Numbers	401		196		205	

Note: Questions ask about feelings and behaviour in past 6 months. Percentages in above tables do not round to 100% since non-responders have been calculated as a proportion of those asked, but not included in table. The proportion not responding can be calculated by subtracting the given proportions from 100.

Table 4.2 Correlations of family, school and other stress with adjustment and suicidality in Chinese adolescents

	Emotional/ somatic disorder		**Conduct disorder/ Hyperactivity**		**Self-esteem**		**Suicidality**	
	M	**F**	**M**	**F**	**M**	**F**	**M**	**F**
	217	205	217	205	217	205	217	205
Family discord (FAD)	.29 **	36 **	.30 **	.36 **	-.36 **	-.33 **	.19 *	.21 **
School stress (harassment)	.25 **	.17 **	.23 **	.04	.04	-.11 *	.06	.13 *
Home/community stress(harassment)	.06	.29 **	.18 **	.21 **	.01	-.19 **	.03	.19 **

Notes

1 'FAD' indicates McMaster Family Assessment Device. 'Harassment' indicates physical and/or sexual harassment.
2 *p <.05>.01. ** p <.01.

measures of family discord (FAD) and of harassment in school and elsewhere have relatively small but statistically significant correlations with one another in the expected direction in both sexes.

In Table 4.3 we show the inter-correlations of the measures of stress and family discord, and the degree to which in combination they predict suicidality, in the Hong Kong sample. Both multiple correlations are significant, the strongest (0.31) being for females. While this correlation explains only some ten per cent of the variance in the measure of suicidality, as correlations go in community psychology, this is quite high (Bagley and Ramsay, 1997).

Discussion and Conclusions

While the levels of suicidal ideation in males across the three national groups show some similarity, the Chinese males are more than twice as likely to report actual acts of self-harm. However, the overall proportions reporting such behaviour is small, and differences could be due to random variations. Chinese females do have significantly higher self-reported rates of deliberate self-harm than their British and Canadian counterparts, including more who 'often' engage in such behaviour as opposed to 'sometimes' engaging in self-harm. The present results also show that females are about twice as likely to report they 'deliberately try to hurt or kill myself' than males in Hong Kong. Such findings are consistent with hospital emergency room-based research on attempted suicide, where a female to male ratio of 3:1 was observed (Chiu, 1989). The present findings are similar to a research study carried out in the United States where the female to male ratio in adolescent attempted suicide is about 3:1 (Canetto, 1997). These findings are consistent with the literature showing significantly elevated rates of completed suicide in young Chinese women, compared with those on Western countries, and Australia (Ruzicka, 1998; Chiang, 2000; Lee, 2000).

In Chinese culture, where female chastity is considered a great virtue, sexual harassment and assault may have severe negative impacts on the victims. The consequences can be traumatic and devastating (Luo, 1998). When physical and sexual harassment happened and the victims did not have positive family support, they became even more vulnerable. These adolescents might resort to using self-harm as a means of releasing anxiety and relieving distress. It is important therefore that suicide prevention programmes should be addressed not only to the specific needs of young males, but also to the needs of young women and adolescents as well. Identifying and reaching adolescents

Table 4.3 Multiple correlation of family, school and other stress from harrassment with suicidality in Chinese adolescents

	FAD stress in: school	home		Correlation with suicidality (217 males)	Correlation with suicidality (205 females)
FAD	–	.06	.21	.19	.21
School stress	.05	–	.23	.06	.13
Home/community stress	.16	.19	–	.03	.19
				Multiple correlation .22	Multiple correlation .31

Notes

1 'FAD' indicates McMaster Family Assessment Device. 'Harassment' indicates physical and/or sexual harassment.
2 In column 2, correlations for females are above the diagonal, for males below the diagonal.
3 *p <.05>.01. **p <.01.

at the stages of suicidal ideation, and self-harm, which does not have lethal intent, is also very important.

For the Chinese adolescents in the present sample, the combinations of family discord, and physical and sexual harassment in school, community and home are in combination, particularly likely to be associated with elevated rates of suicidal ideas and behaviour. While stress due to problems with school work was not measured in this sample, when we consider the findings from the previous chapter it is likely that when school-work stress is added to other forms of stress (family discord, and harassment) higher rates of suicidal ideas and behaviour are particularly likely to occur.

References

Against Child Abuse. (1986). *How Residents in Tung Mun Raise Children*. Hong Kong: Against Child Abuse (in Chinese).

Bagley, C., Bolitho, F. and Bertrand, L. (1995). Mental health profiles, suicidal behavior, and community sexual assault in 2112 Canadian adolescents. *Adolescence*, 32, 361–6.

Bagley, C., Bolitho, F. and Bertrand, L. (1997). Norms and construct validity of the Rosenberg Self-Esteem scale in Canadian high school populations. *Canadian Journal of Counselling*, 31, 82–92.

Bagley, C., Bolitho, F., Bertrand, L. and Mallick, K. (2001). Discrepant parent-adolescent views on family functioning: predictors of poorer self-esteem and problems of emotion and behaviour in British and Canadian adolescents. *Journal of Comparative Family Studies*, in press.

Bagley, C. and Mallick, K. (2000). Prediction of sexual, emotional and physical maltreatment and mental health outcomes in a longitudinal cohort of 290 adolescent women. *Child Maltreatment*, 218–26.

Bagley, C. and Ramsay, R. (1997). *Suicidal Behaviour in Adolescents and Adults: Research, Taxonomy and Prevention*. Aldershot: Ashgate.

Brock, S.E., Sandoval, J. and Lewis, S. (1996). *Preparing for Crises in the Schools: A Manual for Building School Crisis Response Teams*. Brandon, Vermont: Clinical Psychology Publishing Co.

Canetto, S. (1997). Meanings of gender and suicidal behavior during adolescence. *Suicide and Life-Threatening Behavior*, 27, 339–51.

Cheng, S. (1997). Role of perceived social support on depression in Chinese adolescents: a prospective study examining the buffering model. *Journal of Applied Social Psychology*, 27, 800–20.

Chiang, C.W. (2000). *Suicide Figures in Hong Kong 1999*. Hong Kong: The Samaritan Befrienders.

Chiu, L.P.W. (1989). Attempted suicide in Hong Kong. *Acta Psychiatrica Scandanavica*, 79, 425–30.

Dhaliwal, G.K., Gauzas, L., Antonowicz, D.H. and Ross, R. (1996). Adult male survivors of childhood sexual abuse: prevalence, sexual abuse characteristics, and long-term effects. *Clinical Psychology Review*, 16, 619–39.

Garnesfski, N. and Diekstra, R.F. (1997). Child sexual abuse and emotional and behavioural problems in adolescence: gender differences. *Journal of the American Academy of Child and Adolescent Psychiatry*, 36, 323–9.

Kam, K. I., Won, H., Liu, X., Liu, P. and Kitanishi, K. (1997). Students' stress in China, Japan and Korea: a transcultural study. *International Journal of Social Psychiatry*, 43, 87–94.

Koss, M.P. (1993). Rape: scope, impact, interventions, and public policy responses. *American Psychologist*, 48, 1062–9.

Lau, J.T.F., Liu, J.L.Y., Cheung, J.C.K., Yu, A. and Wong, C.K. (1999). Prevalence and correlates of physical abuse in Hong Kong Chinese adolescents: a population-based approach. *Child Abuse and Neglect*, 23, 549–57.

Lee, S. (2000). Suicide in young Chinese women. (Letter). *British Medical Journal*, April 21, 1–2.

Leung, K. and Lau, S. (1989). Effects of self-concept and perceived disapproval of delinquent behavior in school children. *Journal of Youth and Adolescence*, 18, 345–59.

Luo, T. (1998). Sexual abuse trauma among Chinese survivors. *Child Abuse and Neglect*, 22, 1013–26.

Miller, I., Ryan, C., Keitner, G., Bishop, D. and Epstein, N. (2000). The McMaster approach to families: theory, assessment, treatment and research. *Journal of Family Therapy*, 22, 168–89.

Ngai, N.P. and Cheung, C.K. (2000). Family stress on adolescents in Hong Kong and the mainland of China. *International Journal of Adolescence and Youth*, 8, 183–206.

Place, M., Martin, E., Hildreth, A., Wilson, J. and Hulsmeier, J. (1999). Validating the Ontario Child Health Scale in a UK population. *European Child and Adolescent Psychiatry*, 8, 255–9.

Rudzicka, L. (1998). Suicide in countries and areas of the ESCAP region. *Asia-Pacific Population Journal*, 13, 55–74.

Sanford, M., Offord, D., Boyle, M. and Pearce, A. (1992). Ontario Child Health Study: social and school impairments in children aged 6 to 16 years. *Journal of the American Academy of Child and Adolescent Psychiatry*, 199, 60–67.

Social Welfare Department (2000). Statistics on divorce petitions. (Personal communication).

Stepakoff, S. (1998). Effects of sexual victimisation on suicidal ideation and behavior in U.S. college women. *Suicide and Life-Threatening Behavior*, 28, 107–26.

Stewart, S.M., Betson, C.L., Lam, T.H., Chung, S.F., Ho, H.H. and Chung, T.C.F. (1999). The correlates of depressed mood in adolescents in Hong Kong. *Journal of Adolescent Health*, 25, 27–34.

Stewart, S.M., Lam, T.H., Betson, C. and Chung, S.F. (1999). Suicide ideation and its relationship to depressed mood in a community sample of adolescents in Hong Kong. *Suicide and Life-Threatening Behavior*, 29, 227–40.

Tang, C.S.K. (1996). Adolescent abuse in Hong Kong Chinese families. *Child Abuse and Neglect*, 20, 873–8.

Tse, J.W.L. (2000). *Youth Suicide: Facts, Prevention and Crisis Management.* Hong Kong: The Chinese University Press (in Chinese).

Zerin, E., Zerin, M. and Cuiran, Z. (1997). A comparative study of Chinese and American high school students' responses to stress under pressure. *Transactional Analysis Journal*, 27(4), 241–55.

5 The Suicidal Risk Scale for Hong Kong Students

JOHN W.L.TSE, CHRISTOPHER BAGLEY AND
ANTHONY MUK-LEUNG YAU

Summary

In the face of a rising youth suicide rate amongst Chinese youth in Hong Kong, all potential risk factors should be examined, as well as particular psychological indicators of the manifestation of sub-lethal suicidal behaviour, and associated attitudes to self and others, and to suicide itself. Secondary school students frequently experience feelings of suicidality before attempting any such act, and these feelings and associated psychological distress, and the measurement of these feelings along with the identification of potential risk factors is a crucially important task. The identification of pre-suicidal traits and risk factors by means of questionnaires completed by adolescents is the object of the Suicidal Risk Scale (SRS). In constructing a screening instrument for measuring suicidal risk, we explored and adapted several Western instruments. Measures of suicidal risk in the interpersonal environment were academic stress (5 items); family problems (15 items); and interpersonal difficulties (18 items); measures of anger-impulsivity (13 items); depression (11 items); and suicidal ideation (13 items) identified psychological dimensions of suicidal risk. After piloting, these instruments were completed by 595 males and 707 females in forms 1 to 4 of several secondary schools. Females, as expected, displayed more suicidal ideation, planning for suicide, and suicide attempts at some time in the past, than did males. The measures of suicidal proneness and suicidal risk had good internal reliability, and test-retest correlation, and their internal structure was confirmed by principal component analysis. Analysis of variance confirmed that the measures in the SRS strongly discriminated between those with none, occasional and frequent suicidal ideation. Guidelines for the use of the SRS by teachers and school counsellors are outlined, with suggestions for future research.

Introduction

In the past two decades the problem of suicide has aroused considerable public attention and concern in Hong Kong. In 1995, suicide ranked sixth in the leading causes of death in the whole population. With a rate of 4.7 and 1.2 per 100,000, suicide became the first and second leading cause of death in the 15–19 and 10–14 age groups respectively (Yip, 1998). It is a common belief that the rate of teenage suicide is rising rapidly, and that the epidemic of teenage suicide is shifting towards those of a younger age. Others (for instance, Hau, 1993 and Pritchard, 1993) have argued that the suicide rate of children and adolescents has been rather low and stable.

Official data show that in the past twenty years, the rate of teenage and young adult suicide in Hong Kong was rather steady, the average rate being 11.3 per 100,000 population. (Hau, 1993). This rate is not high when compared to other countries (see Diekstra, 1990, and Pritchard, 1993). However, we cannot argue that teenage suicide is not a serious problem. In 1996, for instance, the official data reported that there were 38 completed suicides for persons under 20. The number of 'undetermined' and suspicious cases of death in the under twenty group was 38 (Hong Kong Coroner's Report, 1997). Hence, it is reasonable to suggest that if 'undetermined' cause of death were to be included, the number of teenage suicides would be significantly higher. This view is compatible with Western epidemiological studies, which show that a more accurate rate of suicide is obtained by adding formal suicide verdicts to the numbers of undetermined deaths, and what we have termed 'careless death' resulting in 'accidents' of various kinds (Bagley and Ramsay, 1997).

Unfortunately due to a lack of standard definition of attempted suicide, there are no official reports on attempted suicide among children and adolescents in Hong Kong. In a study by Fong (1993), out of 316 aged 12 to 14 surveyed, 12 (3.8 per cent) reported having had attempted suicide in the past.

Another 88 students (28 per cent) reported having once thought that 'life was not worth living', while 16 per cent currently had such an idea: 32 per cent reported that they had either prior or current suicidal impulses, or both. In another Hong Kong study Ho, Lee and Ho (1994) surveyed 225 adolescents, and found that 132 respondents (58.7 per cent) reported having had thought of suicide while 13 respondents (5.8 per cent) reported that they had engaged in deliberate self-harm.

In a survey of 563 students from 19 secondary schools, 189 students (33.6 per cent) had thought about suicide, with 16 students (2.8 per cent) had frequent thoughts about suicide. Another 60 students (10.7 per cent) reported self-injury (e.g., slashing oneself, deliberately harming oneself), 42 students (7.5 per cent) had a prior suicide attempt, and one student (0.2 per cent) made frequent suicide attempts (Chan, Wong, Ip and Tsui, 1993). In view of these data, it is reasonable to suggest that the official data might have underestimated the rate of teenage suicidal behaviour in Hong Kong and that many children and adolescents are being at high-risk of suicide.

Although many people believe that academic stress and family conflicts are the major contributors to the seemingly rising youth suicide, the causes of suicidal behaviours among the Hong Kong children and adolescents have not been clearly delineated in systematic work. Studies of Western populations generally suggest that suicidal behaviours are related to depressed mood state, negative expectation about the future, rigid thinking style, family conflicts, breakdown of relationships, and loss of significant others (see Brent, 1995, and Shaffer and Piacentini, 1994 for detailed reviews).

Because of obvious cultural differences, it is inappropriate to apply mechanically the findings from Western society to the Hong Kong teenage population. But local studies do suggest that youthful suicidal behaviour in Hong Kong is probably caused or triggered by psychosocial stressors. For example, Fong (1993) found that increased risk of suicidality was associated with self-reported feelings of lacking parental care and understanding, conflicts with parents, non-harmonious family, unhappy school life, having lots of worries, having a swinging mood, becoming tired easily, and absence of emotional support from family and friends. In addition, Ho et al. (1994) reported that among those having suicide ideation in the past two years, 23 per cent reported that the main reason was poor family relationship, while 17 per cent reported love affairs as their main reason, and 11 per cent reported parental neglect as the main reason. In the same study, participants with suicidal behaviour reported that they had displayed certain affective and behavioural symptoms of suicide including depressed state, loss of interests, irritation, confusion, being withdrawn, and trying to communicate their problems to peers and family.

Taking these various research findings together, one can draw an early conclusion that suicidal behaviours among children and adolescents may be triggered basically by psychosocial factors, and that the at-risk children and adolescents are displaying a wide range of detectable, but often neglected, signs and symptoms. In this model teenage suicide is by no means inevitable provided that we could effectively detect the relevant signs of suicidal risk, and then involve the at-risk individuals in an intervention programme which is effective in managing those psychosocial factors triggering their risk of suicide.

The present study attempts to develop an objective and culturally sensitive measurement of suicidal risk. This Chapter deals with the first step in effective prevention of teenage suicide: screening and identification. Psychologists, social workers and teachers could use the assessment scale in large-scale school-based screening of youth in Hong Kong. At present there are no locally developed intruments for assessing the risk of suicide. This lack of a measurement tool has seriously handicapped the efforts of psychiatrists, psychologists, councellors, social workers, and school teachers in trying to design and evaluate prevention and intervention programmes for suicidal youth. The limited instruments that local mental health and education professionals might use are those imported from Western culture, specifically from the United States. Some of the frequently used measures include the Scale for Suicide Ideation (Beck, Kovacs and Weissman, 1979), Beck Depression Inventory (Beck, Ward, Mendelson, Mock and Erbaugh, 1961), Beck Hopelessness Scale (Beck, Weissman, Lester and Trexler, 1974), and Reasons for Living Inventory (Linehan, Goodstein, Nielsen and Chiles, 1983).

One of the problems of using these instruments is the issue of cultural relevance. The instruments were developed in a culture (mainly US culture) very different from that of Hong Kong (basically Chinese culture). Are these measures equally valid to the Hong Kong population? Empirical work on validating these measures in Hong Kong population does exist, for example, the study of Shek (1993) on the Chinese version of Hopelessness Scale, that of Chan (1991) and Shek (1991) on the Beck Depression Inventory, and that of Chan (1995) on the Reasons for Living Inventory. Generally results indicate that these scales are measuring the intended constructs in the Chinese population. Despite these research efforts, many important questions particularly related to the problem of teenage suicide are still left unanswered: How well do the constructs these instruments measure relate to suicidal risk? Are these imported instruments sensitive enough to detect suicide risk factors that are unique to people in Hong Kong? Could these instruments give us any information on how different factors of suicide operate and interact as an integrated system in the context of Hong Kong culture? Developing local measures of suicidal risk seems to be the best solution to these questions.

The need for developing a new and locally sensitive measure of suicidal risk is also emphasised by the fact that school-based screening is lacking. The importance of school-based screening in preventing youth suicide has been asserted by many writers (e.g., Reynolds, 1991; Tse, 1993). The importance of such screening is underlined by the fact that in Hong Kong access to mental health professionals is very limited. Many teenagers with suicidal ideas do not receive the attention of any professional until they have made a serious suicidal attempt. In secondary school, the ratio of students to teacher is so large (42:1) that teachers often fail to recognise any signs of distress their students might display. In many cases the students' suicidal risk states (including non-lethal suicidal gestures) are left unmanaged and may escalate, especially if the students perceive that no one cares. In this regard, a timely school-based screening is necessary to compensate for the inadequacy of the current professional situation, and to effectively identify those most at risk for intervention.

In this chapter, a newly developed suicidal risk measure, the Suicidal Risk Scale for Hong Kong Students (SRS) will be described in terms of its theoretical base, development, characteristics, and its use. This chapter is accompanied by the SRS rating form (Forms I and Form II) and the Score Transformation Table.

The Conceptualisation of Suicidal Risk

The development of the Suicidal Risk Scale of Hong Kong Students (SRS) is based on the conceptualisation of suicidal risk as a multifaceted state of mind in an individual who is experiencing distress or psychological pain. This distress is basically caused by a number of interacting psychosocial factors ranging from negative affect to perceived difficulties in adjusting to the social world. These factors lead to a variety of thoughts and feelings, which are frequently painful, and it is the interplay of such thoughts and feelings (i.e. the multifaceted state of mind) by which the individual in distress is driven toward suicidal behaviours.

The conceptualisation proposed here is not totally new. Many theorists have indeed offered similar ideas on the phenomenon of suicide. For instance, Orbach and his colleagues (Orbach, Gross and Glauman, 1981; Orbach, Feshbach, Carlson, Glaubman and Gross, 1983; Orbach, 1988) constructed a multi-attitudes phenomenological model on childhood suicide (and later generalised it to adolescents) stating that a suicidal tendency is determined by the interplay of four conflicting attitudes. Shneidman (1985, 1993) has suggested that suicide is a multifaceted event and is caused by psychological pain, which he called *psychache*. Leenaars (1996) has discussed a similar view of suicide as a multidimensional malaise, as an intrapsychic drama on an interpersonal stage. This assertion of Leenaars not only is consistent with the idea suicidal risk as a multifaceted state of mind proposed here, but also his idea about 'intrapsychic drama on an interpersonal stage' is consistent with our assertion of the relationship between the suicidal state of mind and psychosocial factors.

The psychosocial nature of suicidal risk has also been suggested in the work of Blumenthal and Kupfer (1988): their threshold model proposes that suicidal behaviour is predisposed by and interacts with risk factors that are largely psychosocial events. The ideas proposed by these theorists are based on much clinical and empirical evidence and these theories have in turn stimulated much scientific research. The models have received considerable empirical support.

In these models, in order to assess suicidal risk, three main classes of psychosocial factors are identified as predictors:

- *Negative affect*: Negative affect is concerned with feelings such as depression, anger, and impulsivity. About two-thirds of suicides are primarily depressive. On the other hand, suicidal behaviour is a violent act which involves certain degree of aggressive energy. Freud argued that suicidality is a kind of disguised murder of introjected objects. Such introjection is particularly likely to occur in younger suicide victims.

- *Negative cognition*: Hopelessness and suicide ideation are common predictors of suicides, and are concerned with cognitive tendency to self-destruction. They may directly motivate the individual to actual suicidal behaviours. It has been estimated that approximately 75 to 80 per cent of suicide victims have given presuicidal clues of their suicidal intention (Maris, 1992).

- *Negative life events*: Persistent undesirable or stressful life events may trigger suicidal attempts. Such events may include interpersonal discord, loss of important relationships, and repeated over-workload. Stressful events may gradually accumulate. Among youngsters in Hong Kong, events surrounding academic stress, peer relationships and family issues are more likely to occur.

To assess suicidal risk is, therefore, to identify the occurrence and intensity of suicide predictors. The SRS in the present study involves also measuring these predictors.

The Suicidal Risk Scale for Hong Kong Students (SRS)

General Description

The SRS is a self-report measure used to assess suicidal risk among secondary school students. The whole scale consists of 75 items which describe the respondent's thoughts, feelings, behaviours, as well as social and interpersonal difficulties that are associated with adolescent suicidal behaviours. The respondents are asked to rate the degree to which the descriptions are true to them. In order to enhance applications of various types, the SRS is divided into two separate forms, including a brief screening form and a more detailed profile form. The students' responses are scored on six sub-scales, namely suicide ideation, anger-impulsivity, depression, academic stress, family problems, and interpersonal difficulties (Table 5.1). The scores of these sub-scales reflect the extent to which the respondents possess corresponding suicidal thoughts and psychosocial disturbances. The scales hence not only assess general suicidal risk but also provide information about the pattern of psychosocial distress the respondents were suffering.

The Sub-scales of the SRS

The construction of sub-scales was based on factor analysis of the original item pool, which reveal that a six-factor solution best interpreted what the whole set of items measured (details of subscale construction are presented in the Scale Development section). In order to enhance interpretation, all sub-scales are scored in a direction that a high score on a particular subscale indicates higher level of malfunctioning or distress, and suggests a higher risk of suicidal behaviours. A full set of scores on these sub-scales provides a psychosocial profile of the respondent, which gives detail information about the respondents' emotional state, and potential risk factors.

The Two Forms of the SRS

In order to facilitate different uses of the scale, the SRS is divided into two separate forms: the Screen Form (Form I) and the Profile Form (Form II). The Screen Form is made up of the Suicide Ideation sub-scale, which consists of 13 items. Because it is brief and the item content is directly related to suicide, it can be used as a quick and effective instrument for screening purpose. The Screen Form is especially suitable for large-scale screening in school.

Table 5.1 SRS sub-scales and descriptions

Sub-scale	No. of items	Description
Suicide ideation	13	Measures suicidal thoughts and impulses, hopelessness, negative attitudes about life and living, positive attitudes about suicide
Anger-impulsivity	13	Measures angry affect, impulsive personality style, lack of personal control, irritable character, aggressive behaviours
Depression	11	Measures depressed mood, loss, grief, guilt feeling, lowered self-esteem, lost of interests, boredom
Academic stress	5	Measures anxiety due to tests and examinations, difficulties in learning, overload of homework assignments
Family problems	15	Measures family coherence, relationship between family members, communication within the family, perceived caring and support from family
Interpersonal difficulties	18	Measures lack of social support, unsatisfactory interpersonal relationship, low level of sociability and popularity, loneliness, isolation from peers

Students with scores high on the Screen Form may be considered at risk of suicide.

The scale user or the counsellor may then arrange for further risk assessment, probably with the SRS Profile Form, and can implement appropriate intervention strategies, including the involvement of peer counselling strategies such as the HITMAN described in a previous chapter.

The sub-scale scores in the Profile Form give more detailed information about the respondents' psychosocial risk pattern. Hence the Profile Form can be used as a further, in-depth assessment of suicidal risk following the screening procedure with the Screen Form. With the psychosocial information provided by the Profile Form, the scale users or the counsellor can have a better understanding of the respondents' problems and may generate hypotheses about the causes of the respondents' suicidal risk. An SRS Scoring Sheet is designed for scoring of the Profile Form together with the Screen Form, so that the sub-scale scores of the whole SRS can be calculated easily, and the profile can be clearly seen.

Purposes and Uses

The scale is intended for use mainly in school, but can also be used in other youth service settings such as youth centre, counselling centre, crisis centre, or suicide prevention programme. Users can be psychologists, school counsellors, school social workers, caseworkers, or other trained paraprofessionals, and referral of less acute cases can be made in a variety of directions, including peer counselling strategies.

Because the SRS has two forms, i.e. the screen form and the profile form and provides six sub-scale scores measuring six suicide-related domains, a variety of applications are possible with the SRS. Firstly, it can be a screening tool to identify high-risk students so that effective intervention can be implemented. The screen form, which contains only 13 items is especially suitable for quick and large-scale screening. For instance, the screen form can be used for school-based screening; and students who are found to be of high-risk can then be referred to counselling service in order to prevent actual suicide attempts. The second type of application of the scale is concerned with assessment during the intervention phase. Suicidal risk can be assessed in order to judge the need or urgency of counselling or psychotherapy. If the risk is high, counselling should be immediately available and more frequent sessions should be arranged. If the risk is so high that suicide attempt is very likely, crisis management procedure is necessary. Thirdly, as the SRS profile form provides a psychosocial profile of the respondents, it may indicate that some further assessment may be considered. For example, if the respondent scored especially high on the depression sub-scale, the counsellor may further assess the student's depressed mood with in-depth interview or other objective measures, say, the Beck Depression Inventory or the Zung Depression Index. Fourthly, the SRS profile also provides information for treatment planning; a high score on Interpersonal Difficulties may imply that treatment focusing on interpersonal style or social skills would be helpful, or a high score on Anger-impulsivity may suggest treatment focusing on emotional release and impulse control training. Finally, risk assessment using the SRS can be used as an index to evaluate how well the counselling or psychotherapy can reduce suicidal risk, and also to evaluate the effectiveness of suicide prevention programme. Such assessment of effectiveness is of great value in the planning and construction of effective suicide prevention programmes and modes of intervention.

Respondent Populations

The SRS is designed for use with secondary school students. Because the standardisation sample is composed of Form 1 to Form 4 secondary school students (ages 12 to 16) validity is not necessarily generalised to students of other grades. Because the SRS is self-rated, respondents need to have the ability to comprehend simple written Chinese. Respondents of SRS should have reading ability normal for his/her age. Students who are intellectually handicapped or disorganised will have difficulties completing the scale. In addition, the self-report nature of SRS could make it prone to conscious faking. The use of SRS is not recommended with students who are unwilling to co-operate, overtly hostile, or suffer from cognitive distortions. Users of SRS should judge whether a particular student is suitable to fill in the scale.

Desired Qualifications of users

Users of the SRS can be a school counsellor, social worker, case worker, and other professionals or trained paraprofessionals who have the basic knowledge of psychological testing. It is important that users are able to judge when and in which circumstances the administration of SRS appropriate, with whom the SRS is suitable, to what extend the obtained results are valid and without bias, and be able to interpret the test results meaningfully. When the scale is used for screening, the users should ensure that follow-up treatment by trained individuals and/or appropriate referral is available for suicidal students.

To ensure the proper use of the SRS, potential users should read through this chapter before administrating the scale, so that they are familiar with the rationale, development, empirical support of validity, administration and scoring procedure, interpretation and limitations of the SRS. Potential users should also have the knowledge of the ethical principles of psychological testing and must conform to these standards (see American Psychological Association, 1992).

Limitations

In the work on normative development for the SRS scales, the following limitations should be noted:

- *Limited sample.* Out of 100 invitations, only five schools participated in the study. The representativeness of the sample in validating the scale may be affected in favour of schools with a more sympathetic approach to student care, and student counselling.

- *Preliminary validation.* The validation tasks of the study are only preliminary. Users of the SRS should judge the validity of individual scores for each respondent.
- *Limitation of self-report format.* Since the assessment format of the SRS is self-administered, response bias is possible. Users should be sensitive to possible distortions.

Administration and Scoring

Prior to administration of the SRS, potential users must check if it is appropriate to use the SRS for the intended purpose, qualification of users are met, and the potential respondents are suitable to take the test.

The context in which test is taken may affect responses of test takers. Therefore, to minimise response biases, testing environment should be carefully monitored when administering the SRS. The most basic rule is that the testing environment should be comfortable for SRS respondents and that any possible distraction should be prevented. For instance, the SRS user could administer the SRS in a quiet room with a desk, which is clean and of appropriate size and height, together with a comfortable chair. The user may put a notice outside the room telling people not to disturb.

If the scale is to be administered in group (e.g., when used in large-scale screening), the user should arrange for a setting with the least distraction from other respondents; for example, respondents should not sit too close to each other, and the administrator of the scale could remind the respondents not to discuss with other respondents while filling the scale.

Another important rule of administration is that the testing environment as well as administration procedure should be standardised. The reason is that the context of testing may have some impact on test responses. Such variation in the effect of context might make comparison between results in various comparisons problematic.

Assessing suicidal risk by the SRS completely depends on honest self-report by the respondents. Therefore, respondents' co-operation and willingness to give true answers is critical to the validity of results. It is desirable that the SRS administrator build a rapport prior to respondents filling the scale. Rapport means a warm and trusting relationship between the administrator and the respondents. With such a relationship, co-operative test taking attitude is more likely, and intentional distortion of responses (i.e. faking) could be reduced. When the scale is administered individually in the process of counselling, the scale administrator (probably social worker or school counsellor) should avoid administering the scale during a too early session. When the SRS is used for school-based screening, the administrator could establish rapport by a warm, caring, and support manner, and could talk with the students about the reasons for doing the scale, and than invite the students to speak freely about their own feelings.

Before administering the SRS, informed consent should be obtained. Potential respondents should be informed about the reasons for testing, type of test to be used, in what way test results would be used, and what and to whom the test information will be released. The scale administrator should then encourage respondents to ask questions if they have anything unclear.

After the respondents are clear about the test and agree to take the SRS, the scale administrator could give the SRS rating form to respondents. As there are two rating forms of SRS, the scale administrator should make sure the appropriate form is given. The ways of using Form I and Form II of SRS could be varied in different situations, and the scale administrator should be careful in using the scale properly. If both Form I and Form II are administered at the same time, respondents should always complete Form I followed by Form II.

When the respondent, or every one of the respondents (if the scale is done in group setting) has the rating form, the administrator should tell the respondents how to complete the scale. No matter which form is being used, the scale administrator should give the standardised instruction as below:

> In this scale is a list of statements which describe your thoughts, feeling, behaviours, or situations. Please read each statement carefully, think if the statement is true to your current or recent situations, then put a (✓) in the appropriate box to indicate your choice.
>
> For example, in the example shown on your rating sheet, there is a statement 'feeling unhappy'. If you think this statement is fairly true to you, that is, you are feeling fairly unhappy, you can put a tick in the box under 'slightly agree'. If you are feeling very unhappy, you tick on the box under 'strongly agree'. In contrast, if you think this statement does not describe your current feeling, you can put a tick in the box under 'slightly disagree' to indicate that you are fairly

> happy. If you feeling very happy, you can put a tick in the box under 'strongly disagree'.
>
> Please rate on all items, do not leave any of them unanswered because all of your responses provide valuable information for us to know more about your situation.
>
> If you are clear about how to fill the scale, you may start. If you have any questions, please let me know.

Make necessary clarification if the respondents raise any queries. After that, respondents can start completing the scale.

When respondents are completing the rating form, they may have various types of problems. They may report that they are unclear about a certain word or concepts that occur in the scale, or have difficulties understanding a certain item. In this case, the administrator should explain the corresponding words or items as naturally as possible. If respondent reports that he/she cannot decide on a particular item, the administrator could encourage him/her to just take the option, which is closest to his/her feeling or situation. Also, remind the respondents to rate the items according to the order they are numbered (i.e. avoid doing item 6 before item 5) and not to miss any item unanswered if possible. In the classroom of the future, where each student has his or her own laptop, computerised administration would be possible, ensuring that all items are answered in a logical order. This type of administration is known to be more successful then pencil-and-paper administration in eliciting information on sensitive issues (Bagley and Tremblay, 1997).

If respondents have finished the scale, ask them to check if there are unanswered items. If there is no problem, the administrator can collect the rating sheet. If the scale is administered in large group, make sure every one has returned the rating form with their name written on it. Filling a scale of suicidal risk may sometimes induce respondents' hidden negative feelings. Therefore, it is recommended the scale administrator pay attention to respondents' immediate reaction (emotional or behavioural) during and after doing the assessment. Immediate action like intervention or referral should be taken if necessary.

Unless the scoring and interpretation is done immediately, tell the respondent when an explanation and discussion of test results would be offered. This would avoid negative feelings due to uncertainty (note that it is the scale user's responsibility to provide scale respondents with an appropriate explanation of test results and recommendations made on the basis of test results in a form that they can understand).

Scoring procedures

Scoring of SRS should be carried out according to the following procedures:

- *First*, make sure the name of respondent and other necessary personal information has been written down;
- *Second*, check if all items are rated and all responses are valid.
- *Third*, write down the item score on the box appearing on the right of the items such that: 1 = strongly disagree, 2 = slightly disagree, 3= slightly agree, 4 = strongly agree.
- *Fourth*, copy the item scores in the corresponding boxes on the Scoring Sheet.
- *Fifth*, on the Scoring Sheet, item with an arrow mark responses which have to be scored in reverse direction (i.e. 1 becomes 4, 2 becomes 3, 3 becomes 2, and 4 becomes 1); just write down the reversed scores next to the box.
- *Sixth*, on the Scoring Sheet, boxes are arranged according to sub-scales. Therefore, just add up all item scores along a column results in sub-scale scores. If the item is reversely scored, add the reversed score instead of the original scores.
- *Seventh*, write the sum of scores along column (i.e. the sub-scale scores) in the box below each column.
- *Eighth*, if a missing or invalid item score exists, an estimated score can be obtained by calculating a mean score of the other items from the same subscale (However, if there are too many missing or invalid item scores, the validity of resulting sub-scale scores should be questioned).
- *Ninth*, from the sub-scale scores, a percentile score can be found for each sub-scale using the Scale Transformation Table (see Appendix D).

- *Tenth*, to do the transformation, users should first choose the appropriate column according to which sub-scale he/she is dealing with. Then they should go down the column to the row where the number indicated in the most left-hand column is just the score the respondent obtained in that sub-scale. The number intersecting that column (sub-scale) and that row (original sub-scale score) is the percentile of that score.

- *Eleventh*, if only Form I is used, there is no need to copy the scores to the Scoring Sheet, all the scoring procedure can be done on the rating form.

After scoring the responses, scale users can go on to the interpretation of scores, which is to be discussed in the next Section.

Interpretation and Implications of the SRS

Respondents to the SRS should obtain scores on the six sub-scales. Each of the scores represent a sub-scale percentile score, which provides the relative positions of the respondents in each domain in comparison with the standardisation sample. For example, if a respondent obtains a percentile score of 80 on the suicide ideation subscale, it means that 80 per cent of the sample scored lower than that respondent according to the Score Transformation Table. This respondent is thus *relatively* more at risk in the domain of suicide ideation than the other 80 per cent of the student population. The score, 80, does not indicate how likely the respondent would be to engage in self-harm in the absolute sense. The same approach of interpretation applies to the other five sub-scales.

Case Illustration

For example, May has completed the SRS assessment and her raw scores are calculated as follows:

Sub-scale	Raw scores	Transformed scores (percentile)
Suicide ideation	36	92
Anger-impulsivity	17	0
Depression	33	95
Academic stress	7	3
Family problems	41	86
Interpersonal difficulties	46	73

In the case of May, although her absolute score of interpersonal difficulties (46) is higher than that of suicide ideation (36), the transformed score of the former is somewhat lower, in percentile terms, than the latter. It implies that interpersonal difficulties is not as crucial as suicide ideation that May is experiencing. On the other hand, level of depression of May is even higher; she is among the top 5 per cent of the normative population in depression.

In this case, May is considered to be at-risk since she is burdened by depression and her suicidal thoughts, feelings and intentions are strong. She needs intervention to reduce her depression and resolve her suicidal ideas. Since her level of anger-impulsivity is 0, it is less likely for her to kill herself suddenly, but rather she will go through a process of consideration and planning. While those with high anger-impulsivity scores need close monitoring to prevent suicide, May needs careful counselling and other intervention tactics to help her resolve her problems. Since May's percentile scores on family problems and interpersonal difficulties are rather high, it would be helpful to start exploring her encounters in these two aspects.

Individual items in each sub-scale are also valuable for assessment. In May's case, it was found that one of the 13 items of suicide ideation scores indicated a strong intention to die. This may imply that May is concerned with some problems which she finds difficult to solve or reluctant to face. So she may attempt or commit suicide as a last resort if problems are not resolved.

Moreover, May also scores high on some items of depression: she 'finds no meaning in life'; she 'is desperate about losing something significant'; 'she wants to cry bitterly'; and she 'feels exhausted'. All these may provide some hints that she has lost something she values so much that it even takes away the meaning of her life, that she is extremely hurt, and that she is already exhausted because of this loss and hurt. Together with the scores on family problems and interpersonal difficulties, interventionists may try to investigate if her loss is concerned with her family or other persons.

Scale Development

Purpose and Rationale

The development of the SRS was prompted by the fact that the completed and attempted suicide rate among school children in Hong Kong had reached an alarming rate. Many at risk of suicidal behaviours were not recognised as having any problems before they attempted to kill themselves. In this regard, an objective screening tool is necessary to identify those who are likely to commit suicide. It is believed that suicide could be prevented if we could identify the at-risk children well before their problems become too severe to cope with.

As discussed in the previous section, suicidal risk is conceptualised as a multi-dimensional phenomenon. Risk of suicide is neither contributed to by a single factor not is itself a single construct. Instead, what we call suicidal risk is the result of an interplay of a broad range of factors including various kinds of subjective distress, difficulties in coping with different socio-environmental stress, and lack of adaptive psychosocial functioning. On the basis of this conceptualisation of suicidal risk, it is meaningless to measure risk of suicide with a single, global index and ignore the heterogeneous nature of suicidal risk; rather, a valid measure of suicidal risk should provide information on not only the degree or intensity of suicidal risk but on the unique pattern of risk factors of the at-risk individual.

Therefore, the SRS attempts to evaluate risk of suicide with a set of psychosocial risk indicators, which are predictive of child and/or adolescent suicide. In other words, the purpose of this study was to establish an instrument with various sub-scales, which measure a variety of factors ranging from psychological disturbances to social stressors, which have been found to be related to teenage suicide. The assumptions are, firstly that the general level of suicidal risk is contributed in a complex additive model combining of these risk factors, i.e. increase in any one of these factors leads to a higher overall suicidal risk. Thus different patterns of these risk factors yield a differential risk of suicidality - for example, if two individuals display different pattern of these psychosocial risk factors, their phenomenological view, their nature of problems, aetiology of suicidal tendency, and treatment needs are different even if their general level of suicidal risk is the same.

Item Construction

The development of SRS is based on a review of literature on suicide risk factors among children and adolescents. A list of risk factors, which were frequently found to predict suicidal thoughts or behaviours was identified. These factors include suicide ideation, hopelessness, lack of life satisfaction, negative attitude toward life, depressive symptoms, angry affect, hostility, impulsive or aggressive personality style, low self-esteem, family dysfunction, lack of social support, loneliness, and incompetence in social situations. The researchers then wrote items to measure these factors.

In order to measure risk factors which are specific to the Hong Kong Chinese culture, some items were rewritten with reference to the locally specific context, and some items were especially written to assess facets which are infrequently mentioned in Western literature but are frequently suspected to be important risk factors of suicide in Hong Kong. Examples of these facets are stressful academic work, problems with congested living environment, rapid pace of life, and certain traditional Chinese beliefs about death or after-life. A total of 190 items were constructed in this phase.

The items were then tested for their readability. Five secondary school teachers who taught Chinese in junior class (Form 1 to Form 3) were asked to read through the items and to judge whether ordinary Form 1 students are able to comprehend those items without difficulties. They were asked to tick against those items, which they thought would be difficult for Form 1 students and also to point out what made the item difficult for students. Most of the items constructed were judged as easily comprehensible by normal Form 1 students. Those judged as 'not comprehensible' were only due to minor problems such as difficult wordings and were revised.

The items were then subjected to a pilot test to see if they were related to suicidal activities in school students. The purpose was to eliminate items, which were clearly of little value in assessing risk of suicide. In the pilot study, 154 secondary students (Form 1 to Form 4) rated on these items according to their current feeling, thinking or situations. They were also asked to give information concerning their suicidal activities, including suicide ideation, past suicide attempts, and self-destructive behaviours. Item responses were then compared across students of varying level of suicide activities. Items which failed to discriminate between suicidal and non-suicidal groups were discarded. As a result 97 items were retained for subsequent test construction procedures.

Other Instruments Used

In addition to the SRS items, the questionnaire used in this study also included the 4-item Suicide Behavior Questionnaire (SBQ, Linehan, 1981), the CES-D (Radloff, 1977), which is a 20-item self-report measure for assessing depressive symptomatology in the general population, revalidated in Hong Kong (Cheung and Bagley, 1998), and the 10-item Rosenberg Self-esteem Scale (Rosenberg, 1979). These measures show satisfactory internal consistency in this study; with the current sample, coefficient alpha is .75, .90, and .81 for the SBQ, CES-D, and Self-esteem Scale respectively.

Further, a set of Semantic Differential scales was included in the questionnaire to assess respondents' attitudes toward suicidal behaviours. This consists of seven pairs of bipolar adjectives, and respondents were asked to rate on a 7-point scale their own feeling or thoughts about suicide. In all pairs of the adjectives one extreme of the pole represented positive feeling toward suicide (e.g., happy, brave, calm) and the other represents negative attitudes toward suicide (e.g., sad, weak, fearful). Two of the items were reversely scored. With the current sample the rating on these bipolar adjectives are highly internally consistent (coefficient alpha .75) with the semantic differential correlating quite strongly with the SBQ (r=.54) and CES-D (r=.59), and negatively with the self-esteem scale (r=-.36), suggesting some construct validity.

The Standardisation Sample

To recruit secondary school students as the standardisation sample, 100 secondary schools were invited to participate in this study. However, only five schools were willing to participate. Form 1 to Form 4 (ages 12 to 19) students of these five schools were then given the questionnaires and were asked to complete the questionnaires during a school period their schools offered. 1,665 questionnaires were distributed to students, and 1,656 of them (99.5 per cent) were returned. Of the 1,656 questionnaires returned, 213 were discarded due to clearly inconsistent responses or too much missing information (rejection rate = 12.9 per cent). Finally 1,443 cases were included in subsequent analyses.

Some characteristics of the current sample are summarised in Table 5.2. Notice that the sum of percentages of sex, father's educational level, and mother's educational level are not equal to zero because some of the respondents did not report on these pieces of information. In Table 5.2, it is shown that male and female participants are of similar proportion, with slightly more girls than boys. Number of participants are evenly distributed across grade. The age of participants ranged from 12 to 19, with a mean age of 14.31, SD of 1.37. Participants' socio-economic status is evaluated by their parents' educational level. In the current sample, father's and mother's educational level are distributed in a way similar to that expected in the general population, as indicated in the 1991 Hong Kong census data (Hong Kong Census and Statistics Department, 1991).

The rates of suicidal activities displayed by the participants are examined in Table 5.3. As shown in that table, most participants reported an absence of

Table 5.2 Sample characteristics

	No.	%
Sex[1]		
Boys	596	41.3
Girls	707	50.0
Grade		
Form 1	357	24.7
Form 2	353	24.6
Form 3	361	25.0
Form 4	370	25.6
Father's education level[2]		
Not educated	57	4.0
Primary	509	35.3
Junior secondary	468	32.3
Senior secondary	280	19.4
Tertiary or above	48	3.3
Mother's education level[3]		
Not educated	90	6.2
Primary	570	39.5
Junior secondary	433	30.0
Senior secondary	249	17.2
Tertiary or above	23	1.6

Notes

1 140 (9.7%) respondents did not report their sex.
2 83 (5.8%) respondents did not report their father's educational level.
3 78 (5.4%) respondents did not report their mother's educational level.

or few suicidal activities ranging from brief suicidal impulse to severe suicidal ideation or past suicide attempts. Roughly three-fourths of the sample were free of any suicidal impulses, thoughts or activities; about one-fifth of the sample reported a mild level of suicidal thoughts, impulse, or ideation; and less than 5 per cent of participants reported having severe from of suicidal activities such as a suicide plan or frequent suicidal ideation. On comparing boys and girls, suicidal activities were more frequently reported by girls. In boys, about one-fifth reported having had suicidal thoughts, impulses or frequent suicidal ideation, whereas in girls, the proportion is as large as one-fourth to one-third. The rate of suicidal ideas and activities the current sample has indicated appears to be within a range we would expect in the general population of Hong Kong, according to the literature reviewed in Chapter 1.

Table 5.3 Rate of suicidal ideas and actions in lifetime, in the present sample

	Boys		Girls	
	No.	**%**	**No.**	**%**
Suicidal activities[1]				
None	479	81.0	460	65.6
Suicidal thoughts	103	17.4	208	29.7
Had a plan	8	1.4	22	3.1
Attempted suicide	1	0.2	11	1.6
Suicide ideation[2]				
Never	435	73.6	386	54.9
Few times	103	17.4	187	26.9
Sometimes	47	8.0	107	15.2
Often	5	0.8	20	2.8
Very frequent	1	0.2	3	0.4
Suicidal impulse[3]				
Never	456	76.8	449	63.6
Sometimes	138	23.2	257	36.4
Frequent suicide ideation[4]				
No	527	88.4	576	81.6
Yes	69	11.6	131	18.5

Notes

1 χ^2 [3, N=1292] = 41.64, p <.0001.
2 χ^2 [4, N=1294] = 51.32, p <.0001.
3 χ^2 [1, N=1300] = 26.45, p <.0001.
4 χ^2 [1, N=1303] = 12.03, p <.001.

Item Selection

With the purpose of developing a multi-dimensional scale of suicidal risk, which consist of reliable and internally consistent sub-scales, only items which constitute a single factor of suicidal risk were adopted in the SRS. Therefore the original 97 items were first subjected to factor analysis. Principal-components analysis with oblique rotation (Direct Oblimin) was conducted on the whole set of items. A series of different solutions were inspected and it was found that the six factor solution was the most interpretable and was thus chosen. The six factors accounted for 38.4 per cent of variance of the whole 97-item scale. Items with factor loading of .30 or greater on a given factor were viewed as indicators of that factor. Sixteen items were excluded from the scales due to equally high factor loadings on more than one factor.

The remaining items were grouped into six clusters, yielding six preliminary sub-scales. Item-subscale correlation was derived for each item. In order to ensure internal consistency of items, items which failed to correlate highly with the corresponding sub-scales were rejected. On this basis, six items which correlate lower than .30 with the corresponding sub-scales were discarded. To check whether the items discarded are indeed valid in differentiating between suicidal and non-suicidal despite the fact that they did not constitute a single reliable sub-scale, responses on the rejected items were compared between participants displaying varying degree of suicidal activities. The results show that these items did not discriminate very well between suicidal and non-suicidal participants. Finally, 22 items were discarded and 75 items were retained in the scale.

Constructing Sub-scales

Principal-component factor analyses with oblique rotation were conducted again on the 75-item scales. The factor structure was very similar to that of the 97-item scale and again yielded a six-factor solution. These six factors accounted for 43.1 per cent of total variance (see Table 5.5 later in this chapter). According to the factor loadings of items (items with factor loading of .30 or higher on a particular factor were viewed as an indicator of that factor), six sub-scales were constructed by grouping items which contribute to the same factor. For each sub-scale, scores were calculated by simply adding item scores, and internal consistency was then evaluated by computing alpha. The factors thus formed were named suicide ideation (13 items, α=.92), anger-impulsivity (13 items, α=.82), depression (11 items, α=.84), academic stress (5 items, α=.71), family [roblems (15 items, α=.91), and interpersonal difficulties (18 items, α=.89). These sub-scales show good face validity and internal consistency (see Appendices for sub-scale items).

Testing SRS Sub-scale Validity

Based on respondents' self-report, respondents were classified as suicidal or non-suicidal (Ss who reported 'have not thought of suicide at all' were classified as non-suicidal; Ss who reported 'have thought of suicide', 'have a suicide plan' or 'have attempted suicide' were classified as suicidal). SRS sub-scale scores were then compared between suicidal and non-suicidal respondents with the t-test. The results of t-tests are presented in Table 5.7. Mean scores of all SRS sub-scales significantly differ between suicidal and non-suicidal students at $p < .001$.

Respondents were also classified as non-suicide ideators, occasional suicide ideators, and frequent suicide ideators according to their reports of suicidal thoughts frequencies. These three groups of respondents were then compared on SRS sub-scales scores. A series of univariate ANOVAs were conducted with frequency of suicide ideation as IV and SRS sub-scales scores as DV. In Table 5.8, it is shown that ANOVAs on all sub-scales yield F-values significant at $p < .0001$, and that all sub-scales discriminate between every two levels of suicide ideation frequencies (with the only exception that Academic stress did not differ between occasional and frequent ideators). In conclusion, the findings provide evidence supporting the validity of all SRS sub-scales in measuring suicidal risk.

Development of the SRS Screen Form and the SRS Profile Form

During the process of constructing the SRS, we aimed at developing a suicidal risk measure, which could be used in large-scale, school-based, quick screening administered by teachers or school social workers. The SRS should be brief enough for quick screening; it should also be easy to administer and easy to interpret so that it can be properly managed by teachers and school social workers who might have only limited knowledge in psychological testing. Moreover, the SRS should provide information on the unique pattern of suicidal risk any individual displays so that the scale users could know more on the individual's distress and suffering and thus be able to plan treatment strategies more appropriately.

With respect of the above purposes, we attempt to divide the SRS into two forms, which can be administered separately. One of the two forms would be especially suitable for quick and large-scale screening, the other focusing on a more detailed and comprehensive profile of the respondent's suicidal risk.

There are two ways to construct the screen and profile forms. One is to select from each sub-scale items that are most predictive of suicide and this subset of items can form the screen form of SRS which could measure suicidal risk equally well as the whole SRS in general. In this approach the screen form would be a brief, summary version of the full form. However, the drawback with this approach is that if the screen form consists of items which are each measuring a different factor, interpretation of the overall score becomes problematic. In other words, it would be difficult for the scale users (who are likely to have minimal testing experience) to interpret a scale which is itself heterogeneous in nature.

An alternative approach is to select one subscale of SRS to be the screen form. It must be noted that to construct the screen form this way, we need to make sure that the sub-scale used is adequate in providing information for estimating general suicidal risk and that the meaning of this sub-scale will be straightforward to scale users. Thus, a sub-scale can be accepted as the screen form only if it is brief enough, internally consistent, has content clearly related to suicide to make interpretation easy, and is of satisfactory validity in measuring suicidal risk independently of other sub-scales. To test if any of the SRS sub-scales met these criteria, each SRS sub-scale was examined on their number of items, face content, internal consistency, and validity. In addition to studying the sub-scales' relative contribution on measuring suicidal risk, multiple regression analysis were conducted with the six SRS sub-scales as the independent variables (IVs) and the SBQ scores as the dependent variable (DV). These analyses revealed that the Suicide Ideation scale is brief (only 13 items), shows the highest internal consistency (α=.92), has face content which is clearly related to suicide and thus is easy to interpret, and discriminates strongly between students of different level of suicidal activities.

The regression analysis also shows that the suicide ideation sub-scale accounts for a large proportion of variance of the SBQ mean scores among all SRS sub-scales. These results point to the fact that the suicide ideation sub-scale can adequately assess suicidal risk even when used independently of other sub-scales. Based on these findings, the suicide ideation sub-scale has been used as the screen form and the other five sub-scales have been used as the profile form.

Thus the present SRS is divided into two forms which can be administered separately. Form One is the 13-item screen form (also called Form I of SRS) which constitutes the suicide ideation sub-scale of SRS, and is to be used for quick and large-scale screening. The other is the 62-item profile form (also called Form II of SRS), which is made up of the depression, anger-impulsivity, academic stress, Family problems, and Interpersonal difficulties sub-scales, and is to be used for obtaining detailed psychosocial profiles concerning suicidal risk.

Transformation of Sub-scale Scores

In order to facilitate interpretation, the final sub-scale scores are transformed so that the meaning of a particular score is more interpretable, and comparisons between sub-scale scores are possible. Since the SRS is intended to be used by individuals who may have only basic knowledge of psychological testing, it is more appropriate to employ this transformation method which is not only easy to perform, but is also a simple and straightforward way of interpreting the transformed scores.

Given the above consideration, the percentile method was chosen among other transformation techniques because it is very easy to understand, even for those without any training in statistics. Moreover, as the SRS is to be used mainly in school settings, the concept of percentile would be extremely familiar with those schoolteachers who used to evaluate their students on a 100-point scale. The implications of a percentile is easy to understand – for example, a percentile of 85 means that in the sample there are 85 per cent of respondents who scored lower than this point, suggesting that the respondent's level of suicidal risk is within the top 15 per cent of the population.

A table has been prepared for doing the sub-scale scores transformation (the SRS Score Transformation Table, see Appendix D). Based on the standardisation sample, each sub-scale percentile of each corresponding score was derived and summarised into the Score Transformation Table. In the table, the original sub-scale scores define the rows and the six SRS sub-scales define the columns. To do the transformation, users first choose the appropriate column according to which sub-scale he/she is dealing with, and then search the number down the column to the row where the number indicated in the most left column is just the score the respondent obtained in that sub-scale, and the number intersecting that column (sub-scale) and that row (original sub-scale score) is the percentile of that score.

Psychometric Properties of the SRS

Internal consistency Scale and factor internal consistency were high for all sub-scales and individual items. Cronbach alphas (a) for the six sub-scales ranged from .71 (academic stress) to .92 (suicide ideation) (Table 5.4). Item sub-scale correlations were also satisfactory, ranging from .32 to .78 (Table 5.5).

Split-half consistency Split-half consistency for all sub-scales were also

Table 5.4 Sub-scale reliability and intercorrelation

	Suicide ideation	Anger-impulsivity (AI)	Depression (DP)	Academic stress (AS)	Family problems (FP)	Interpersonal difficulties (ID)
Sub-scale intercorrelation						
AI	.49	–				
DP	.60	.46	–			
AS	.34	.31	.42	–		
FP	.61	.46	.53	.34	–	
ID	.49	.36	.49	.27	.51	–
Reliability						
Alpha	.92	.82	.84	.71	91	.89
Split-half	.88	.74	.76	.58	.87	.82
Test-retest	.72	50	.58	.61	.76	.70

Table 5.5 Factor structure of SRS and item – sub-scale correlation

Item number	Suicide ideation	Interpersonal problems	Family problems	Angry-impulsive	Depression	Academic stress
11	.66					
6	.63					
8	.69					
2	.54					
1	.58					
12	.65					
13	.52					
5	.70					
10	.76					
9	.72					
4	.67					
7	.55					
3	.44					
60		.71				
56		.73				
36		.73				
48		.71				
30		.66				
47		.62				
50		.37				
21		.44				
31		.55				

Table 5.5 continued

Item number	Suicide ideation	Interpersonal problems	Family problems	Angry-impulsive	Depression	Academic stress
19		.35				
25		.49				
20		.40				
45		.47	-.30			
71		.46				
44		.64				
22		.43				
42		.32				
18		.40				
27			-.74			
62			-.71			
29			-.66			
65			-.69			
14			-.70			
43			-.77			
49			-.69			
69			-.73			
73			-.67			
66			-.48			
51			-.40			
28			-.39			
61			-.35			
68			-.44			

Table 5.5 continued

Item number	Suicide ideation	Interpersonal problems	Family problems	Angry-impulsive	Depression	Academic stress
15				.33		
52				.35	-.30	
24				.44		
33				.51		
16				.62		
41				.57		
40				.67		
72				.70		
17				.60		
34				.35		
35				.47		
57				.43		
33				.46		
63					-.55	
75					-.53	
67					-.57	
32					-.60	
23					-.47	
74					-.55	
37					-.55	
54					-.60	
59					-.44	

Table 5.5 continued

Item number	Suicide ideation	Interpersonal problems	Family problems	Angry-impulsive	Depression	Academic stress
38					-.40	
58					-.40	
70						.59
55						.63
39						.38
64						.47
46						.55

Note: The present factor solution is the result of Principal Components Analysis of 75 items with Direct Oblimin rotation. Only factor loadings higher than .30 are shown.

analysed. This ranged from .58 (academic stress) to .88 (suicide ideation). The relatively lower consistency for academic stress may be attributed to its smaller number of items (only five items were included in academic stress sub-scale) (Table 5.4).

Test-retest reliability A one-month interval of test-retest was applied to 71 respondents equivalent to two classes of one of the schools randomly selected from the five respondent schools. They were administered the same questionnaire. Test-retest reliability of the sub-scales of the SRS were: suicide ideation, .72 (p=.000); anger-impulsivity, .50 (p=.000); depression, .58 (p=.000); academic stress, .61 (p=.000); family problems, .76 (p=.000); interpersonal difficulties, .70 (p=.000). These results indicate that the SRS is generally reliable instrument since it yields relatively stable scores.

Construct Validity

The six factors extracted from the SRS were computed for factor analysis by Principal Component Analysis with oblique (Oblimin) rotation (Table 5.5). These factors accounted for 43 per cent of total variance. Items loading higher than .30 on a particular factor were considered as being indicative of that factor. Almost all items load highly on just one individual factor (except for item 45 and 52). The pattern of factor loadings clearly demonstrated that items were clustered in six sets, which measure six different factors.

Sub-scale intercorrelations were satisfactory among the six factors (Table 5.4). They ranged from .27 (between interpersonal difficulties and academic stress) to .61 (between family problems and suicide ideation). All correlations were in the hypothesised directions, supporting the construct validity of the SRS.

Overall, hypotheses that correlations between the six factors and SBQ, CES-D, semantic differential, and SE are high were supported (Table 5.6). The most obvious set of correlations was that between suicide ideation and the above four constructs, yielding r= .73, .70, .58, -.56, respectively.

Discriminant Validity

Comparison between suicidal and non-suicidal students The differences among the mean scores between suicidal and non-suicidal students in the six factors are highly significant with t-values ranging from -8.84 to -23.26 (p<.001) (Table 5.7).

Table 5.6 Correlations between SRS sub-scales and other measures

	Suicide ideation	Angry-impulsive	Depression	Academic stress	Family problems	Interpersonal problems
SBQ	.73	.42	48	.28	.48	.33
CES-D	.70	.53	.74	:52	.66	.63
SE	-.56	-.43	-.54	-.40	-.50	-.55
Semantic differential	.58	.33	.30	.14	.38	.29

Note: SBQ = Suicide Questionnaire; SE = Rosenberg's Self-esteem Scale (scored in the direction of better self-esteem); semantic differential measures positive attitudes to suicide. All correlations are significant at the 1% level or beyond.

Table 5.7 Comparison between non-suicidal and suicidal students

	Non-suicidal (n=1043)		Suicidal (n=389)		
	M	*SD*	*M*	*SD*	*t-value*
Suicide ideation	19.28	5.89	30.11	8.33	23.26
Anger-impulsivity	29.30	5.93	33.85	6.15	12.71
Depression	20.59	5.39	25.71	5.69	15.57
Academic stress	12.05	3.11	13.67	2.98	8.84
Family problems	28.19	8.19	36.53	8.97	16.50
Interpersonal difficulties	38.80	8.33	44.12	9.18	10.30

Note: All *t*-values are significant at $p<.001$. Degrees of freedom for above analyses range from 1392 to 1426.

Comparison between students with varying levels of suicide ideation Mean scores between students with none, occasional, and frequent suicide ideation in the six factors are also differ significantly yielding F-values from 57.01 to 602.94 ($p<.0001$) (Table 5.8). The factor, suicide ideation, has the greatest significance in each of the comparison, yielding $t=-23.26$, $p<.001$, and $F=602.94$, $p<.0001$, in the above two comparisons respectively.

Gender comparison on SRS sub-scales Mean scores between boys and girls in the six factors are significantly different, except for family problems. T-values ranged from 1.97, $p=.049$ (interpersonal difficulties) to -3.11, $p=.002$ (suicide ideation) (Table 5.9). While the issue of family problems is similarly important to both boys and girls, girls may experience more suicide ideation and academic stress and depression, while boys may be more impulsively angry and find it more difficult in handling interpersonal matters.

Educational level comparison on SRS sub-scales It is found that existing grade of study produces little effect on the six factors, except academic stress ($F=26.99$, $p<.0001$). Thus the higher the grade of study, the stronger the academic stress.

Directions for Future Research

Though suicidal tendencies are difficult to detect by observation, suicidal behaviour is associated with acute personal stress and manifestations of poor mental health. It is therefore crucial that other indicators of suicidal risk be discovered as early as possible. Objective and scientific assessment devices might be reliable tools for early detection, especially for teachers handling a large number of students. The SRS developed in this study enables assessors to evaluate suicidal risks of adolescents with a significant degree of accuracy, at the same time establishing some of the major contributor(s) to the risks. Further refinement of the SRS would be concerned with the validation and perhaps the extension of the scales.

Predictive Validity

The SRS could be further validated with a longitudinal study to test its predictive validity. This might be done by investigating the behaviours of a high-risk group. However, one obvious ethical difficulty is that the high-risk

Table 5.8 Comparison between students with none, occasional, and frequent suicide ideation

	Non -ideators *(n=911)* *Mean (SD)*	**Occasional ideators** *(n=322)* *Mean (SD)*	**Frequent ideators** *(n=201)* *Mean (SD)*	***F*-value**
Anger-impulsivity	28.84_a (5.82)	32.50_b (5.87)	35.09_c (6.03)	114.98
Depression	20.12_a (5.22)	23.91_b (5.39)	27.27_c (5.54)	173.39
Academic stress	11.86_a (3.10)	13.40_b (2.86)	13.94_b (3.05)	57.01
Family problems	27.42_a (7.87)	33.88_b (8.52)	38.81_c (8.74)	191.77
Interpersonal difficulties	38.36_a (8.28)	42.12_b (8.14)	45.87_c (9.73)	72.26

Note: All *F*-values are significant at $p<.0001$. Means with different subscript are significantly different from all others at $p<.05$ or beyond in post hoc analysis.

Table 5.9 Comparison between boys and girls on SRS sub-scales

	Boys *Mean (SD)N=590*	**Girls** *Mean (SD)N=701*	*t-value*	*Significance*
Suicide ideation	21.32 (7.85)	22.74 (8.43)	-3.11	.002
Anger-impulsivity	30.85 (6.22)	30.13 (6.17)	2.07	.039
Depression	21.55 (5.93)	22.35 (5.82)	-2.44	.15
Academic stress	12.24 (3.19)	12.73 (3.06)	-2.8	.005
Family problems	30.27 (8.77)	30.58 (9.43)	0.62	NS
Interpersonal difficulties	40.73 (8.48)	39.76 (8.99)	1.97	.049

Table 5.10 Comparison of SRS sub-scale scores across grade

	Grade				
	Form 1	**Form 2**	**Form 3**	**Form 4**	***F-value***
Suicide ideation	21.78 (7.84) $_{a}$	23.52 (8.63) $_{b}$	21.76 (8.73) $_{a}$	21.73 (7.40)	4.09 *
Anger-impulsivity	29.72 (6.74)	30.88 (6.50)	30.57 (6.47)	30.89 (5.77)	2.69
Depression	21.41 (5.57) $_{a}$	22.42 (6.02) $_{ab}$	21.48 (6.26) $_{a}$	22.62 (5.70) $_{b}$	4.01 *
Academic stress	12.10 (3.32) $_{a}$	12.03 (2.99) $_{a}$	12.10 (3.04) $_{a}$	13.74 (2.92) $_{b}$	26.99 **
Family problems	29.56 (8.69)	30.82 (9.39)	30.87 (9.90)	30.57 (8.63)	1.56
Interpersonal problems	39.86 (9.72)	40.35 (8.96)	40.19 (9.07)	40.55 (7.84)	0.37

Note: Means with different subscripts indicate significant post hoc differences at a) p<.05 or b) .01. * p<.01 ** p<.0001.

group identified should be dealt with immediately. Long-term follow-up after emergency treatment would be feasible however.

Construct Validity of Sub-scales

The construct validity of the six factors of the SRS could be further tested by correlating each sub-scale (e.g., academic stress) with other existing measures.

Cut-off point

A criterion group of attempted suicide cases could be developed as a reference of screening for establishing a cut-off point for the scale. A cut-off score may then be set for identifying emergent cases.

References

American Psychological Association (1992). Ethical principles of psychologists and code of conduct. *American Psychologist*, 47, 1597–661.

Bagley, C. and Ramsay, R. (1997). *Suicidal Behaviour in Adolescents and Adults: Research, Taxonomy and Prevention*. Aldershot: Ashgate.

Bagley, C. and Tremblay, P. (1997). Suicidal behaviors in homosexual and bisexual males. *Crisis: Journal of Crisis Intervention and Suicide Prevention*, 18, 24–34.

Beck, A.T., Kovacs, M. and Weissman, A. (1979). Assessment of suicide ideation: The Scale for Suicide Ideation. *Journal of Consulting and Clinical Psychology*, 47, 343–52.

Beck, A.T., Ward, C.H., Mendelson, M., Mock, J. and Erbaugh, J. (1961). An inventory for measuring depression. *Archives of General Psychiatry*, 12, 57–62.

Beck, A.T., Weissman, A., Lester, D. and Trexler, L. (1974). The measurement of pessimism: the Hopelessness Scale. *Journal of Clinical Psychology*, 42, 861–5.

Blumenthal, S. and Kupfer, D. (1988). Overview of early detection and treatment strategies for suicidal behavior in young people. *Journal of Youth and Adolescence*, 17, 1–23.

Brent, D. (1995). Risk factors for adolescent suicide and suicidal behavior: mental and substance abuse disorders, family environmental factors, and life stress. *Suicide and Life-Threatening Behavior*, 25(Suppl.), 52–63.

Chan, D.W. (1991). The Beck Depression Inventory: what difference does the Chinese version make? *Psychological Assessment*, 3, 616–22.

Chan, D.W. (1995). Reasons for living among Chinese adolescents in Hong Kong. *Suicide and Life-Threatening Behavior*, 25, 347–57.

Chan, K.C., Wong, S.P., Ip, T.C. and Tsui, K.C. (1993). *The Values of Secondary School Students and Self-Destructive Tendencies in Hong Kong*. [In Chinese]. Hong Kong: Breakthrough Research Group.

Cheung, S.-K. and Bagley, C. (1998). Validating an American scale in Hong Kong: the Center for Epidemiological Studies Depression Scale (CES-D). *Journal of Psychology*, 132, 169–86.

Diekstra, R. (1990). An international perspective on the epidemiology and prevention of suicide. In S. Blumenthal and D. Kupfer (eds), *Suicide Over the Life Cycle*. Washington, DC: American Psychiatric Press.

Fong, S.Y.Y. (1993). A study on suicide ideation and attempted suicide in 316 secondary school students. *Hong Kong Journal of Mental Health*, 22, 43–9.

Hau, K.T. (1993). Suicide in Hong Kong 1971–1990: age trend, sex ratio and method of suicide. *Social Psychiatry and Psychiatric Epidemiology*, 28, 23–8.

Ho, K.W., Lee, M.C. and Ho, W.S. (1994). *A Study on Adolescent Suicidal Pathways in Hong Kong*. [In Chinese]. Hong Kong: Hong Kong Playground Association.

Hong Kong Census and Statistics Department (1991). *Hong Kong 1991 Population Census: Summary Results*. Hong Kong: Census and Statistics Department.

Hong Kong Coroners (1997). *Hong Kong Coroner's Report 1996*. Hong Kong: Hong Kong Government Printer.

Leenaars, A.A. (1996). Suicide: a multidimensional malaise. *Suicide and Life-Threatening Behavior*, 26, 221–36.

Linehan, M.M. (1981). *Suicidal Behaviors Questionnaire*. Seattle: University of Washington.

Linehan, M.M., Goldstein, J.L., Nielsen, S.L. and Chiles, J.A. (1983). Reasons for staying alive when you are thinking of killing yourself: the Reasons for Living Inventory. *Journal of Consulting and Clinical Psychology*, 51, 276–86.

Maris, R.W. (1992). Overview of the study of suicide assessment. In R.W. Maris, A.L. Berman, J.T. Maltsberger and R.I. Yufit (eds), *Assessment and Prediction of Suicide*. New York: The Guilford Press.

Orbach, I. (1988). *Children Who Don't Want to Live*. San Francisco: Jossey-Bass.

Orbach, I., Gross, Y. and Glauman, H. (1981). Some common characteristics of latency-age suicidal children: a tentative model based on case study analyses. *Suicide and Life-Threatening Behavior*, 11, 180–90.

Orbach, I., Feshbach, S., Carlson, G., Glaubman, H. and Gross, Y. (1983). Attraction and repulsion by life and death in suicidal and in normal children. *Journal of Consulting and Clinical Psychology*, 51, 661–70.

Pritchard, C. (1993). A comparison of youth suicide in Hong Kong, the developed Western world and the People's Republic of China. *Hong Kong Journal of Mental Health*, 22, 6–16.

Radloff, L.S. (1977). The CES-D Scale: A self-report depression scale for research in the general population. *Applied Psychological Measurement*, 1, 385–401.

Reynolds, W.M. (1991). A school-based procedure for the identification of adolescents at risk for suicidal behaviors. *Family and Community Health*, 14, 64–75.

Rosenberg, M. (1979). *Conceiving the Self.* New York: Basic Books.
Shaffer, D. and Piacentini, J. (1994). Suicide and attempted suicide. In M. Rutter, L. Hersov and Taylor, E. (eds), *Child and Adolescent Psychiatry.* (3rd edn) (pp. 407–24). London: Blackwell Scientific.
Shneidman, E. (1985). *Definition of Suicide.* New York: Wiley.
Shneidman, E. (1993). *Suicide as Psychache.* Northvale, NJ: Aronson.
Shek, D.T. (1991). What does the Chinese version of the Beck Depression Inventory measure in Chinese students – general psychopathology or depression? *Journal of Clinical Psychology*, 47, 381–90.
Shek, D.T. (1993). Measurement of pessimism in Chinese adolescents: The Chinese Hopelessness Scale. *Social Behavior and Personality*, 21, 107–19.
Tse, J.W.L. (1993). 36 ways of preventing suicide in school. In J.W.L. Tse (ed.), *Prevention of Teenage Suicide in Schools* (pp. 53–74). Hong Kong: City Polytechnic of Hong Kong.
Yip, P.S.F. (1998). The epidemiological profile of youth suicides. In P.S.F. Yip (ed.), *Youth Suicides in Hong Kong.* Hong Kong: Samaritan Befrienders International.

Appendix A

The Full Suicide Risk Scale in Chinese

學童自殺風險量表 （表一）

填卷指示

以下是一些描述你個人的想法或感受的句子。請小心閱讀每句，想想每句所說的是否切合你現在的想法或感受，然後用「✓」選出最適合你的答案。

例如：

	非常不同意	有點不同意	有點同意	非常同意
1. 我覺得不快樂。			✓	

請回答所有題目：

	非常不同意	有點不同意	有點同意	非常同意
1. 我認爲繼續在這世界生活，實太不值得。				
2. 我覺得生命十分可貴。				
3. 我實在無法改善現在的情況，真想放棄了便算。				
4. 我覺得死沒甚麼大不了。				
5. 我想死了或者會比現在還好。				
6. 有時，我會有種衝動要了結自己的生命。				
7. 我覺得那些自殺的人都很愚蠢。				
8. 我時常會想到自殺。				
9. 有些問題是只有死才能解決的。				
10. 我認爲死亡是一種解脫。				
11. 想起那些自殺而死的學生，我也有尋死的衝動。				
12. 我真想結束一切，好讓我不用再承受痛苦。				
13. 我想若我死了，別人會好過得多。				

--- 表一完 ---

學童自殺風險量表 （表二）

填卷指示

以下是一些描述你個人的想法或感受的句子。請小心閱讀每句，想想每句所說的是否切合你現在的想法或感受，然後用「✓」選出最適合你的答案。

例如：

	非常不同意	有點不同意	有點同意	非常同意
1. 我覺得不快樂。			✓	

請回答所有題目：

		非常不同意	有點不同意	有點同意	非常同意
14.	我認為家裏沒有人真正明白我。				
15.	對於身邊某些事情，我有一種莫名的憤怒。				
16.	若有人攻擊我，我定必予以還擊。				
17.	我常不自覺地對人發脾氣。				
18.	學校裏的同學都十分友善。				
19.	絕大部份我認識的人都是不值得信任的。				
20.	我覺得我的朋友其實都不明白我。				
21.	我感到別人欣賞真的我。				
22.	我感覺自己與別人格格不入。				
23.	我感到生活空虛苦悶。				
24.	我想我是個憤怒少年。				
25.	我有可以傾訴的對象。				
26.	我感到我爸爸很關懷我。				
27.	我和家人的關係很親密。				
28.	我因為家境貧困而承受著很大壓力。				
29.	我感到我沒有家庭溫暖。				
30.	我覺得我在朋友心目中有頗重要的地位。				

		非常不同意	有點不同意	有點同意	非常同意
31.	若我遇到困難，我的朋友會樂意幫助我。				
32.	我完全陷入自己的思想感覺中，而對身邊發生的事完全失去興趣。				
33.	我很少會發脾氣。				
34.	我頗能控制自己的情緒和行爲。				
35.	我總是一想到甚麼就去做，而很少考慮到其後果。				
36.	我覺得大多數人都很樂意和我交朋友。				
37.	我很憎恨自己。				
38.	我真想痛哭一場。				
39.	我認爲學校的功課太繁重。				
40.	若有人惹怒了我，我定必雙倍還他。				
41.	爲了保護自己，我會使用暴力。				
42.	我想若我要離開，沒有人會掛念我。				
43.	我覺得我的家人都不支持我。				
44.	我十分慶幸我有許多好朋友。				
45.	我感到很多人深切地關心我。				
46.	我擔心自己沒能力再升學。				
47.	在朋輩中我得到甚多人的欣賞。				
48.	我很容易跟別人結交成朋友。				
49.	在家中，我好像做甚麼都不能令人滿意。				
50.	我覺得自己並不孤獨。				
51.	家中的居住環境甚擠逼，使我不勝其煩。				
52.	生活上許多事情都能令我氣憤。				
53.	我一感到煩躁或憤怒，就想破壞物件、或者亂擲東西。				
54.	我感到自己有很多嚴重的錯失。				
55.	由於無法理解課堂所教授的，我面對測驗和考試加倍吃力。				

		非常不同意	有點不同意	有點同意	非常同意
56.	我十分受朋友或同學的歡迎。				
57.	我做甚麼都三思而後行。				
58.	我覺得若別人真的認識我，便不會喜歡我。				
59.	我痛失了一些對我很重要的東西。				
60.	我有許多朋友。				
61.	因爲要分擔家務，我感到很大壓力。				
62.	我很享受和家人共處的時刻。				
63.	我幾乎對任何事情都失去了興趣。				
64.	我覺得自己追不上功課，又沒有人能幫助我。				
65.	我覺得自己在家裏沒有被尊重。				
66.	我很容易與父母爭吵。				
67.	我感到疲倦和沒精打采。				
68.	我想過離家出走。				
69.	我無法與家人溝通。				
70.	學校內的測驗和考試，令我非常焦慮。				
71.	我沒有知心的朋友。				
72.	我覺得自己頗爲衝動。				
73.	我感到我媽媽很關懷我。				
74.	我認爲自己應該受到懲罰。				
75.	我再也無法作出任何決定。				

--- 表二完 ---

Appendix B

Suicidal Risk Scale (Short Form) for Secondary School Students (Applicable to students between ages 12 and 16)

Below is a list of statements concerning personal feelings or thinking. Please read each statement carefully and think about it in relation to the current feelings or thinking. Please circle the answer.

SD = Strongly disagree
D = Disagree
A = Agree
SA = Strongly agree

	SD	D	A	SA
I believe it is worthless to continue to live in this world.	1	2	3	4
I feel that life is precious.	1	2	3	4
I cannot improve existing conditions and feel like giving up.	1	2	3	4
I feeling that dying is no big deal.	1	2	3	4
I think being dead may be better than what it is now.	1	2	3	4
Sometimes, I have the impulse to kill myself.	1	2	3	4
I think those who kill themselves are foolish.	1	2	3	4
I often think about suicide.	1	2	3	4
Some problems can only be resolved by death.	1	2	3	4
I believe that death is a kind of relief.	1	2	3	4
Thinking about the students who committed suicide, I also have the impulse to die.	1	2	3	4
I really want to put an end to all this so that I don't have to continue to bear the pain.	1	2	3	4
I think if I were dead, others might feel better.	1	2	3	4

Appendix C

The Full Suicide Risk Scale – English Translation (SRS-E)

Suicide ideation

11 Thinking of students who completed suicide, I have an impulse to kill myself.
6 Sometimes I have an impulse to kill myself.
8 I often think of committing suicide.
2 I think life is very precious.
1 I think it's not worth continuing to live in this world.
12 I really want to end all this so that I don't have to suffer any more.
13 I think if I were dead, other people would be much better of.
5 I think it may be better to die than to live as I do now.
10 I think death is a kind of release.
9 Some problems could be solved only by death.
4 I think death is no big deal.
7 I think the people who commit suicide are very foolish.
3 I really want to give up, as I cannot improve the present situation.

Anger-impulsivity

15 I feel angry at many things in my life.
24 I think I am an angry person.
33 I seldom get into a temper.
16 If someone attacks me, I will fight back.
41 I would use some aggression in order to protect myself.
40 If someone makes me angry, I will give him/her twice in return.
72 I feel I am rather impulsive.
17 I often get into a temper with other people.
34 I can control my own emotion and behaviours quite well.
35 I always do whatever I think of and seldom consider the consequences.
57 I always think thoroughly before I do anything.
53 Once I feel irritated or angry, I feel like I want to damage or throw things.

Depression

63 I have lost interest in almost everything.
75 I can no longer make any decision.
67 I feel tired and listless.
32 I get into my own feelings and thoughts so much that I completely lose interest in things around me.
23 I feel that my life is empty.
74 I think I should be punished.
37 I hate myself.
54 I feel I have made many serious mistakes
59 I have lost something that is very important to me.
38 I really feel like crying
58 I think people wouldn't like me if they really knew me.

Academic stress

70 The tests and exams in school makes me very anxious.
55 As I could not understand what is taught in class, I feel it hard to face the tests and exams.
39 I think my schoolwork is too much.
64 I feel I lag behind in my schoolwork but nobody can help me.
46 I am worried that I am unable to pursue my studies further.

Family problems

27 My relationship with my family is good.
62 I enjoy the time I spend with my family.
29 I don't feel warmth in my family.
65 I think I am not respected in my family.
14 I feel no one in my family really understands me.
43 At home, I feel like that everything I do is not good enough.
69 I can hardly communicate with my family.
73 I feel that my mother cares a lot about me.
26 I feel that my father cares a lot about me.
66 I quarrel with my parents easily.
51 I am irritated by the crowded environment at home.
28 I am under great pressure because my family is poor.
61 I feel great pressure since I have to share the load of housework.
68 I have thought of leaving home.

Lack of social support

60 I have many friends.
56 I am popular among my friends and schoolmates.
36 I feel that many people are happy to make friends with me.
48 I can make friends with other people easily.
30 I feel that I am important to my friends.
47 I am admired by many people among my peers.
50 I feel that I am not alone.
21 I feel that people appreciate my real self.
31 If I'm in trouble, my friends will always help me.
19 Most of the people I know are trustworthy.
25 There is someone I can talk to.
20 I feel that my friends actually do not understand me.
45 I feel that many people are concerned about me deeply.
71 I don't have any close friend.
44 I'm very glad that I have many good friends.
22 I feel that I do not fit in with other people.
42 I feel that if I left, nobody will miss me.
18 My schoolmates are quite nice.

Appendix D

The Full Suicide Risk Scale: Transformation of Sub-scale Scores

Raw scores	Percentile					
	Suicide ideation	Anger-impulsivity	Depression	Academic stress	Family problems	Interpersonal difficulties
5	–	–	–	0	–	–
6	–	–	–	1	–	–
7	–	–	–	3	–	–
8	–	–	–	7	–	–
9	–	–	–	11	–	–
10	–	–	–	16	–	–
11	–	–	0	25	–	–
12	–	–	2	35	–	–
13	0	0	4	49	–	–
14	11	0	8	61	–	–
15	19	0	11	75	0	–
16	26	0	15	86	3	–
17	33	0	20	89	5	–
18	38	1	25	94	7	0
19	42	2	30	97	9	0
20	47	3	36	99	13	0
21	50	5	41	–	15	0
22	54	7	47	–	19	0
23	58	9	53	–	22	1
25	65	16	66	–	28	3
26	70	21	71	–	31	3
27	73	26	77	–	36	5
28	75	32	81	–	40	6

Raw scores	Percentile					
	Suicide ideation	Anger-impulsivity	Depression	Academic stress	Family problems	Interpersonal difficulties
29	78	38	86	–	44	9
30	81	44	88	–	48	11
31	83	50	92	–	52	14
32	85	56	94	–	56	17
33	86	63	95	–	60	20
34	89	69	97	–	63	23
35	90	74	98	–	68	26
36	92	79	98	–	72	30
37	93	84	99	–	74	34
38	94	86	99	–	77	38
39	95	89	99	–	79	43
40	96	91	99	–	83	48
41	97	93	99	–	86	52
42	97	95	99	–	87	57
43	97	95	99	–	89	61
44	98	97	99	–	91	65
45	98	97	–	–	92	69
46	98	98	–	–	93	73
47	98	98	–	–	94	76
48	99	99	–	–	95	80
50	99	99	–	–	96	85
51	99	99	–	–	97	87
52	99	99	–	–	98	89
53	–	–	–	–	98	92
54	–	–	–	–	99	93
55	–	–	–	–	99	94
56	–	–	–	–	99	95
57	–	–	–	–	99	95
58	–	–	–	–	99	96
59	–	–	–	–	99	96
60	–	–	–	–	99	97

Raw scores	Percentile					
	Suicide ideation	Anger-impulsivity	Depression	Academic stress	Family problems	Interpersonal difficulties
61	–	–	–	–	–	97
62	–	–	–	–	–	98
63	–	–	–	–	–	98
64	–	–	–	–	–	98
65	–	–	–	–	–	99
66	–	–	–	–	–	99
67	–	–	–	–	–	99
68	–	–	–	–	–	99
69	–	–	–	–	–	99
70	–	–	–	–	–	99
71	–	–	–	–	–	99
72	–	–	–	–	–	99

6 How Chinese Adolescents Cope with Parental Death

CATHERINE TSANG YUK-CHUN

Summary of Findings

Bereavement produces intense and enduring emotional stress and its impact on adolescents is likely to be particularly traumatic. Adolescent bereavement has been addressed as a serious life crisis (Fleming and Balmer, 1996). The loss of a parent during adolescence might interfere with the completion of the developmental tasks and the transitions to young adulthood (Balk, 1991; Fleming and Adolph, 1986). Yet, not all youngsters who lose a parent will become maladjusted or profoundly depressed. An adolescent's ability to cope with the loss is an indicator of a more general psychological resilience (Mireault and Compas, 1996). As little research on this topic has been done and this issue has never been explored with Chinese adolescents in Hong Kong, a qualitative study using the grounded theory approach was conducted in order to explore the potential depth and richness of the phenomenon under consideration. The aims of the study are to examine the impact of the death of parent on adolescents, and the coping strategies adopted by them in managing this situation. Seven adolescents, who have experienced the loss of a parent between six months to two and a half years before, ranging in age from 14 to 19 years were interviewed. *Insecurity* was identified as the core theme of the impact of parental death on adolescents, while *self-reliance* was identified as the core category of their coping with parental death. After portraying the phenomenon the future direction of palliative care service and research regarding adolescent bereavement are also discussed.

Adolescence and Parental Loss: Review of Previous Studies and a Theoretical Formulation

Introduction

Adolescence refers to the age of transitions between childhood and adulthood (Elder, 1990), and is a particularly challenging period of the life span (Herman-Stahl et al., 1995). During this period adolescents are confronted by changes in different aspects of their lives, including cognitive development, changes of body image, development of identity, achieving independence from the family while staying connected, fitting into a peer group, and fulfilling the requirements of schooling (Chan, 1995; Deveau, 1990; Frydenberg, 1997). When the death of a parent superimposes itself on these numerous transitions, it is likely to precipitate an extreme life crisis for the adolescent. It may produce intense and enduring emotional stress, affecting many areas of an adolescent's life, and can impair successful completion of developmental tasks, presenting obstacles to the transition to young adulthood (Balk, 1991; Fleming and Balmer, 1996). It is believed that among all the key relationship changes for adolescents, the death of a parent is likely the greatest loss (Raphael, 1996). Most western researchers agree that losing a parent is a major developmental and emotional challenge to an individual. In Chinese societies, where the Confucian philosophy of filial piety still prevails, parental loss could no longer fulfil their social responsibilities and moral obligations of taking care of the parent (Chan and Mak, 2000).

The experience of the death of a parent is not uncommon for adolescents in many cultures. Research studies reflect the fact that about 10 to 15 per cent of adolescents up to 16 years old have lost one parent due to death (Floerchinger, 1991; Silverman and Worden, 1992), while 47 per cent of the undergraduate population have experienced a close family member's death (Balk, 1996). However, studies concerned adolescents' parental loss are few, and the majority of literature has focused on parental responses to the death of a child, adult loss of spouse and children's reactions to parental death. The non-normative aspect of death and bereavement in adolescence, and the difficulties in dealing with death may lead researchers to avoid investigating such issues (Balk, 1991). It is only until recently that adolescent bereavement has been addressed in more focused studies (Ann, 1991; Fleming and Adoph, 1986; Fleming and Balmer, 1996).

Some studies have linked parental loss with several forms of psychopathology, such as adult depression, sociopathic personality, and unspecified psychoneurosis (Balk, 1991; Dietrich, 1984; Silverman and Worden, 1992; Tyson-Rawson, 1996). In Gray's study (1987), she found that parental death resulted in greater feelings of depression in adolescents, while other studies showed that the risk of major depression was over seven times greater for early adolescents after the death of a parent (Tyson-Rawson, 1996). Freudenberger and Gallagher (1995) also addressed the loss of parent in adolescence as a traumatic event, resulting in feelings of abandonment and depression in adolescents, with risk of long-lasting deleterious effects on the personality development and functioning of the individual. The problems they faced included forced maturity, incredible stress, a sense of confused identity and alienation, and distortions of ego. It has been observed that 'the loss of parent while the individual is still immature inflicts a massive trauma from which it is very difficult to recover' (Freudenberger and Gallagher, 1995, p. 150).

However, Mireault and Compas (1996) indicated that the adolescents they studied who experienced loss were not more distressed than the non-bereaved adolescents. Instead, bereavement experience during adolescence led to greater maturity, but not psychological disturbance. It may accelerate the psychological growth of adolescents and result in positive outcomes such as increased sense of strength and self-reliance, greater caring for loved ones, including younger siblings, strengthened emotional bonds with others, searching for meaning in one's life, developed emotional strength, increased empathy for others, more general quickening to life and deeper appreciation of existence (Balk, 1991; Balk and Corr, 1996; Hogan and Balk, 1990; Hogan and Greenfield, 1991; Oltjenbruns, 1991).

It has been asserted, perhaps tautologically, that whether parental loss can evoke growth or harm depends on how adolescents cope with it (Balk, 1996). 'Death of one parent during adolescence presents dangerous opportunities. This crisis can evoke growth and maturity, or presage maldevelopment, depending on how adolescents respond to and cope with it' (Balk and Corr 1996, p. 5). Studies have shown that the presence of effective coping is especially important for adolescents who are having to deal with multiple changes in their lives (Compas, 1987; Herman-Stahl et al., 1995; Herman-Stahl and Peterson, 1996). Effective coping may eliminate the effects of negative life events on psychological well being. There are certain styles of coping that might lead to better adaptation, while ineffective coping may exacerbate the effects of stress on adjustment (Herman-Stahl and Peterson, 1996; Phelps and Javis, 1994). Therefore, examination of adolescent coping in parental bereavement is important to those who are concerned about the adolescent welfare and psychological development. Knowledge development in this field should help us to anticipate the possible outcomes of their bereavement, and the support they may need.

Stress Theory and Coping with Bereavement

Bereavement is the set of reactions to the loss of a close relationship, which include physical, spiritual, intellectual, social, emotional reactions, and their mediation by cultural experiences (Weiss, 1994). Worden (1991, 1996) has also stressed that besides the loss of the person, the adjustment one has to make involves many aspects of life. These secondary stressors often require much effort to overcome, but have not been specifically recognised in conventional grief theories (Stroebe, 1996).

With reference to the literature on coping with stressful events, according to Folkman and Lazarus's cognitive stress theory, an individual experiences stress when the demands of a given situation are seen as exceeding psychological resources, in ways which endangers well-being and health (Lazarus and Folkman, 1984). Coping therefore is defined as the person's cognitive and behavioural efforts to manage specific external and/or internal demands that are appraised as taxing or exceeding the person resources (Folkman et al., 1986). This account of stress focuses on effortful or purposeful reactions to stress (Compas, 1987). Coping actions mobilised to master the stress are classified into problem-focused and emotion-focused types of coping. The problem-focused coping is aimed at doing something to change the stress, while the emotion-focused coping is aimed at reducing or managing the emotional distress associated with the situation (Carver, Weintraub and Scheier, 1989; Folkman et al., 1986a; Moos and Billings, 1982). There is no single coping strategy to fit all circumstances because a coping strategy that is adaptive for one situation may be maladaptive in another context. Success of coping depends on the match between the strategy and the coping demands of a situation (Compas, 1987; Glyshaw, Cohen and Towbes, 1989).

A number of studies have shown that both problem- and emotion- focused coping were used by adolescents and both were important in successful adaptation to various kinds of stress (Compas, Malcarne and Fondacaro, 1988; Hoffman et al., 1992). Their coping behaviour varied significantly with different circumstances (Compas et al., 1987; Frydenberg, 1997) and the importance of these two types of coping may vary in different types of stressful encounter and in different points in time (Compas, 1987). For instance, psychological symptoms will be higher when people use more emotion-focused coping with controllable events and more problem-focused coping with uncontrollable events (Compas, Malcarne and Fondacaro, 1988, p. 410).

However, this theory has three limitations in explaining reactions to bereavement. Firstly, it does not describe a process of concurrent appraisal and coping with different stressors which are associated with the bereavement process, but rather offers appraisal and coping associated with one specific stressor. Secondly, it does not reflect the dynamic interplay of approach and avoidance between the various stressors (Stroebe, 1999). Thirdly, it has not been determined which strategies are most effective in coping with which types of stress and at what points in time (Compas, 1987). Many studies showed that adolescents' coping behaviour varies significantly with different circumstances (Compas, 1987; Compas et al., 1987; Frydenberg, 1997), and that family stresses seem to elicit different coping behaviours. Adolescents would use more emotion-based coping with family problems than with school-related problems, suggesting that family-based problems are particularly difficult circumstances for adolescents to handle (Frydenberg, 1997). However, how adolescents cope with the death of a parent and to what degree the above findings can be generalised to coping with parental death have not been specifically explored in available studies.

In traditional Chinese societies, the mourning period was a rather lengthy one. In modern day Hong Kong, the mourning period is drastically shortened to the extent that it might negatively affect the grieving process of adults and adolescents alike. It is a custom for family and relatives to gather together and observe the rituals, for instance, having some monks to pacify the soul in the 7th as well as 49th day after death. In the 49th day, with the burning of mourning ropes as the 'closing ceremony', the grieving process is to be completed. However, such rituals are seldom closely observed which means that the mourning period is often too hastily finished. Future research should study the impact of this artificial shortening of bereavement period on adolescents' mental health.

Theories of Bereavement

A number of writers have discussed how a bereaved individual works through the process of bereavement. Among the key conventional theories of grief explaining how people cope with the loss, are theorists amongst whom Lindemann, Bowlby, Parkes and Worden are the most frequently quoted. These theorists imply that in order to adapt to loss and recover successfully, one must confront the experience of bereavement, work through or process what has happened, as well as overcoming denial of the implications of the loss (Stroebe and Schut, 1999; Wortman and Silver, 1989). This theoretical model of grief work is defined as a 'cognitive process of confronting a loss, of going over the events before and at the time death, of focusing on memories and working toward detachment from the deceased. Fundamental to current conceptions is the view that one needs to bring the reality of loss into one's awareness as much as possible and that suppression is a pathological phenomenon' (Stroebe, 1992, pp. 19–20).

While Freud and Lindemann described a bereavement process requiring the bereaved to deal with the pain of grief, release the lost person, and readjust to the world by forming a new identity with new relationships and roles (Sanders, 1989), Bowlby also argued that one has to work through the loss actively, meaning redefinition of self and situation. This would involve the realisation and reshaping of one's internal representational models to align with the changes that have occurred. For Parkes, his 'psychosocial transition' also emphasises the importance of grief work, describing the process of bereavement in four stages: numbness, searching and pining, depression, and recovery. In the process of bereavement the bereaved has to rearrange an old set of assumptions about affective roles, and adopt a new internal working model of thoughts, cognitions and feelings (Parkes, 1994; Strobe, 1992–93). Another scholar, Worden (1991), also argued that adaptation to loss involved four tasks of accepting the reality of the loss, working through the pain of grief, adjusting to an environment in which the deceased is missing, emotionally relocating the deceased and moving on with life. Lack of completion of these grief tasks was likely to impair further emotional growth and development.

However, as more empirical evidence accumulates, the notions of these theories have been challenged. Firstly, Wortman and Silver (1989) questioned the assumption that one had to 'work through' one's grief, since they found that bereaved people who failed to feel distress were not less likely to cope in the long run. Secondly, Margaret Stroebe (1992) also highlighted that there was no significant overall relationship between working through grief and adaptation to loss. Thirdly, more recently Stroebe and Schut (1999), in their Dual Process Model, argued for the recognition of the range of stressors and the multiplicity of losses embedded in the bereavement experience. They emphasised that bereaved individuals had both to grieve over their loss (loss-orientation) and also had to attend to other stresssors (such as restoration-orientation) other than the lost relationship itself. The so-called secondary stressors add considerable burden to the bereaved person's burden of loss and cause additional anxiety and upset. While such practical tasks are being attended to, grief has to be sidelined. The bereaved thus experience fluctuation of attention in the dynamic coping process, which is described as oscillation. In other words, bereavement consists of an oscillation between confronting and avoiding different stressors associated with bereavement, and this is a dynamic and back-and-forth process (Stroebe and Schut, 1999; Walter, 1996). The extent to which the conventional notion of grief work and Streobe and Schut's proposition of oscillation processes apply to adolescent bereavement after parental loss have not been explored.

Adolescent Development and Coping in Bereavement

A number of scholars have stressed that the major grief theories outlined above have been inadequate in explaining adolescent bereavement. They emphasised that adolescents' grief reactions may differ in many ways from those of adults because their distinct developmental differences can affect how adolescents approach and accomplish the tasks of grieving (Balk, 1991; Raphael, 1996; Fleming and Balmer, 1996). '... it differs because of its increased affective intensity, a product of the interaction of the loss and the developmental context within which it occurs' (Tyson-Rawson, 1996, p. 157).

Research on bereavement and grief studies carried out in Hong Kong focused on elderly widows (Lin, 1999) and young widows (Leung, 1966; Tsang, 1966). The way that Chinese adolescents cope with bereavement has not yet been explored. On the other hand, even in the west, grief theory for explaining adolescent bereavement has been scarcely developed. Fleming and others have developed a model that links adolescent development with adjustment to loss (Fleming and Balmer, 1996), and some scholars have also tried to apply existing theories to understand adolescent bereavement (Balk, 1996; Worden, 1996). This model is distinguished from other grief theories by its appealing developmental grounding for understanding adolescent bereavement, and the extension by these writers of the model of Fleming and Adolph (1986) is therefore favoured by the present researcher. Fleming and Adolph identify both tasks and conflicts for adolescents coping with bereavement. When adolescents attempt to resolve their bereavement experience, there is an interplay with the tasks and conflicts of each maturational phase of adolescence. This model defines adolescence as the years from 11 to 21 with three maturational periods: early, middle and late. Passing through each phase, adolescents have to face three developmental tasks: 1) emotional separation from their parents; 2) development of mastery and competence; 3) development of intimacy with individuals outside of their immediate family circle.

Alongside these tasks, they propose that bereavement requires adolescents to cope with five core issues that differ according to the maturational phase of the adolescent, which include predictability of events, mastery/control, belonging, a sense of fairness/justice, and development of self-image:

> *During adolescence, the loss of a profound relationship - whether an internalised object or a person in the external world - may interfere in what seems to be the natural progression of intellectual-emotional-psychological 'growing up.' Changes that are normally expected may be averted, avoided, or may not even take place. Such an arrest of developmental unfolding may put the adolescent 'on hold' in one phase, and thus inhibit the energy and skills necessary to meet subsequent phase-appropriate demands. A developmental arrest may also have the opposite effect, that is, of increasing the intensity of prior phase-specific behavior in a following phase.* (Fleming and Adolph, 1986, pp. 101–102)

Since the methodology of the research reported below is based in the process of 'grounded theory' which seeks to generate fresh hypotheses through the narrative process of elaborated case histories, no initial assumptions or hypotheses are made, although the previous literature on bereavement has influenced what questions have been asked in the open-ended interviews.

Methods of Research

Design

This study has adopted qualitative research design which is regarded as a good method when little empirical examination has been conducted for the issue being studied and an exploratory descriptive approach is required (Creswell, 1994; Davies, 1991; Glaser, 1996; Chenitz and Swanson, 1986). Grounded theory was chosen as the research method of this study because it is a systematic method for the collection and analysis of qualitative data, particularly useful for use in preliminary, explanatory, and descriptive studies (Glaser, 1992). It can help to provide means to exploit the richness of human experience, to identify the core variable or the process reflecting the characteristics of a particular condition and the relationship between the process (Artinian, 1986; Chenitz and Swanson, 1986).

Subjects

Co-operation was invited from the bereaved adolescents whose parent had died in the researcher's hospice in Hong Kong. To be selected for participation, subjects needed to have experienced a parent's death between six months to two and a half year prior to the commencement of the study, were between 12 to 17 years old when their parents died, and came from families that were intact before the death of parent. Extended interviews have been conducted with seven adolescents whose ages ranged from 14 to 19 years old at the time of interview. Their average age was 14.5 years when their parents died. One subject experienced the loss of father while the other six experienced the loss of mother. Three were male and four were female. The time elapsed since death of parent ranged from one to 2.5 years (average is 2 years). Of the adolescents initially approached, some 40 per cent agreed to participate.

Selection of Subjects

Theoretical sampling is a useful method in the context of grounded theory (Sandelowski, 1998): subjects are chosen progressively during the research process. Theoretical sampling is 'the process of deciding on analytic grounds what data to collect next and where to collect it by sampling particular groups of people according to their significance to the development and testing of the emergent theory' (Bartlett and Payne, 1997, p. 191). In the research process, the researcher used the codes to direct further data collection, based on a theoretical premise in order to determine whether new units and data are necessary. Each potential participant would produce information which might lead to the selection of the next subject.

For example, in the present study one subject was invited to participate because his elder sibling revealed that he had a rather different coping style; it was considered that his participation therefore might enrich the data of the study. Sampling ceased when the study was felt to have reached a theoretical saturation, when inclusion and analysis of new units did not appear to produce new data (Sandelowski, 1998).

Initially, several sampling parameters were considered as 'research employing grounded theory typically begins with a selective sampling strategy aimed at phenomenal variation and then proceeds to theoretical sampling'

(Sandelowski, 1995, p. 182). The selection criteria could help to reduce the minimum sample required for this single research project, while still producing credible findings.

Data Collection Procedures

As parental loss is a very personal and sensitive issue for adolescents, semi-structured interviews were used as it is a primary tool to obtain an account of the richness of human experience, through the participants' own words and frames of reference (Bartlett and Payne, 1997). An interview guide was adopted to elicit the data from the participants as adolescents are likely to have greater difficulties in disclosing their feelings, and reflecting on experiences (Douglas, 1984). However, the content and sequence of the interview guide was not rigidly adhered to as it was more important to follow the flow of participant's major concerns or viewpoint during the interview. The interviewer aimed at: being supportive, communicating warmth, putting the participants at ease, giving permission to talk about private issues (Swanson, 1986).

As 'the major considerations of the interview setting are the convenience of the site to the respondent ... and the setting should assure privacy and should be free from interruptions and distractions' (Swanson, 1986, p. 73), respecting the choices of subjects and their parents was emphasised in the selection of the interview site. Travelling time and avoidance of pain involved in revisiting the hospice were key considerations in the choice of interview setting. Among the seven interviews, two were conducted at participants' homes and four were conducted in the hospice's community day centre, and only one subject chose to come back to the hospice.

The audio-taped interviews lasted from one hour to one and a half-hours, depending on the response of the participants. As the interview may be incomplete and more information may be needed, the closure of the interview was treated as tentative (Swanson 1986). Participants were informed that a further second face-to-face interview and phone contact additional information might be needed. Based on the participants' choice, all additional data was collected through half-an-hour phone interviews.

Data Analysis

The qualitative method of constant comparative analysis was adopted for the data analysis. The initial step of constant comparative analysis was open coding, starting with a completely open mind i.e. no precoded categories were created (Glaser, 1992; McKenzie, Powell and Usher, 1997). Then, the data was broken down into pieces by reading the data line by line and paragraph by paragraph. Each piece of conceptual data may represent a specific incident or fact. It was then coded as a concept or abstraction from the data. Categories were then gradually developed from open coding. Similar concepts were categorised and labelled, and these conceptual categories were at a higher level of abstraction than the initial and individual concepts of a category (Corbin, 1986). Categories are the major unit of analysis in the grounded theory method (Corbin, 1996).

Types of categories in this study include core category, major categories and sub-categories. As comparisons of data were an important strategy for discovering and building categories, concepts, categories or incidents were constantly compared with one another to look for similarities and differences, in order to ensure the validity and reliability of the analysis (Corbin, 1986). In this process, based on the data each category has to be constantly verified and refined or rejected (Bartlett and Payne, 1997).

When most of the categories emerged and developed, the researcher made linkages among the categories, if possible. After the categories have been built and linked, core category was identified. Glaser (1992, p. 75) states that the core category accounts for most of the variation in a pattern of behaviour, and serves several important functions of integration, density, saturation and completeness. Through this analytic process, two strategies of writing memos and diagramming were employed in line. In this process, as Glaser (1992) has emphasised, the researcher tried to immerse herself into the data by going from incident to incident, with patience and trust to allow emergence of codes (Corbin, 1986; Glaser, 1992). The availability of space and time was very important in this process. This is because impatience may lead to preconception. In conclusion, 'The grounded theorist should simply constantly code and analyse categories and properties with theoretical codes which will emerge and generate their complex theory of a complex world! And in turn they will produce simple or complex explanations along the way of the processing of the concerns of a substantive area' (Glaser, 1992, p. 71).

Results[1]

Impact of Parental Death

Insecurity was identified as the major category for the impact of parental loss. The loss has shattered the equalibrium of the adolescents' lives, and has demonstrated to them that they have only little control over events and circumstances. The five subcategories of this core category are emotional disequilibrium, disruption of family system, change of identity, alienation as well as lack of control (see Figure 6.1).

Emotional Disequilibrium

Adolescents experienced *emotional turmoil* upon and after the moment of parental death. The emotional features being expressed included separation grief, longing, helplessness, guilt and fear.

Separation grief here refers to the emotion an adolescent possesses when his/her parent died. Adolescents particularly felt grieved at the moment of death because the separation was forever. Despite the fact that there was forewarning of death, they still had feelings of shock and numbness, and feelings of sadness, ambivalence and unwillingness to let the loved parent go were common.

> *... I was very tearful ... I grasped mother's hand and refused to let her go. I was afraid that if I let her hand go, she would leave me forever and would never return.*

> *Although father had told me before that mother's illness was incurable and she would die some day, I was still shock and unable to accept when that moment came.*

Longing

Longing refers to the feeling of missing the deceased, which is usually accompanied with memories and reunion wishes.

> *After the loss, everyday I thought of how father had treated me in the past ... he had accompanied me going to school, defending for me when mother scolded me.*

> *I want to hear her voice, she had a beautiful voice ...*

Several adolescents expressed the opinion that longing for the deceased parent affected their functioning – school performance is a typical example. But the

Figure 6.1 Adolescents' challenges in time of parental death

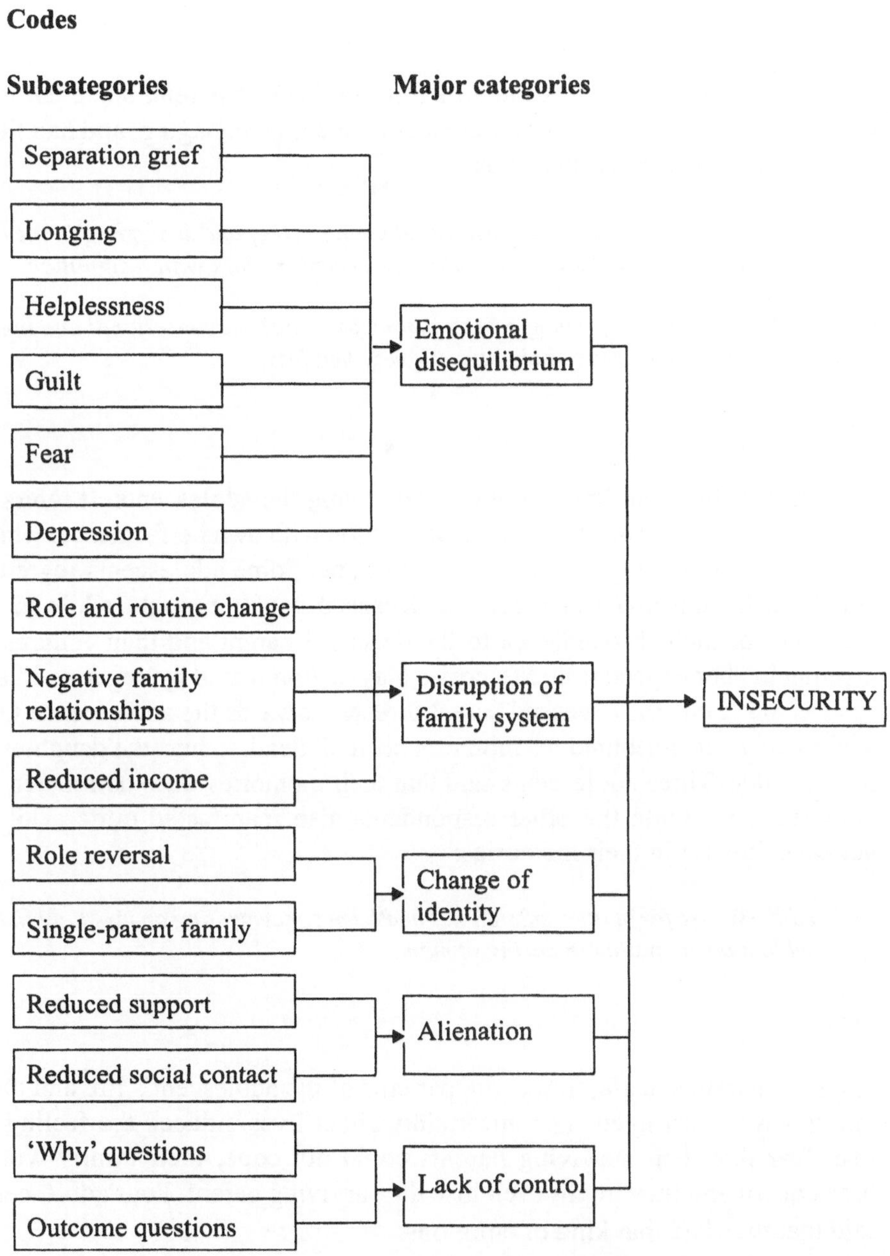

interference was found to be rather short-term, usually not longer than a few weeks.

Helplessness

A sense of helplessness was induced from the loss of parent, since the loss made adolescents feel that they were incompetent in managing, and had little or no control over individual events.

> *It was really helpless to have witnessed mother dying and struggling in the last five minutes before death ... I could only accept the loss with resignation.*

> *Father is the most grieving person among us ... he's very emotional and upset, but I don't know how to help him. It's very helpless!*

Guilt

Guilt is a feeling that frequently existed among the adolescents. It refers to the regret or self-reproach due to dissatisfaction with own performance, which can be something that one has or has not done. Some adolescents regretted about not having loved or cared the deceased parent enough, while many regretted for their disobedience to the deceased parent and their failures in meeting his/her expectation. Memories may be dominated by negative issues such as the blame the deceased parent directed towards the adolescents. One adolescent even attributed his mother's difficult death to her (the daughter's) poor attitude. Three adolescents said that their memories were dominated by guilt feelings, while the other respondents also manifested quite a lot of negative thought in their memories.

> *I did not care for mother enough ... I had been concentrating on my study ... but seldom participating in caring of mom.*

Fear

After the parent's death, the secure patterns of the adolescent's life and their families were disrupted. The uncertainty about lives induced the feeling of fear, fear that their surviving parents could not cope, their family would break down and they might even lose the surviving parent. Four adolescents said that they had that kind of emotions.

> *Father was very grieved and depressed after mom's death ... I was upset about this, and was afraid of losing father and our family as well.*

> *I wonder whether my family can overcome these problems or not? I am very puzzled ...*

Depression

While 'depression' has often been equated with mental illness, a looser sense is adopted here. It refers to the presence of sadness, unhappiness or blue feelings for an unspecified period of time after the parent's death. Two adolescents in the study were obviously affected by these emotions for quite a long time. Another adolescent boy who was very active before, indicated that he had become more quiet and withdrawn after the death of his mother. Even after a year since the death, he felt that he hadn't fully recovered his previous level of enthusiasm.

> *After mother died, I became more moody and self-isolated. I had no interest to make friends as in the past ...*

Disruption of Family System

The loss of a parent resulted in great changes in the family: both structure and relationships of the family were affected internally and/or externally. The impact includes role and routine change, negative family relationship and reduced income, resulting in worries among the adolescent.

Role and Routine Change

All adolescents felt that the death of their parents has resulted in reallocation of family roles and responsibilities. An obvious change they observed is the increasing responsibilities of the surviving parent. Besides, the change of roles also involved other family members. One adolescent girl felt sorry for the great stress and burden imposed on her elder sister, which she thought was even heavier than that of her surviving parent.

> *In the past, all family routine was looked after by mother (with sadness), now father has to shoulder all of them ... he was not very used to it and seems difficult to adjust.*

> *... it's too much for father. He's tired after father comes back from work, but he has to clean up the house, and arrange activities with us.*

Besides the reallocation of roles, established family routines were also disrupted. An adolescent boy expressed in exasperation:

> *I miss mum's delicious meals ... I love eating and mum's cooking was fantastic. But now I have to depend on lunch box ... Besides, the house had been very neat and tidy in the past, it is more messy now.*

> *Father is not clear about the household matters and therefore always turns to us for information ... such adjustment is a bit difficult to me.*

With more preparation and a transitional period, the adolescents could adapt to the changes in an easier way. An adolescent boy, whose mother had been hospitalised for quite a long time before death, expressed the idea that he didn't find it very difficult to adapt to the change as he had already learned to depend on himself.

Negative Family Relationships

Loss of a loved one affected family members' emotions, which in turn brought adverse impact on communication and interaction between each of them. All adolescents said that the loss had upset the family members, especially the surviving parent.

> *Mother is very hurt, she washes her face with tears every night.*

> *Father is very grieved, he always sits numbly on sofa and cries a lot.*

The emotions of surviving parent or other members may undermine existing relationships and subsequently resulted in secondary or double loss to adolescents. In addition, the loss may lead to blame and conflicts among family members.

> *... my relationship with father is not as good as the past ... we have less communication, poorer relationship. He smokes more heavily, becomes more silent, irritable, bad-tempered and unreasonable.*

My younger brother has suddenly become very quiet after mum's death ... he refused to talk to me and kept himself isolated for about one year ...

In this time of family grief, mutual support in the family was unsatisfactory. Family members seldom shared the loss and emotions among each other. The overall family atmosphere was described as deteriorating.

... our family is not as happy as before. We had more conversation and laughter previously. If mother were alive, all of us would be happier.

... We had less communication during that time because all of us were upset by the death of mum.

Reduced Income

Four adolescents reported that the death of their parents has resulted in greater financial constraint on their families since their surviving parents had to stop working and depend on government allowances for livelihood. Henceforth, they had to reduce their social activities and were continuously worried about family finances.

Change of Identity

Feelings of low self-worth, lack of self-respect and feelings of inferiority among adolescents occurred as part of the change of identity after the parental loss. The change of identity was related to role reversal and status of being a single-parent child.

Role Reversal

Adolescents were often expected to take up the role of caring for and supporting to others after the death of parent, and had to shoulder many more family responsibilities. This phenomenon was more prevalent among adolescents who were the elder children among siblings. The various roles included being a supporter to the surviving parent or affected family members, mediator for conflicts among members, and co-parent of the surviving parent.

Father was very grieved after mom's death, I therefore had to suppress my emotions and to comfort father. I was very ambivalent ...

> *Father told me that when I was young I could have mum's and daddy's love, but now my young brother could only have him, therefore I should give more to my brother ... as my father feels helpless in parenting my young brother, he expects me to discipline him.*

With the increasing responsibilities and expectation, adolescents became more stressed.

> *... If my mother was here, I would have had more personal time, perhaps I would sleep more, I love sleeping very much.*

> *When my mum was there, my responsibilities are not that heavy ... no matter what happens, my parents will help me ... there is less stress. But now it is totally different!*

Single-parent Family

The status of single parent family has different meanings to the adolescents. Some associated the change of this status with increase in responsibilities, but some regarded this a stigma and resulted in feelings of inferiority. This feeling discouraged the adolescents from sharing the loss with her peer.

> *... I have lost others' concern. Since we have become a single parent family and depended on government allowance, other people begin to stigmatise us ... and do not want to have the relationship with me.*

> *Days are more difficult and stressful now ... more duties to fulfil, higher academic expectation to meet, but less concern ... I am a bit jealous of my schoolmates.*

Alienation may occur, andrefers to the feeling of isolation and loneliness among adolescents, a result of the deprivation of the needs for care and opportunities of social contact after the death of parent. It has the following elements.

Reduced Support

With the loss of parent, the adolescents have lost the blessings in their relationship with the deceased parent, such as love, protection, fun and laughter. They were expected to carry out their roles and responsibilities by themselves independently.

> *As mother died, I have to handle all the things by myself, no one can help me anymore. I have to stand up on my own feet if I fell down.*

> *I shared everything with my mum in the past, just like close friends ... She protected me, looked after me, listened to me, taught me many things and even how to be a person ...*

> *When mum was here I could talk to her, share things related to school and peers with her, but now I have got nobody!*

Unfortunately, adolescents had no substitute for these losses. All the adolescents in this study expressed the idea that they could not get sufficient care and concern from others. Many adolescents felt their relationship with the surviving parent was mostly dominated by expectations of better academic performance and more family duties.

> *My greatest loss resulting from mum's death is care and concern. This is a big difference from the past. I wish I could have more concern ... I am not happy with it.*

> *If mum was still alive, there would be more communications among us, more happiness, and more warmth and care to me ... mother is not replaceable.*

The adolescents felt family support was crucial to them. They wished they could have a better family relationship. In addition, the quality of family relationship could help the adjustment of the loss. An adolescent mentioned the improvement of his relationship with a sibling had helped to reduce his negative memories.

> *I hoped that I could communicate more with father, like talking about happy school events, ... but I don't know how to talk to him! ... and if we could share more about the loss of mother, I think both of us would be less upset.*

Reduced Social Contact

More than half of the adolescents said that social opportunities were diminished as they got less freedom and fewer social activities after the loss. The main reasons were due to the financial constraint, increasing household responsibilities, and greater expectation on their study from surviving parents. In addition, as mentioned before, the reduced social contact may be the result of the depressed emotions of the adolescents.

I am an active girl, however, I have to reduce my activities as father now has high expectation on my academic performance. I am quite unhappy about this.

If my mother was alive, I think I would have more leisure moments. I like camping, outdoor activities, and organising programmes ... Now, there is less feasibility.

Lack of Control

The loss and separation made adolescents feel that they had very little control over their life, leading to feelings of helplessness and powerlessness.

Why Questions

'Why?' questions emerged from adolescents as they tried to understand the death and why it happened. More than half posed the question of why bad luck happened to good people or why chose their parents. Feelings of unfairness, anger and resignation were usually associated with these questions.

There are so many smokers in the world, I don't understand why it took away my father's life so early? ... Why did it happen to me?

I couldn't understand and accept that mother would become sick suddenly, and why choose my mum ... it's unfair and unreasonable!

Outcome Questions

Some adolescents raised questions of long-term outcomes. An adolescent girl expressed she had become more fatalistic and she was unconfident that her endeavour could make any impact on her future.

I had been very optimistic towards my future before, but I have become pessimistic after my mum's death ... I think my future is decided by fate and I have no choice ... . I believe my future will be more difficult than before.

Coping with Challenges

Being self-reliant has emerged as a core category (see Figure 6.2), which describes a situation in which adolescents try to master the challenges of

Figure 6.2 Adolescents' coping following parental death

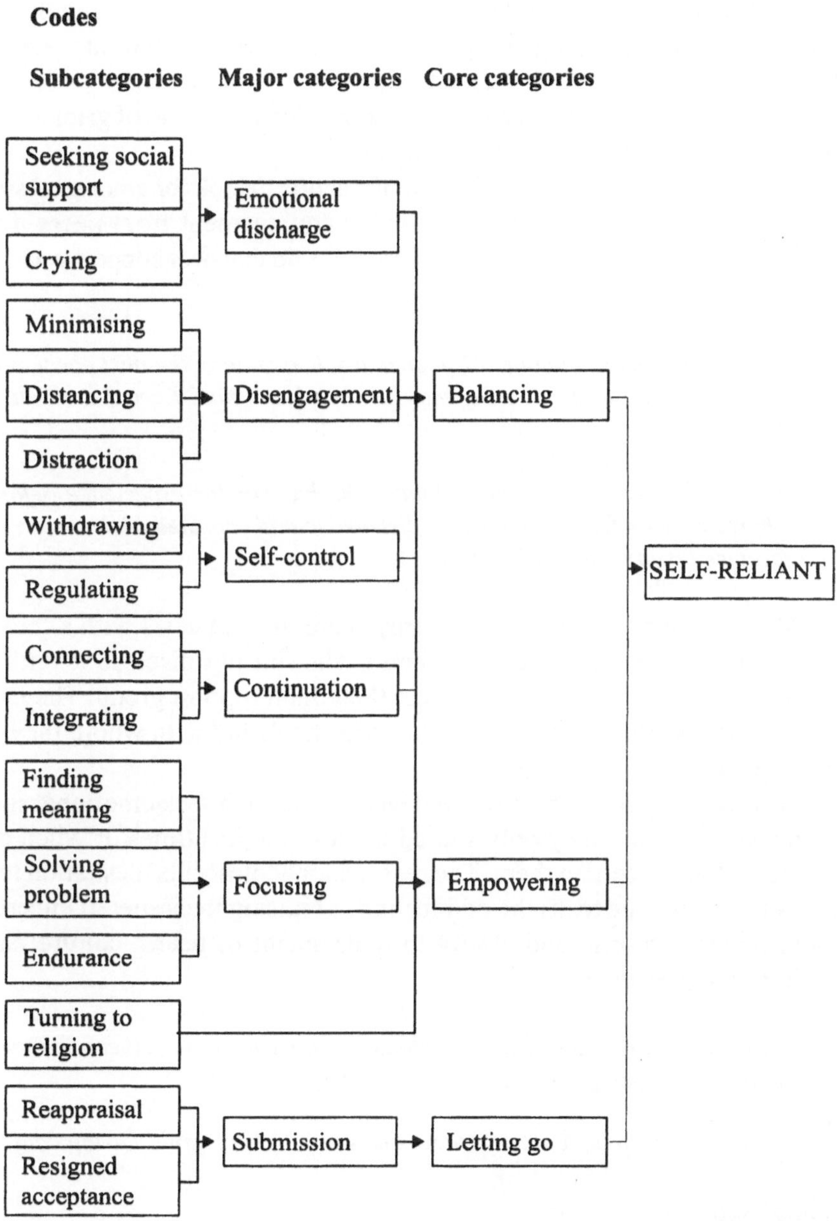

parental death mostly by themselves. This self-reliant process will be discussed in relation to three minor categories: balancing, empowering and letting go.

Balancing refers to the efforts that the adolescents use to regulate their emotional turmoil during the parental loss. There are two subcategories: emotional discharge and disengagement.

Emotional discharge is seen as the expression or release of grief emotions either in front of others or when being alone.

Seeking social support is defined as the action to look for emotional support such as reassurance, understanding and encouragement from peers, family, teachers or other helpful persons. Adolescents said that peer support was crucial and helpful to them.

> *After mom died in midnight, I phoned a schoolmate in the next early morning and asked him to accompany me, ... when I met him, I cried and felt better then.*

> *I had talked to an elder schoolmate who has similar experience before. We shared how we felt about the loss, listened to and consoled each other ... and I became less afraid and insecure.*

Most of the adolescents would only share the bad news with a few good friends, but there were two adolescents who did not disclose it until their friends asked them. Schoolmates were their main support group. They would choose friends who had the ability to understand, and with whom they had a close relationship.

However, the adolescents indeed were not used to seek emotional support from peers. Usually they only shared the loss for few times or when others expressed the concern to them. The reasons for adolescents' hesitation to seek peer support are due to: a) the odd feelings of raising the issue; b) uncertainty about peers' response and ability to understand; c) peers' culture; and d) adolescents' personality.

> *... I am not sure whether they would understand me or not, since we do not talk about such kind of issue in our daily dialogue ...*

> *I did not want to talk about it, it was no use ... I don't think sharing could help!*

School Support

Besides schoolmates, four adolescents shared the loss with those teachers who had taken the initiative to approach them. But the conversation was described as superficial, except by a girl who felt her form-mistress had given her continuous encouragement in her time of loss. According to most of the adolescents, the conventional teacher-student relationship may hinder them from seeking support. The teachers' friendliness, initiative and rapport (or the lack thereof) were emphasised as important.

> *When my father died, I was still in primary school. The teachers in primary school were more distant ... I thought this is not a topic between teachers and students, since it is a family issue.*

Adolescents rarely got support from people outside school, unless they already had some external affiliation. Only two adolescents who had prior involvement in social service organisation or church could get support from other resource persons such as a social worker or church fellows.

Family Support

Despite the significance of family in the growth of adolescents, most of the adolescents did not seek emotional support from their parents or siblings. The reasons for this passivity were due to: a) the surviving parent was overwhelmed by their own grief; b) the family did not have the cultural value of sharing the loss issue; and c) rapport with the surviving parent was not strong enough.

> *I am not used to communicate with my father, ... and I have grown-up, I am able to look after myself, and there is no particular difficulty ...*

> *Father was very tired and busy with the arrangement of schooling and child care issues for younger brother during that time. It was unrealistic to expect him to listen to me ... and I guessed my family did not want to recall this unhappiness.*

> *Mom was more grieved than us, it should be our responsibility to support her.*

Among these various sources of help, peers have provided the greatest support, despite the fact that teachers, social workers and church people were often supportive. Adolescents treasured these various kinds of support, especially when family members were too devastated themselves to provide emotional help.

> *Yes, although the support is not very great, at least I feel that there is somebody to care and help me.*

> *Father was very busy during that time ... It is good to have a friend to listen to me.*

Crying

Crying is another type of emotional discharge, although not all of the adolescents released their emotions through crying. Upon the moment of death, all of the adolescent girls were crying and one adolescent boy was sobbing. The adolescent girls in the study cried more than boys. But, both males and females usually cried privately as they did not like crying in front of others. The adolescents felt that crying was helpful, as it helped to relieve themselves from negative emotions.

> *I am not used to cry. I do not want to be seen when I cried. It is embarrassing, shameful ... I am afraid of teasing by others.*

> *I would choose a private place to cry ... I hope that I could carry on my life bravely ... If they see my tears, they may think that I am not tough enough.*

Disengagement

Disengagement refers to the cognitive or the behavioural attempt through which adolescents stabilise their emotions, detach and protect themselves from the grief. This coping works in opposite direction to the emotional discharge, and was adopted more frequently than the emotional discharge by the subjects. There were six skills identified for this subcategory.

Minimising is the cognitive skill adopted by adolescents to deny or to eliminate the seriousness of the loss including the wishful thought.

> *As mom had been hospitalised for quite a long time before her death, the loss does not have much impact on us.*

> *Attending funeral is to say a temporary goodbye to mother, like seeing somebody off in the airport and we would meet again ... I feel mom is on a long trip now, just I cannot contact her...*

Distancing describes adolescents making cognitive efforts to detach themselves from the situation using strategies such as trying not to think about the problems, asking 'why' questions, ruminating on the impact of the loss on their lives, and so forth.

> *It is useless to compare myself with peers. Although I wish I could have what they have, it's impossible ... As comparison doesn't help but only results in admiration, I rarely make comparison with them.*

> Researcher: *Have you ever thought about what would be different if your mom had not died?*

> *Occasionally, but I would stop thinking about it very soon. This seems a nonsense thought ... and perhaps I am trying to avoid the sadness. I think life should be happier.*

Distraction refers to the adolescents' behavioural or cognitive actions to draw their attention away from the unwelcome situation. The behavioural actions include relaxation activities, sleep, engaging in alternative tasks like schoolwork or family duties and so on.

> *Usually shortly after I get upset, I will get something else to occupy me like doing homework, studying books, or going out. Then I would forget the unhappiness soon.*

> *After the death of my mom, I wasn't affected. I was busy a school project during the following week after the death ... I enjoyed my job very much and I just forgot the death of my mom.*

The cognitive actions draw one's attention away from the loss include thinking about other caring tasks, recalling positive memories. Some adolescents said that positive memories could help to distract them from negative emotions like guilt feelings.

> *I like to recall memories of happy moments with mother because I did not want to upset myself. This is more comfortable and it helps me to feel better.*

Self-control

Self-control relates to the efforts of the adolescents in regulating their emotions at a desired level, so that the overt expression of grief is usually avoided.

Self-control involves 'regulating' which refers to the adolescents' attempt at keeping their emotions under control. Many adolescents tried to keep their feelings to themselves and to present themselves as emotionally stable to others.

> *I tried to be calm and normal in front of my classmates during the days after my mum's death ... I did not want them to know I was upset and my family had such a big change.*

> *I behaved as usual in school after my father died. I was afraid of revealing my emotions to my school-mates, because I used to be cheerful in front of them.*

Two adolescent boys indicated that they withheld their emotions upon the moment of death. They remained calm when mother passed away, although they were very grieved about the loss and were also affected.

> *I have had some tendency to cry upon the moment of my mom's death, but I did not, not even a drop of tear ... I do not like crying, this is my personality.*

> *I did not want her die ... in order to neutralise the event and my emotions, I told myself that mom did not want me to be so upset.*

Another type of self-control strategy involves withdrawing, isolating oneself from people by reducing social activities, showing less involvement during social contact, making less attempt to seek support or share their situation with others.

> *... I became less involved in activities. My schoolmates asked me to play sport, but I did not join them.*

Empowering

Empowering is a minor category and describes adolescents' attempt to strengthen themselves to master the challenges of parental loss, psychologically and instrumentally. The three subcategories in relation to self-empowering are: continuation, focusing on and turning to religion.

Continuation is a way of developing bonding and maintaining a sense of the presence of the deceased parent in adolescents' lives. This continuity of relationship gives strength to adolescents to go on with their lives.

Connecting refers to the attempt to maintain an ongoing emotional attachment with the deceased parent. Feeling the presence of the lost parent in their lives helped adolescents gain assurance, encouragement and courage to press on.

> *Although mom has died, I feel that she was still with me. No matter what would happen, she would be there to support me ... Therefore, when I am depressed, I need not to be frightened because mom would stand by me. This is a great help to me, because mom is the person I love most.*

> *... spiritually, I feel that mother is still with me ... This feeling could help me a bit, even though it gives some pressure too. It encourages and urges me to make some improvements.*

Adolescents used several ways to connect themselves with their deceased parents. An adolescent boy refused to move to a new flat and chose to stay at the original flat for certain period because the house gave him strong sense of affiliation with mother.

> *I have visited mom's cemetery several times in the first half year. No other way could make me feel closer to mom than this ... In the cemetery, I felt I was close to mom again. I cleaned the place and talked to her. I was very upset when I arrived, but I felt very happy when I left.*

> *My family still go to that park on every Christmas, as we did with mom in the past. I like to go there because this brings back lots of happy memories about mom and us.*

Besides visiting places, adolescents also acquired the sense of connection through positive memories about the deceased parent. An adolescent boy enjoyed recalling the memories very much because through which he could regain the closeness and relationship with her mom.

> *Since my mom's diagnosis, we have going through lot things together. I am very glad that I could remember them in details ... just like enjoying a video show.*

Integrating

Integrating refers to the internalisation of the lost parent's expectations about their lives as a goal or direction. As a compensation for their lost parent, adolescents wanted to fulfil the parent's unfinished wishes for themselves and their families. Integrating could be important to the establishment of adolescents' identity as this helps them to resolve negative feelings related to the loss as well as building their self-esteem.

> *After the death of mom, I forced myself to study harder, ... I wanted to get a better result for mom because I know she would be glad of this.*

> *... do what mom expected me to do and to improve ... perhaps this is a way to compensate and help me to accept the loss.*

Internalisation of deceased parent's expectation would also affect how adolescents cope with the loss. An adolescent boy who appeared to be very calm and resilient after the death of mom adopted this method of coping according to the deceased parent's wish.

> *From the very beginning, I was always asking what did mom expect me to do, because I wanted to make her more happy ... Since she wanted me to carry on my life happily, I tried to do it.*

Focusing

Focusing refers to the adolescents' actions in dealing with the current situation. This includes understanding the problem and identifying solutions. Being able to work on their problems, adolescents could have greater sense of control over their lives. The skills involved were finding meaning, solving problems, and endurance.

Finding meaning refers to the adolescents' attempt to identify the goals of their lives, even small goals. This can help adolescents deal with the feelings of loss, the emptiness or the guilt after the parental death. Usually they ascribed meaning to their life according to the expectations of their deceased and surviving parents. The two main dimensions are their study and family responsibilities.

> *... the past has gone. I hope I could reflect to care for my family, to look after my siblings, to keep healthy, to take care of my daddy, as a compensation to my mom.*

Solving problems is defined as the attempt or action to arrive at solutions and to take direct action to correct the problem. It was rather difficult for the adolescents to be exact about what concrete solutions they had employed to solve the problem. For instance, one adolescent girl described how she had supported her surviving parent, which included helping father to do the household tasks, sitting with him watching TV, and chatting with him. Due to the increasing life stress, some adolescents adopted a more constructive attitude in problem solving.

> *It is important to identify positive methods to help myself, in order not to make other people worried about me ... If I feel I am inadequate in dealing with some problems, I should join some programmes to learn more skills, and to be open in making attempt.*

> *I have more initiative than before. Now I am more active to seek teachers' help on my study problems ... and I have joined more activities in social service centre ... I am aware that I could not depend on others much.*

Endurance concerns the strategies the adolescents used to make themselves keep going instead by giving up, and maintain commitment in the situation despite of the difficulties. Adolescents who suffered from greater stress seemed to have put more emphasis on this coping.

> *... no matter how difficult it is, I have to bear it, I cannot stay back or give up ... I have to carry on.*

> *... if you think it is important, you have to bear and keep going as usual.*

Turning to religion refers to the action of seeking spiritual support from one's faith. An adolescent girl mentioned that her faith has given her great support in dealing with the parental loss. While she rarely seeks support from others, she could express herself freely in prayer, in which she obtained lot of reassurance and strength to face her life.

> *I pray to God, talk to Him, tell Him that why I was unhappy, and all kinds of things ... just like communication, He gives me lots of encouragement, and helps me to reduce my conflicts with younger sister.*

> Researcher: *What do you think is the most helpful coping strategies in your time of parental loss?*

> *... it's my involvement in church, it is God!*

Letting Go

Letting go is a major category and describes the coping strategy that adolescents address the loss as a reality with acceptance, absence of unresolved anger, blame or guilt. Its subcategory is submission.

Submission refers to the acceptance of what come to them as the adolescents realised the unchangeable reality. The two strategies of submission are reappraisal and resigned acceptance.

Reappraisal

Reappraisal refers to the cognitive strategy adopted by adolescents to make sense of unanticipated crisis in their lives. Firstly, in response to their 'why' questions and the feelings of anger or unfairness, some adolescents tried to give a good justification to this bad experience, for example by making comparisons with individuals who are unfortunate, by noting that things could be even worse, and/or by seeing good things coming out of their difficulties.

> Researcher: *Do you regret for being unable to visit mom more before the death due to the preparation for examination?*
>
> *No. I believed if mom was conscious during that time, she would also prefer me to pay more time on studying.*
>
> *I do not feel things are unfair now. Although some people do not lose their mother at such an inappropriate time, they may not have a mother as wonderful as mine. This has been my blessing, and she will be always in my mind. Therefore, I am even more grateful than them.*
>
> *Although we are not as financially sufficient as my schoolmates, but we could still go out and enjoy meeting with them, and we have learnt to manage the money better.*

Accepting responsibility is another way of reappraising the event. An adolescent girl who has been angry with fate for taking her father away, acknowledged that being a smoker, her father may have been somewhat responsible for the illness.

Resigned Acceptance

Resigned acceptance is defined as adolescents coming to terms with the loss and accepting it as it is, and submitting to 'certain fate' as the basic circumstance cannot be altered.

> *I don't ask why now ... death is part of life, and there is misfortune everyday.*

> *... forgetting what my life had been and carry on, then you would not ask for addition ... This is not my wish, however, once I could not change it, I have to accept it.*

Discussion

Impact of Parental Death on Adolescents

Insecurity is identified as the core theme of the impact of parental death on adolescents. Not only does this study identify the grief for the deceased parent, but also substantial changes that incurred after the loss were identified. These include the disruption of family system, increase in family responsibilities and expectation from the surviving parent, changes in roles and family relationships, inadequate emotional and practical support, and reduced social contact and feelings brought by these changes.

These findings support the proposition of Streobe, which emphasises that in bereavement there are other aspects of adjustment than changes in relationship alone. She has defined these stressors as restoration-orientation (Stroebe and Schut, 1999).

The present study shows that adolescents possess grief reactions similar to the adults reported in other studies. Their emotions include shock, numbness, ambivalence, yearning, helplessness, guilt, fear and depression (Balk, 1983; Davies, 1991; Murray, 1986–87). Although their emotional responses to the loss would likely be diminished in time, the feelings of guilt, depression, loneliness and helplessness persist for lengthy periods. Even two years after the death, many adolescents still recalled their parental loss in pain. Tears, sobbing, and avoidance of talking about certain issues were not uncommon during the interviews. Parental death may affect Chinese adolescents for a longer period of time and counsellors have to be aware that there are unrealistic societal expectations about the adolescent's recovery from the bereavement.

Indeed, some studies have showed that there can be considerable variability in the length of time it may take to recover from a loss (Wortman and Silver, 1989).

However, it must be noted that the adolescents who participated in this research did not usually manifest open expression of their grief, and many indicated that after the death of a parent they did not experience intense and prolonged distress. Their grief reactions were generally diminished after a few weeks. This finding challenges the conventional notion that early distress after loss is inevitable, and also challenges the idea that failure to become distressed following the loss is indicative of problems or indeed of pathology. Such insistence on distress following loss has been labelled as the 'requirement of mourning' (Wortman and Silver, 1980).

Despite the forewarning of death, the adolescents still had feelings of shock and numbness at the time of death. Nevertheless, preparation is still important in helping adolescents to face the irreversibility and permanence of death, and it helps to make the death scene less traumatic for adolescents (Gray, 1987; Mireault and Compas, 1996; Worden, 1996). The adolescent who was less aware of the poor prognosis showed greater feelings of shock at the death moment than the adolescents who had been prepared for the death.

Guilt is very common among the adolescents. This is consistent with findings of previous studies (Bloom, 1980; Crenshaw, 1990) and can be explained by two factors. Firstly, ambivalence and conflicts in the parent-child relationship are particularly evident in adolescence (Raphael, 1996), and guilt may ensue for adolescents who have had some conflict with their parent. Secondly, it may relate to a latent negative self-image. The self-image of an individual in adolescence is not well established, and it has been suggested in one study that Chinese adolescents in Hong Kong have a greater sense of failure than adolescents in other regions (Chan, 1991). Since guilt feelings following bereavement may lead to a lowered sense of self-worth, it is extremely important that the adolescents should be reassured by others about their positive identity (Gray, 1987). However, guilt feelings may exist in a more implicit way, as adolescents attempt to suppress negative emotional responses. Two adolescents in the present study said that they did not share their guilt feelings with peers because they felt these emotions were unacceptable and shameful to confront it.

Most of the adolescents in the study had 'why' questions after the parent's death. Some even lost confidence in their ability to control their future and accomplish their identified goals. These questions of doubt, feelings of anger, decline in confidence, and the development of feelings of helplessness have shaken adolescents' internal assumptions about their world, and threaten their self-confidence and self-image. This may therefore affect or inhibit the core developmental task of development of identity in adolescence, as defined by Fleming and Adolph (1986).

Literature on bereavement suggests that the bereaved adolescent may react to the loss with anger and aggression (Fleming and Balmer, 1996). However, the adolescents in this study did not present themselves in this way. Two reasons may account for this. Firstly, it may be due to the cultural difference in expression of feelings. Chinese adolescents have higher depression scores on a standardised instrument (the Beck Inventory) than US adolescents and Chinese young adults, and they adopt more avoidant and withdrawal coping strategies as well (Chan, 1994). Secondly, perhaps it is because this study could not recruit adolescents who have more anger and aggression, since adolescents who may have more difficulties in adjusting to the loss and different style of coping might be less willing to join the study.

In general, family support for the adolescents was found to be inadequate. This is consistent with other findings that death of a parent affected the whole family system (Balk, 1983), in which adolescents were faced with a shattered family environment following, and perceived their family support to be poor (Raphael, 1996). Many of the adolescents wished that their families could be more concerned about them. In this respect our findings are similar to those of Worden (1996), which highlighted the fact that better family support, nurturance and structural continuity could help counter the adolescents' emotional disequilibrium following parental death.

The present study contradicts previous findings that adolescents rated their surviving parent as the helpful person with whom they could openly, share feelings and talk at length about the loss. While some studies find that adolescents could talk about the loss with their family members (Berman et al., 1988; Gray, 1989; Silverman and Worden, 1992; Worden, 1996), all of the adolescents in the present study disconfirmed these findings from Western studies.

Several reasons may account for this. Firstly the father-child relationship may precipitate the difficulty of providing support to adolescents. Most of the adolescents in this study had lost their mother. Previous research has indicated that comments about father as the surviving father are more negative, since they are less emotionally accessible than mothers. Secondly, the surviving parent may be preoccupied with their own grief work. In addition, Chinese society is reticent about death issues and emotions. The adolescents interviewed felt the need to improve family communication, as they thought that talking about the loss would be helpful since this could improve their mutual understanding and support and could address various concerns. However, they are not comfortable in initiating discussion. As one adolescent revealed, 'It is good to talk, but how to talk is difficult.'

Coping Strategies

Self-reliance has been identified as the core theme in adolescents' coping, meaning that the adolescents often relied on their own emotional resources. This study found that adolescents rarely sought support from family members. Similar to other studies' findings (Bird and Harris, 1990; Hogan and De Santis, 1994; McNeil, 1986), they turned more to friends for support as their main coping strategy. The adolescents regard peers as their main source of support during difficult times: they appreciate their peers listening to them, sharing their grief and giving comfort. However, the younger adolescents in this study sought less peer support than the older adolescents. They tend to feel insecure about peers' response and felt that the loss issue did not fit within their usual dialogue. Developmental maturity in older adolescents may have enabled them to discuss their grief with peers.

Most adolescents in the study verbalised the idea that sharing the loss with others was a helpful coping skill. Although two younger adolescent girls did not share the loss with their classmates, they still believed that sharing could relieve their grief emotions and they would have liked to talk to peers about this. For those who had shared their emotions with others, they felt that the availability of a friend was of vital importance. Their openness in the interviews implies that with sensitivity and encouragement, adolescents would be willing to share their emotions surrounding the bereavement issue. This finding invites those who are concerned about adolescents to initiate the contact and give them support during their difficult time.

While social support is very important to adolescents, the nature of support needs further investigation. While some of the adolescents in this study suggest that rapport, security and the person's ability to understand them are their key concerns in sharing the loss with others, some prefer others to give them support through natural conversation instead of focusing on their emotions or the loss-related issues. This emphasises the importance of developing appropriate, culturally specific methods of support.

This study supports Gray's finding (1989) that school personnel play little role in supporting the adolescents following bereavement. Although many of the teachers knew about the adolescents' loss, they only talked to them once or twice, and some offered no help at all. This suggests that the teachers may not understand that the impact of the loss on adolescents is likely to be long lasting. Since school plays a significant role in adolescents' growth and development, it is important for teachers and school social workers to provide more emotional or instrumental support to the adolescents.

Compared with the coping method of emotional discharge, the adolescents in this study used the coping of mental disengagement and self-control more often, and the older adolescents seem to employ greater variety of these skills to deal with the loss. The strategies of mental disengagement and self-control of emotions may be more efficacious since the adolescents are powerless and helpless in face of the situation. In view of the irreversibility of the loss, most of the adolescents resolved their grief through reappraising and accepting the event. Nevertheless, the death of mother had shattered one adolescent girl's 'internal assumptive world', resulting in feelings of lack of control, incompetence, hopelessness and helplessness. Another adolescent girl who had been disturbed by 'why' questions for about two years after her father's death, but became relieved after she had worked through the issue with the help of a school social worker.

Similar to previous research's findings (Silverman and Worden, 1992), the adolescents' efforts to maintain a relationship with the deceased parent is also emphasised in this study. The parent was dead, but the relationship did not die. The connection serves as comfort and security, since it helps the adolescents to regain happiness, identify the goals for themselves like striving to perform their schoolwork or fulfilling family roles as a compensation. This is particularly vital to the adolescents since the family support is often insufficient.

Furthermore, this study also found that religious faith was a helpful resource in coping for the adolescents, but was not adopted by those who had no prior religious faith. In what ways the major religious belief can help adolescents deal with the loss of their parent needs further exploration. The psychological coping characteristics of adolescents in this study are similar to the description of Stroebe (1999, p. 213): 'This alternation between loss and restoration-oriented coping occurs ... at times when the bereaved will be confronted by their loss and at other times they will avoid memories, be distracted, or seek relief by concentration on other things, and have to attend to the additional stressors ... Early on in bereavement, loss orientation dominates, later on, attention turns more and more to other sources of upheaval and distress.' This dynamic process of bereavement has been described as oscillation and is important to successful coping.

The benefits of denial are acknowledged provided that denial is not extreme or persistent. Adolescents who solely adopt this strategy to cope with the loss may experience problems, since those using continuous avoidance or denial were found to be more depressed and as previous writers have suggested, are more vulnerable (Herman-Stahl, Stemmler and Peterson, 1996; Herman-Stahl et al., 1995; Hoffman et al., 1992; Holahan et al., 1995). For example, an adolescent boy in the present study who had isolated himself from siblings and peers in the first year after his mother's death, commented that persistent isolation was not beneficial, since it led to depression.

In conclusion, findings of this study concerning adolescents' coping are summarised as the following:

- The loss of a parent affects many aspects of the adolescents' lives, but they receive little support for their grief and difficulties.

- The adolescents have emotional reactions similar to adults, and its impact may last longer than expected.

- The feelings of guilt and helplessness, and questions about life and fate are evident in adolescents; but anger and aggression are not identified in this study.

- The family system experiences many changes, adolescents are often assigned many new responsibilities, and family support for the adolescents is insufficient.

- The adolescents sought more peer support than family support, but they were not used to strategies of sharing loss with peers. No substantive differences among boys and girls in the use of seeking support were found. Both boys and girls go through the bereavement in a rather private way.

- The adolescents often used disengagement or avoidant coping strategies to detach themselves from their pain of grief.

- The adolescents resolved the loss through reappraisal of the event, resigned acceptance, and developing a connection with the deceased parent through which they gained assurance, strength and sense of direction.

- Age seems to be a discriminator of adolescent coping, since older adolescents adopt a greater variety of coping skills.

Implications for Palliative Care Services

The major implications which have emerged from the study are as follows:

- The loss of a parent affects many aspects of adolescents' lives: they need support during this time of intense changes. Health care professionals should recognise this impact on adolescents, and should be sensitive in offering them support.

- Professionals should provide a safe and caring environment in which adolescents can address their death-related concerns, providing emotional support with particular attention given to underlying feelings such as guilt, depression, helplessness and loneliness; and assistance in dealing with the multiple stressors associated with the loss. When providing emotional support to the adolescents, particular attention should be given to underlying feelings of guilt, depression, helplessness and loneliness.

- The adolescents are often reticent, and it requires adults to take the lead in supporting them, listening actively and perceptively.

- We need to develop services to strengthen the adolescents' coping skills, and help them acquire sense of confidence and direction during the process, including help with the expression of thoughts and feelings, problem-solving skills, stress management, accommodation of the deceased parent in their current lives.

- We need to commence intervention for the family before the death if possible, strengthening parent-adolescent communication, helping the surviving parent understand the needs of adolescents and how to support them.

- As the family system undergoes change the surviving parent may be overwhelmed with their own grief after the loss, so that outside resources may be required. The importance of not over-burdening the adolescents with excessive responsibilities and expectations should be emphasised.

- We need to promote the societal understanding of bereaved adolescents, especially educating school personnel about the reactions and needs of the adolescents after the parent's death so that more support can be provided to them.

Recommendations for Future Research

Based on the findings of this study, future research on the following topics should be considered:

- A longitudinal study on adolescent coping at different points of time in the bereavement process should be undertaken. This could minimise the weaknesses of a retrospective study and provide a better understanding of the relationship between coping and adaptation.

- A study on the impact of the loss in relation to adolescents' self-image, sense of mastery/control, life values and attitudes could lead to an understanding of how much the loss might affect the completion of the adolescents' developmental tasks.

- As family is an important mediator of adolescents' adaptation to the loss, a study to explore the relationship between family coping and adolescent coping after the death of a parent could help in enhancing care provided to the family.

- Since social support plays important role in mediating the effect of crisis, a study is needed to understand the nature of adolescents' needs for social support and their behaviour in seeking social support could help in providing support for adolescents.

- As the long-term outcome of bereavement was not the focus of this study, it is worth considering future studies on the relationship between the outcome of bereavement and different coping strategies, factors affecting the length of time in recovery from the parental death, and mediating factors that may promote or impede psychosocial recovery.

Note

1 Interviews were conducted in Cantonese. Colloquial Cantonese does not translate well into English, and the force of adolescents' comments has been captured in the quotations by literal translations.

References

Artinian, B. (1986). The research process in grounded theory. In W. Chenitz and J. Swason (eds), *From Practice to Grounded Theory*. New York: Addison-Wesley.

Balk, D. (1983). Adolescents' grief reactions and self-concept perceptions following sibling death: a study of 33 teenagers. *Journal of Youth and Adolescence*, 12, 137–61.

Balk, D. (1991). Death and adolescent bereavement: current research and future directions. *Journal of Adolescent Research*, 6, 7–27.

Balk, D. (1996). Models for understanding adolescent coping with bereavement. *Death Studies*, 20, 367–87.

Balk, D. and Corr, C. (1996). Adolescents, developmental tasks, and encounters with death and bereavement. In C. Corr and D. Balk (eds), *Handbook of Adolescence and Bereavement*. New York: Springer.

Balk, D., Tyson-Rawson, K. and Colletti-Wetzel, J. (1993). Social support as an intervention with bereaved college students. *Death Studies*, 17, 427–50.

Bartlett, D. and Payne, S. (1997). Grounded theory – Its basis, rationale and procedures. In G. McKenzie, J. Powell and R. Usher (eds), *Understanding Social Research: Perspectives on Methodology and Practice*. Brighton: The Falmer Press.

Berma, H., Cragg, C. and Kuenzig, L. (1988). Having a parent die of cancer: adolescents' reactions. *Journal of Adolescence*, 15, 159–63.

Bird, G. and Harris, R. (1990). A comparison of role strain and coping strategies by gender and family structure among early adolescents. *Journal of Early Adolescence*, 10, 141–58.

Bloom, M. (1980). *Adolescent-Parental Separation*. New York: Gardner Press.

Carver, C., Scheier, M. and Weintraub, J. (1989). Assessing coping strategies: a theoretically based approach. *Journal of Personality and Social Psychology*, 56, 267–83.

Chan, D. (1995). Depressive symptoms and coping strategies among Chinese adolescents in Hong Kong. *Journal of Youth and Adolescence*, 24, 267–79.

Chenitz, W. (1986). Getting started: the research proposal for a grounded theory study. In W. Chenitz and J. Swason (eds), *From Practice to Grounded Theory*. New York: Addison-Wesley.

Chenitz, W. and Swanson, J. (1986). Qualitative research using grounded theory. In W. Chenitz and J. Swason (eds), *From Practice to Grounded Theory*. New York: Addison-Wesley.

Compas, B.E. (1987). Coping with stress during childhood and adolescence. *Psychological Bulletin*, 101, 393–403.

Compas, B.E., Malcarne, V.L. and Fondacaro, K.M. (1988). Coping with stressful events in older children and young adolescents. *Journal of Consulting and Clinical Psychology*, 56, 405–11.

Compas, B.E., Slavin, L.A., Wagner, B.M. and Vannatta, K. (1986). Relationship of life events and social support with psychological dysfunction among adolescents. *Journal of Youth and Adolescence*, 15, 205–21.

Compas, B.E., Davis, G.E. Forsythe C.J. and Wagner, B.M. (1987). Assessment of major and daily stressful events during adolescence: the Adolescent Perceived Events Scale. *Journal of Consulting and Clinical Psychology*, 55, 534–41.

Crenshaw, D. A. (1990). *Bereavement: Counseling the Grieving Throughout the Life Cycle*. New York: Continuum Publishing.

Creswell, J.W. (1994). *Research Design: Qualitative and Quantitative Approaches*. London: Sage.

Davies, B. (1991a). Long-term outcomes of adolescent sibling bereavement. *Journal of Adolescent Research*, 6, 83–96.

Davies, B. (1991b). Responses of children to the death of a sibling. In D. Papadatou and C. Papadatos (eds), *Children and Death*. New York: Hemisphere Publishing.

Deveau, E.J. (1990). The impact on adolescents when a sibling is dying. In J.D. Morgan (ed.), *The Dying and the Bereaved Teenager*. Boston: Charles Press.

Deveau, E.J. (1995). Perceptions of death through the eyes of children and adolescents. In D. Adams and E. Deveau (eds), *Beyond the Innocence of Childhood: Factors Influencing Children and Adolescents' Perceptions and Attitudes toward Death*. San Francisco: Baywood Publishing.

Dietrich, D.R. (1984). Psychological health of young adults who experienced early parent death: MMPI trends. *Journal of Clinical Psychology*, 40, 901–8.

Douglous, B. (1985). *Creative Interviewing*. New York: Sage.

Fleming, S. and Balmer, L. (1996). Bereavement in adolescence. In C. Corr and D. Balk (eds), *Handbook of Adolescence and Bereavement*. New York: Springer.

Fleming, S.J. and Adolph, R. (1986). Helping bereaved adolescents: needs and responses. In C.A. Corr and J.N. McNeil (eds), *Adolescence and Death*. New York: Springer Publishing.

Floerchinger, D.S. (1991). Bereavement in late adolescence: interventions on college campuses. *Journal of Adolescent Research*, 6, 146–56.

Folkman, S., Lazarus, R.S., Dunkel-Schetter, C., DeLongis, A. and Gruen, R.J. (1986). Dynamics of a stressful encounter: cognitive appraisal, coping, and encounter outcomes. *Journal of Personality and Social Psychology*, 50, 992–1003.

Folkman, S., Lazarus, R.S., Gruen, R.J. and DeLongis, A. (1986). Appraisal, coping, health status, and psychological symptoms. *Journal of Personality and Social Psychology*, 50, 571–79.

Freudenberger, H.J. and Gallagher, K.M. (1995). Emotional consequences of loss for our adolescents. *Psychotherapy*, 32, 150–53.

Frydenberg, E. (1997). *Adolescent Coping: Theoretical and Research Perspectives*. London: Routledge.

Garber, B. (1983). Some thoughts on normal adolescents who lost a parent by death. *Journal of Youth and Adolescence*, 12, 175–83.

Glaser, B.G. (1992). *Basics of Grounded Theory Analysis*. Mill Valley, MD: Sociology Press.

Glyshaw, K., Cohen, L.H. and Towbes, L.C. (1989). Coping strategies and psychological distress: prospective analyses of early and middle adolescents. *American Journal of Community Psychology*, 17, 607–23.

Gray, R.E. (1987). Adolescent response to the death of a parent. *Journal of Youth and Adolescence*, 16, 511–25.

Gray, R.E. (1989). Adolescents' perceptions of social support after the death of a parent. *Journal of Psychosocial Oncology*, 7, 127–44.

Herman-Stahl, M.A., Stemmler, M. and Petersen, A.C. (1995). Approach and avoidant coping: implications for adolescent mental health. *Journal of Youth and Adolescence*, 24, 649–63.

Herman-Stahl, M.A. and Petersen, A.C. (1995). The protective role of coping and social resources for depressive symptoms among young adolescents. *Journal of Youth and Adolescence*, 25, 733–53.

Hoffman, M.A., Levy-Shiff, R., Sohlberg, S.C. and Zarizki, J. (1992). The impact of stress and coping: developmental changes in the transition to adolescence. *Journal of Youth and Adolescence*, 21, 451–67.

Hogan N.S. and Balk, D.E. (1990). Adolescent reactions to sibling death. *Nursing Research*, 39, 103–6.

Hogan, N.S. and Greenfield, D.B. (1991). Adolescent sibling bereavement symptomatology in a large community sample. *Journal of Adolescent Research*, 6, 97–112.

Hogan, N.S. and DeSantis, L. (1994). Things that help and hinder adolescent sibling bereavement. *Western Journal of Nursing Research*, 16, 132–53.

Hogan, N.S. and DeSantis, L. (1996). Adolescent sibling bereavement. In C. Corr and D. Balk (eds), *Handbook of Issues in Adolescent Bereavement*. New York: Springer.

Holahan, C., Valentiner, D. and R. Moos (1995). Parental support, coping strategies, and psychological adjustment. *Journal of Youth and Adolescence*, 24, 633–47.

Leung, W.Y.B. (1996). *Adaptation to bereavement of young widows with dependent children in Hong Kong*. Unpublished MA Thesis. Department of Applied Social Studies, Hong Kong Polytechnic University.

Lin, J.F. (1999). Secondary losses in bereaved children when both parents have died: a case study. *Omega*, 39, 297–314.

Mahon, M. (1999). Secondary losses in bereaved children when both parents have died: a case study. *Omega*, 39, 297–314.

McNeil, J. (1986). Talking about death: adolescents, parents, and peers. In C. Corr and J. McNeil (eds), *Adolescence and Death*. New York: Springer.

Mireault, G. and Compas, B. (1996). A prospective study of coping and adjustment before and after a parent's death from cancer. *Journal of Psychosocial Oncology*, 14, 1–18.

Moos, R. and Schaefer, J. (1986). Life transitions and crises. In R. Moos and J. Schaefer (eds), *Coping with Life Crises: An Integrated Approach.* New York: Plenum Press

Murphy, P. (1986–87). Parental death in childhood and loneliness in young adults. *Omega*, 17, 219–29.

Oltjenbruns, K. (1991). Positive outcomes of adolescents' experience with grief. *Journal of Adolescent Research*, 6, 43–53.

Parkes, C. (1972). *Bereavement: Studies of Grief in Adult Life.* New York: International Universities Press.

Parkes, C. (1993). Bereavement as a psychosocial transition. In D. Dickenson and M. Johnson (eds), *Death, Dying, Bereavement.* New York: Sage.

Petersen, A., Sarigiani, P. and Kennedy, R. (1991). Adolescent depression: why more girls? *Journal of Youth and Adolescence*, 20, 247–69.

Phelps, S.B. and Jarvis, P.A. (1994). Coping in adolescence: empirical evidence for a theoretically based approach to assessing coping. *Journal of Youth and Adolescence*, 23, 359–71.

Raphael, B. (1996). *The Anatomy of Bereavement.* London: Routledge.

Sandelowske, M. (1995a). Sample size in qualitative research. *Research in Nursing and Health*, 18, 179–83.

Sandelowske, M. (1995b). Qualitative analysis: what it is and how to begin? *Research in Nursing and Health*, 18, 371–5.

Sanders, C. (1989). *Grief: The Mourning After – Dealing with Adult Bereavement.* Boston: Wiley-Interscience.

Seiffage-Krenke, I. (1995). *Stress, Coping, and Relationships in Adolescence.* New Jersey: Lawrence Erlbaum Associates.

Siddique, C. and D'Arcy, C. (1984). Adolescence, stress, and psychological well-being. *Journal of Youth and Adolescence*, 13, 459–73.

Silverman, P. and Worden J. (1992). Children's reactions in the early months after the death of a parent. *American Journal of Orthopsychiatry*, 62, 93–103.

Silverman, P., Nickman, S. and Worden, J. (1992). Detachment revisited: the child's reconstruction of a dead parent. *American Journal of Orthopsychiatry*, 62, 494–503.

Stroebe, M. (1992–93). Coping with bereavement: a review of the grief work hypothesis. *Omega*, 26, 19–42.

Stroebe, M. and Schut, H. (1999). The dual process model of coping with bereavement: rationale and description. *Death Studies*, 23, 197–224.

Tsang, W.H.W. (1996). *Attitudes towards 'life' and 'death and dying' in Chinese bereaved widows.* MSW Thesis. Hong Kong: University of Hong Kong.

Tyson-Rawson, K. (1996). Adolescent responses to the death of a parent. In C. Corr and D. Balk (eds), *Handbook of Adolescence and Bereavement.* New York: Springer.

Weiss, R .(1986). Growing up a little faster. In R. Moos and J. Schaefer (eds), *Coping with Life Crisis: An Integrated Approach.* New York: Plenum Press.

West, S.G., Sandler, I., Pillow, D.R., Baca, L. and Gersten, J.C. (1991). The use of structural equation modeling in generative research. *American Journal of Community Psychology*, 19, 459–80.

Worden, W. (1996). *Children and Grief.* New York: Guilford.

Wortman, C. and Silver, R. (1989). The myths of coping with loss, *Journal of Consulting and Clinical Psychology*, 57, 349–57.

7 Stress, Social Support and Quality of Life of Bereaved Spouses

BANNY BING-YEE CHENG AND JOYCE LAI-CHONG MA

Summary

This chapter reports the results of a survey of 70 bereaved spouses in Hong Kong, which aims to identify the stressors commonly faced, the levels of perceived stress, the types of social support received, their quality of life and the types of service most needed. Data were collected through face-to-face interviews using a structured questionnaire. Stressors commonly faced by the respondents were: dual parenting roles, the sense of an incomplete family, decision making without support, upsetting situations, loneliness and financial difficulties. Six respondents (8.6 per cent) felt very or quite stressed in bereavement. Almost half of the respondents perceived quite strong overall support from their families, friends and helping professionals. The respondents' overall quality of life was moderately high. Counselling service and financial aid remained a higher priority of the respondents' service need in different periods of bereavement. The results suggest that different packages of bereavement services should be developed to meet the needs of these clients. The fact that younger bereaved spouses experienced the most distress also has implications for counselling and support for their young children and adolescents.

Introduction

Bereavement service is an integral part of hospice service, which has been promoted in Hong Kong since the 1980s. Hitherto, knowledge on the bereaved spouses' stress, social support and their quality of life is scant. Only Chow,

Koo, Koo and Lam's study (2000) can be identified in this field, examining the impact of a group intervention for bereaved spouses.

In view of this knowledge gap, the researchers have carried out a study in Hong Kong with the aim of understanding the stressors commonly faced by bereaved spouses, the levels of their perceived stress, the types of social support received, their quality of life and the types of service they need most. This Chapter reports the findings of this study and discusses the implications for clinical practice, policy formulation and research in future.

Literature Review

Bereavement is the state of having suffered from a loss of the loved one (Rando, 1988), in our instance, the spouse. As a stressor itself, bereavement arouses anxiety and generates secondary stressors such as physical illnesses (Elliott and Eisdorfer, 1982; Osterweis et al., 1984), depression (Lazarus and Folkman, 1984; Jacobs and Kim, 1990), disruption of friendship with other couples, changes of social status that lead to role and identity conflicts (Horowitz, 1980), deterioration of social functioning, and loneliness (Glick, Weiss and Parkes, 1975), financial difficulties, and declining support relationship with the deceased spouse's family (Lopata, 1979).

Lazarus and Folkman (1984) viewed the perceived stress as a more pronounced impact on the quality of life of people encountering the negative life event than the stressors themselves. Perceived stress refers to the subjective appraisal or perception of the bereaved spouses about their experience. They feel inadequate to cope with and face changes in social roles, identities and life difficulties. Their need for intimate and social relationships can no longer be fulfilled. Having inadequate coping skills or lacking personal resources, they feel distressed. Utilising social resources to meet the needs of these bereaved spouses is important.

Cultures differ in response to death and bereavement. For instance, to an Asian Indian, death may be seen as just one more phase in a life cycle that includes many rebirths (McGoldrick and Giordano, 1996). Hong Kong is a cosmopolitan city with 97 per cent of the population being Chinese. Hong Kong people are strongly influenced by traditional Chinese cultural norms and beliefs. Their experience in bereavement may be different from the west. However, empirical study on bereaved spouses is rarely found in Hong Kong. Helping professionals in Hong Kong are often ignorant of how this distress will affect the quality of life of the bereaved spouses.

Social support has been found to be associated with a reduced risk of psychopathology (Cohen and Wills, 1985; Kessler and McLeod, 1985) for people in the face of negative events in general, and for the bereaved spouses in particular (Lehman et al., 1986; Shinn et al., 1984; Caserta et al., 1989). It is an important factor in adapting to the loss of the beloved and in recovery of one's function, identity and status (Bankoff, 1983; Osterweis, Solomon and Green, 1984; Dimond, Lund and Caserta, 1987). An understanding of the types of social support that people wish to receive from different sources (namely, families, friends and helping professionals) is a first step to the understanding of the impact of social support on the bereaved spouses' quality of life.

There are two perspectives in conceptualising social support: the structural and the functional. The structural perspective focuses on the objective indicators of social support such as the size, the frequency of contact and the number of confidants, while the functional perspective focuses on the respondent's subjective perception of social relationship (House and Kahn, 1985; Wortman and Dunkel-Schetter, 1987). Social support has different functions to play in people's life: the provision of tangible assistance, information, emotional support and company. Based on these functions, social support in turn can be grouped into four types: emotional, informational, instrumental and affiliational support.

Because of the cost and time constraints, only two components of social support, namely, source and function, have been examined in this study. Family (immediate family members or in-laws), friends (peers, colleagues, supervisors, church-mates or neighbours), and helping professionals (social workers, clinical psychologists, nurses or doctors) have been identified as the most important sources of support for the bereaved spouses.

Despite its positive contribution to recovery from the loss, social support, if given at an inappropriate time in an inappropriate manner from an inappropriate source, can have negative effects on adjustment to bereavement (Gottlieb, 1983; Lehman, Ellard and Wortman, 1986; Clayton, 1974; Vachon et al., 1982). Also, the work of Wellman (1981), Littlewood (1983), Lehman et al. (1986), and Caserta, Van Pelt and Lund (1989) indicates that not all supportive attempts are necessarily perceived by their recipients as helpful. Therefore, this research also studied negative social support, namely, those aspects of support that the respondents perceived as not helpful.

The quality of life is not a unitary concept. Fallowfield (1990) listed four core domains of quality of life: psychological, social, occupational and physical. Baker, Jodrey and Intagliata (1992), in a study of 729 severely mentally ill adults, examined people's satisfaction in life in 15 domains ranging from basic material comforts to health and leisure activities. Socio-culture forces shape people's subjective definition of the quality of life. Taking into account the Hong Kong Chinese culture, Ho (1991) conceptualised the quality of life as an individual's overall well-being and satisfactory functioning along six dimensions: health and illness, human relations and support, living and interest, psychological well-being, philosophical well-being, and fulfillment and completion of task.

In this study, the researchers employed Ho's (1991) conceptualisation to understand the quality of life of the bereaved spouses, as it is comprehensive and culturally relevant.

Methodology

Research Design

Due to limited time and resources, this study adopted a one-time survey as a research design. A pilot study was carried out to assess the appropriateness of the length and content of the questionnaires.

The research population consisted of the surviving spouses six months to two years after bereavement. This target group was selected because past studies (Lehman, Ellard and Wortman, 1986; Stroebe and Hansson, 1988) have shown that the majority of the bereaved spouses recover over a two-year period. Nine hundred and seven potential respondents were provided by 11 hospitals and one territory-wide clinic. As these bereaved spouses would not be expected to be very responsive, all were invited to participate in this study by letter. As predicted, the response rate was low (7.8 per cent, N = 71). Finally we succeeded in interviewing 70 bereaved spouses, as one respondent was too depressed to complete the questionnaire during the interview.

Respondents

Among the 70 respondents, 25 (35.7 per cent) were male and 45 (64.3 per cent) were female, a male-to-female ratio is approximately 1: 2. Fifty-six respondents (80 per cent) were young or middle-aged adults (under or at age 55). Fifty-two (74.3 per cent) received education of or below junior secondary level. Thirteen (18.6 per cent) completed senior secondary education. Only five (7.2 per cent) were university/college graduates or above. All the respondents' spouses had died of cancer, except one who had died of heart disease. Forty-nine (70 per cent) respondents had religious beliefs. Fourteen (20 per cent) practised ancestor worship; 15 (21.4 per cent) believed in Buddhism, and 13 (18.6 per cent) were Christians.

Thirty-five (50 per cent) respondents were in paid employment. Among the 'non-working' respondents, 19 (54.3 per cent) relied on the Comprehensive Social Security Assistance (a financial assistance provided by the Hong Kong SAR Government for the poor); 10 (28.6 per cent) were receiving financial support from their relatives, while 6 (17.1 per cent) relied on their pension or saving. The median monthly income of the working respondents was HK$9,500, somewhat higher than that of the whole population (Hong Kong Government, 1996). Half were living in public housing, and 34 (48.6 per cent) were living in rented or private housing.

Forty-nine respondents (70.0 per cent) had dependent children at or below the age of 15, and 62 (88.9 per cent) lived with their children. However, only 13 (18.6 per cent) lived with relatives who helped to take care of their children. Twenty-three (32.8 per cent) of their relatives contacted them at least once a week. Most of the respondents (71.4 per cent) had contacts with their friends regularly. Only seven (10 per cent) had sought help from helping professionals.

Measures

The data of this study were gathered with the aid of a structured questionnaire, which comprised two parts: socio-demographic characteristics (gender, the number of children, employment status, the sources of social support, the number of confidants, the frequency of contacts) and the measuring scales.

a) Stress of Bereavement Scale

This self-constructed scale comprised two parts, with one measuring the stressors and another measuring the perceived stress of the bereaved spouses. Each sub-scale consists of 13 items, which measure different dimensions of stress including the physical, the psychological and the social. The respondents were asked to respond to both the objective and the subjective measures. The statements in the objective and the subjective measures are the same, but the questions are differently stated. In the first part of the measure, the question on top of each statement was asked in the following way: 'How often did the following stressors occur to you during the last three months?' The answer to these questions ranged from 'frequently' (5), 'quite often' (4), 'sometimes'

(3), 'seldom' (2) and 'never' (1). In the second part of measure, the question on top of the statements was asked as followed: 'How stressful did you feel about the following stressors during the last three months?' The answers of the subjective measure ranged from 'very stressful' (5), 'quite stressful' (4), 'somewhat stressful' (3), 'slightly stressful' (2) and 'not stressful' (1). The Cronbach's alphas of the Stressor and the Perceived Stress Sub-scales were 0.82 and 0.85 respectively, indicating that their internal consistency was satisfactory.

b) Social Support Scale

Adapted from Ma's (1996a) study, the Perceived and Desired Social Support from Family, Friends and Helping Professionals scale consists of three sub-scales, measuring the respondents' degree of satisfaction with and desire for the support of their family, friends and helping professionals. The reliability of the overall desired and perceived social support ranged from .83 to .93 (Ma, 1996a). Minor modifications were made as follows.

The content of the informational support was changed from advice for cancer patients to advice, guidance or information relevant to the bereaved spouses, while the affiliational support was explained with examples.

1. The term 'health professionals' in Ma's (1996a) scale was changed and replaced by the term 'other helping professionals, namely social workers and clinical psychologists' because of their contributions in bereavement care.
2. The sub-scales were converted from the original 4-point Likert scale into a 5-point Likert scale to avoid a skewed distribution of the responses. The scale ranged from strongly desired or satisfied (5) to strongly not desired or not satisfied (1). Higher scores denote a stronger desire for or satisfaction from the three main sources.
3. Preferences for social services in different periods of bereavement (immediate after the death, the first six months, and from six months to two years) were asked.
4. Questions on the negative effects of social support from family, friends and the helping professionals were added.

The Cronbach's alphas of the desired social support from family, friends and helping professionals were 0.73, 0.77 and 0.80 respectively. However, as the number of responding cases on the perceived social support was not large enough, the reliability test of the perceived social support was not performed.

c) Quality of Life Scale

Ho's (1991) quality of life scale assessed the adjustment outcome of the bereaved spouses. In order to cater to bereaved spouses' situations, Question 3 was changed from 'your living, ability, movement/action, interest' to 'your participation in activities, cultivating interest'. Higher score denoted better quality of life of the respondents. The Cronbach's alpha of this scale was 0.89.

Data Collection and Statistical Analysis

Three social workers and one counselling teacher were recruited as interviewers of this study. The data were gathered via face-to-face interviews. Home visits were conducted from early April 1996 to May 1996.

The mean scores summarised the respondents' level of stress, social support and their quality of life. T-test, ANOVA and Pearson's correlation were employed to examine the impact of the demographic data on the perceived stress, the perceived and the desired social support, and the quality of life.

Results

Types of Stressors

Table 7.1 summarises the frequency distribution of the 13 stressors faced by the respondents. The six common stressors that were frequently faced by the respondents were identified in descending order as: (i) stress of dual parenting roles (N = 33, 47 per cent); (ii) the sense of an incomplete family (N = 33, 47 per cent); (iii) upsetting situation or thing (N = 27, 39 per cent); (iv) financial difficulty (N = 24, 34 per cent); (v) loneliness (N = 23, 33 per cent); and (vi) making decisions alone without support (N= 21, 30 per cent).

Frequency of Occurrence of the Stressors on the Respondents

The mean score of the Stressor Sub-scale in this study was 2.58 (standard deviation of .71), indicating the moderate frequency of occurrence of these stressors. The mean scores of the respondents ranged from 1.08 to 4.38.

Table 7.1 Frequency distribution of stressors faced by the respondents (N = 70)

Item	Frequently No. (%)	Often No. (%)	Sometimes No. (%)	Seldom No. (%)	Never No. (%)	NA No. (%)
1 Poor health and vulnerability to diseases	0 (0%)	18 (25.7%)	21 (30%)	10 (14.3%)	21 (30%)	0 (0%)
2 Depressed mood	3 (4.3%)	8 (11.4%)	34 (48.6%)	9 (12.9%)	16 (22.9%)	0 (0%)
3 Loneliness	5 (7.1%)	18 (25.7%)	33 (41.7%)	6(8.6%)	8 (11.4%)	0 (0%)
4 Financial difficulty	5 (7.1%)	19 (27.1%)	16 (22.9%)	7 (10%)	23 (32.9%)	0 (0%)
5 Lack of experience in managing finance	2 (2.9%)	4 (5.7%)	11(15.7%)	2 (2.9%)	22 (31.4%)	29 (41.4%)
6 Fear of relating to other couples	1 (1.4%)	6 (8.6%)	14 (20%)	8 (11.4%)	40 (51.7%)	1 (1.4%)
7 Loss of sense of security	4 (5.7%)	5 (7.1%)	15 (21.4%)	4 (5.7%)	42 (60%)	0 (0%)
8 The sense of an i ncomplete family	6 (8.6%)	27 (38.6%)	21 (30%)	8 (11.4%)	8 (11.4%)	0 (0%)
9 Decision-making without support	7 (10%)	14 (20%)	21 (30%)	9 (12.9%)	19 (27.1%)	0 (0%)
10 Difficulty in relating to children	1 (1.4%)	6 (8.6%)	23 (32.9%)	10 (14.3%)	30 (42.9%)	0 (0%)
11 Stress of dual parenting role	6 (8.6%)	27 (38.6%)	15 (21.4%)	3 (4.3%)	15 (21.4%)	4 (5.7%)
12 Upsetting situation or thing	4 (5.7%)	23 (32.9%)	25 (35.7%)	9 (12.9%)	9 (12.9%)	0 (0%)

The frequency of occurrence of the stressors on the respondents was categorised into three groups: the low group (mean value from 1 to 2.33), the moderate group (mean value from 2.34 to 3.66), and the high group (mean value from 3.67 to 5). There were 25 (35.7 per cent) respondents in the low group, indicating that they seldom or never faced the stressors listed; 40 respondents (57.1 per cent) were in the moderate group. Five respondents (7 per cent) were in the high group, indicating that they often faced the stressors listed.

Magnitude of Stress and Impact of Demographic Characteristics on Perceived Stress

The mean score of the Perceived Stress Sub-scale in this study was 2.57, with a standard deviation of .77. The ranking order of items (the common stressors and the perceived stress) of both sub-scales did not differ significantly. A similar result was also found in ranking by mean value. Six (8.6 per cent) respondents fell within the range 3.67–5.00, indicating that they felt very or quite stressed in the face of the stressors listed. Twenty-eight (40 per cent) respondents fell within the range 1.00–2.33, indicating that they did not feel any stress from bereavement.

Demographic characteristics of the respondents did not impact on the overall perceived stress, except gender (t value = 1.43, $p<0.005$) and age. The female respondents (mean = 2.67, S.D. = .51) perceived higher stress than the males (mean = 2.40, S.D. = .87). Female respondents perceived markedly higher stress than male respondents in the loss of a sense of security; t-value = 4.75, $p<0.01$, and in maintenance of family materials, t-value = 5.37, $p<0.01$.

Higher perceived stress correlated with younger bereaved spouses ($r = -.32$, $p<0.01$). Specifically, the younger respondents perceived higher stress in taking up dual parenting roles than the older respondents ($r = -.51$, $p< 0.01$).

Social Support of the Respondents: Size and Frequency of Contact with the Social Network

The size and the frequency of contact with the social network are shown in Table 7.2. Different sizes of social networks do not make any difference in social support perceived by the respondents. However, the respondents' frequency of contact with their friends showed a positive correlation with their perceived overall social support from friends ($r = .48$, $p <0.01$, N =46), affiliational support from friends ($r = .38$, $p < 0.05$, $N = 46$) and emotional support from friends ($r = .36$, $p < 0.05$, $N = 47$). The results indicate that the more frequently the respondents contacted their friends, the more satisfied they felt with these two types of support received.

Perceived Helpfulness from Family, Friends and Helping Professionals

Seventeen respondents (24.3 per cent) had no family support at all; 18 (25.7 per cent) respondents perceived their siblings as most helpful to their adjustment to bereavement; 14 (20 per cent) viewed their children as most helpful; 12 (17.1 per cent) named their parents and nine (12.9 per cent) named other relatives as most helpful.

The friends of 59 (84.3 per cent) respondents helped them face the bereavement. Eleven respondents (15.7 per cent) did not have any help from their friends.

Perceived Social Support from Family and Friends

Among the four types of support, the family provided most satisfaction in affiliational support ($N = 37$, 52.8 per cent) and emotional support ($N = 31$, 44.3 per cent). The respondents ($N = 18$, 25.8 per cent) felt least satisfied with the informational support provided by their family.

Overall, 38 (54.3 per cent per cent) respondents were either very satisfied or satisfied with the support from friends, but only 29 (47.1 per cent) respondents perceived their friends as very or quite helpful in tackling their difficulties. Among the four types of social support, the respondents felt most satisfied with affiliational support ($N = 43$, 61.4 per cent) provided by friends, followed by emotional support ($N = 40$, 57.1 per cent). The respondents felt least satisfied with the instrumental support ($N = 18$, 25.7 per cent) received from friends.

Perceived Social Support from Helping Professionals

Eighteen (25.7 per cent) respondents were either very satisfied or satisfied with the support from helping professionals, but only 12 (17.4 per cent) respondents perceived helping professionals' support as helpful to them when facing the difficulties. Among the four types of social support, 26 respondents (37.1 per cent) felt most satisfied with the emotional support provided by helping professionals, followed by informational support ($N = 23$, 32.9 per

Table 7.2 Social contact/support of tespondents

Item	Number	%	Item	Number	%
Frequency of contacts with relatives			**Frequency of attendance**		
At least one every 3 days	9	12.9	At least once every 3 days	5	7.2
Once a week to 2 weeks	23	32.9	Once a week	18	25.7
Once a month or less often	21	29.9	Once every 2 weeks	2	2.9
Irregular/don't know	8	11.4	Once a month or less often	20	28.6
No relatives contacted	9	12.9	Did not attend any organisations	25	35.7
No. of friends in contact			**Consulted helping professionals**		
None	17	24.3	Yes	7	10.0
One	8	11.4	No	63	90.0
Two	17	24.3			
Three	10	14.3	**Frequency of contacts with helping professionals**		
Four	4	5.7	Once every 2 weeks	1	1.4
Five	3	4.3	Once a month	1	1.4
More than 5	11	16.0	Once every 2–3 months	5	7.1
			Did not contact any helping professionals	63	90.0
No. of relatives living together			**Regular attendance in organisation**		
None	57	81.4	Yes	40	57.1
One to three	13	18.6	No	30	42.9

Table 7.2 continued

IItem	Number	%	Item	Number	%
No. of relatives in contact			**Types of organisation**		
None	8	11.4	Religion organisation	26	37.1
One	10	14.3	Bereavement/single parent group	8	11.4
Two	10	14.3	Community centre/women's association	6	8.6
Three	7	10.0	Did not participate any organisations	30	42.9
Four	9	12.9			
Five	5	7.1			
More than five	21	31.0			
Frequency of contacts with friends					
At least once every 3 days	17	24.3			
Once a week	13	18.6			
Once every 2 weeks	8	11.4			
Once a month or less	14	20.0			
No friends contacted	17	24.3			

cent). Nineteen respondents (27.1 per cent) felt least satisfied with the instrumental support received from helping professionals.

In sum, 31 (45.7 per cent) respondents perceived 'very strong' or 'quite strong' overall support from their families, friends and helping professionals. Only 14 respondents (20 per cent) perceived little or no support from them.

Social Support from Family

Among the types of support from family that the respondents wished to receive, emotional support was strongly desired (N= 43, 61.4 per cent), followed by affiliational support (N = 40, 57.1 per cent); and instrumental support was least desired (N = 30, 42.85 per cent). There is no difference between the perceived and desired social support from the families of the respondents.

Twelve respondents (17.1 per cent) did not wish to receive emotional support from their families. Eleven respondents (15.7 per cent) did not wish to receive informational support from their families. Thus, the bereaved spouses may tend to approach people other than their family members from whom they think it is appropriate to get the support.

Desired Social Support from Friends

Among the four types of support from friends that the respondents wished to receive, emotional support was strongly desired (N = 43, 61.4 per cent), followed by affiliational support (N = 40, 57.1 per cent) and informational support (N = 39, 55.7 per cent); the instrumental support was least desired (N = 22, 31.4 per cent). Among the four types of support, only the respondents' perceived affiliational support (mean = 4.0) exceeds their desired affiliational support (mean = 3.75); t-value = 2.17, $p<0.05$.

Desired Social Support from Helping Professionals

Among the types of support from helping professionals that the respondents wished to receive, informational support was strongly desired (N = 35, 50 per cent), followed by instrumental support (N = 29, 41.4 per cent); affiliational support was least desired (N = 6, 8.6 per cent).

The overall perceived social support from helping professionals (mean = 3.79) was higher than the overall desired social support from helping professionals (mean = 3.23); t value = 3.96, $p<0.001$. Among the four types of support from helping professionals, the perceived emotional support (mean

= 3.88) and the perceived affiliational support (mean = 3.96) were higher than the desired emotional support (mean =3.30); t value = 3.12, $p<0.01$ and the desired affiliational support (mean = 2.70); t value = 5.99, $p<0.001$. The findings suggest that the respondents' degree of satisfaction towards the professional help in the overall social support, emotional and affiliation support was greater than their degree of expectation.

Demographic characteristics (e.g., age, and gender) did not have any impact on both the respondents' perceived and desired social support from the three main sources.

In brief, the respondents wished to receive emotional support from their families and friends, and to receive informational support from helping professionals.

Inappropriate Support from Family, Friends and Helping Professionals

Among the 70 respondents, 16 (22.9 per cent) perceived what they felt was inappropriate or unhelpful advice/support from their families or relatives, with eight (11.4 per cent) respondents feeling most distressed for being blamed for having contributed to their spouses' death.

Thirteen (18.6 per cent) respondents perceived inappropriate or unhelpful advice or support from their friends, with six (8.6 per cent) respondents being advised to forget their spouse, and another six (8.6 per cent) being advised to seek another partner, making them most distressed. Two (2.9 per cent) respondents perceived inappropriate or unhelpful advice or support from helping professionals. They complained that the social security officer reduced the financial assistance after their spouses' death; they did not inform the bereaved spouses on their right to have telephone charges reimbursed.

Expressed Needs of Social Services in Different Periods of Bereavement

The respondents had prioritised different service needs at different stages of bereavement (Table 7.3). Counselling service and financial aid remained a higher priority of the respondents throughout the three phases of bereavement. However, their need for counselling decreased as time passed by, while their need for social recreational activity increased. Forty respondents (57.1 per cent) did not know where to obtain the above service, and only 14 (20 per cent) were satisfied with the service rendered.

Table 7.3 Expressed service needs of the bereaved spouses at different periods of bereavement

Just after death of their beloved spouse			
1st priority	Counselling (37.1%)	Financial aid (21.4%),	Funeral service (8.6%)
2nd priority	Financial aid (15.7%),	Counselling (12.9%)	Funeral service (5.7%)
3rd priority	Counselling (5.75)	Financial aid (5.7%)	Funeral service (4.3%)
Within six months of spouse's death			
1st priority (8.6%)	Counselling (27.1%)	Financial aid (11.4%)	Social recreational activities
2nd priority (4.3%)	Counselling (10%)	Financial aid (5.7%)	Social recreational activities
3rd priority	Counselling (4.3%)	Social and recreational activities (4.3%)	
Recent month (after at least half a year following spouse's death)			
1st priority	Social recreational and financial aid (15.7%)	Counselling (12.86%)	Compassionate rehousing (8.57%)
2nd priority	Social recreational activities (12.9%)	Compassionate rehousing (4.3%)	Counselling (2.9%) Financial aid (2.9%)
3rd priority	Counselling (7.1%)	Social recreational activities (4.3%)	Nil

Quality of Life

The mean scores of the respondents on the quality of life ranged from 3 to 8.78. The mean score of the Quality of Life Scale in this study was 6.20, with a standard deviation of 1.21. Three (4.3 per cent) respondents fell within the range of 1–4 (poor quality of life); 28 (40 per cent) fell within the range of 4.1–6 (fair quality of life); and 39 (55.7 per cent) fell within the range of 6.1–9 (good quality of life). The results show that the overall quality of life of the respondents was moderately good.

Comparatively speaking, the mean score of Item 2, that is, relationship with family (mean = 7.12) was the highest, and Item 3, that is, participation in activities and cultivation of interest (mean = 5.41) was the lowest among all the items of the scale. Demographic characteristics of the respondents did not affect the quality of life.

Discussion

This study has taken a first step in understanding the stress, social support and the quality of life of bereaved spouses in Hong Kong. In addition, it attempted to understand the service needs expressed by these bereaved spouses in different stages of bereavement.

Nevertheless, there are five limitations of this study. First, due to practical constraints, random sampling has not been employed. The results of this study may not be generalised and applicable to other bereaved spouses in Hong Kong. Second, the respondents were interviewed six months to two years into bereavement as it may not be ethical or feasible to interview them earlier. The duration might have allowed some respondents to adjust to new living; and the changes experienced by them over time and during the early months of bereavement have not been thoroughly examined.

Third, bereaved spouses in their low mood might not be ready to participate in the study; hence, there may be a risk of biased sampling. Fourth, as a one-time study, this study fails to capture changes in the subjective experiences of the respondents throughout the bereavement process. Fifth, one has to acknowledge that the measure of the perceived social support may not be reliable since its reliability could not be assessed due to the limited number of responding cases.

The data indicate the strong need of the younger bereaved for social support, in comparison with the older respondents. The younger respondents perceived higher stress than the older ones in the following areas: the loss of a sense of security, difficulty in relating to children, maintenance of family's material culture, and dual parenting roles. This suggests that the younger bereaved spouses were not capable of coping with the heavy family responsibility, as their children were still young and dependent.

A majority of the respondents had no relatives living with them (81.4 per cent), and the frequency of contact with their relatives was not high (only 32.8 per cent had contacts with their relatives at least once a week). This is in line with the fact that the nuclear family constitutes more than 60 per cent of the family structures in Hong Kong (Hong Kong Government, 1996). Two types of families may deserve special professional care and support in bereavement: families whose breadwinner had died, and families whose surviving spouses have never assumed the child care responsibilities in the past.

The more frequently the respondents contacted their friends, the higher the level of their perceived social support, suggesting that friends may be the appropriate source of comfort and support for the bereaved spouses. This points to a need for the development of peer support service. Nine respondents had no contact with their relatives and 17 respondents had no contact with their friends. Thirty respondents did not regularly participate in any organised activities. These respondents may need other forms of social relations provided in society, such as social clubs and self help groups.

Most respondents were satisfied with the social support from family, friends or helping professionals. Specifically, affiliational support from family and friends, and emotional support from helping professionals were usually perceived as satisfactory. However, emotional support was most desired by the respondents from family and friends, and informational support from helping professionals.

These results suggest that Hong Kong people generally understand that the workload of helping professionals is heavy and the extent of help they can offer may be limited. Therefore, the respondents dared not expect to receive affiliational or emotional support from helping professionals. They rather preferred to obtain informational support from helping professionals. There were a considerable number of respondents who did not desire informational support from family. They might think that their family members were not capable of doing so.

Although emotional support from families was most desired, a considerable number of respondents chose not to seek emotional support from the family. These people might be afraid to place additional burdens on their family members.

Another possible explanation is that the other family members were also in grief; they might lack the emotional capacity to nurture and take care of others. As indicated by Reed's study (1993), a few of the severely grief-stricken bereaved might cope with the loss by detaching from the family.

The respondents least desire instrumental support. A significant number (18.6 per cent) did not want to receive instrumental or material support from the family; perhaps either the respondents, despite their own needs, feared putting too much burden on their families, or perhaps there were insufficient resources within the family. Hence, social workers in Hong Kong need to help these bereaved persons to fulfill their need for instrumental and material support by referring them to appropriate service agencies, if needed.

A number of respondents perceived inappropriate support from their family or friends. As death is still a taboo in Hong Kong, and death education has not been promoted, people may be ignorant of the needs of the bereaved and may not be capable of giving them appropriate advice. Eight (11.4 per cent) respondents were most distressed at being blamed. This result may reflect a tendency among the traditional Chinese family to attribute an unfortunate event to the fault of the victim. This might well induce feelings of guilt in the bereaved.

The inappropriate responses from the significant others may be in part related to a lack of social norms and guidelines for behavior for those interacting with the bereaved spouses and for the bereaved spouses. Thus, it is worthwhile to promote death education. It may help to change the attitude of the relatives and friends around the bereaved and to develop new social norms and behaviors to heal the bereaved. Also, the inappropriate support of the helping professionals should not be overlooked, because the bereaved would feel frustrated and refrain from seeking help from them.

In different periods of bereavement, the bereaved spouses wished to receive tangible aids such as financial assistance, funeral advice, and counselling or informational support. The need for counselling service within six months after the death of their spouses was strongly indicated, reflecting the need of the respondents in resolving their grief in this period. As time passes, the need for social recreational activities increases.

Perhaps they had gradually re-gained the energy to become involved in social activities and to develop new personal relations. Six months after the death of their spouse, the counselling service was given a lower priority by the bereaved. The result suggests that those in later stages of bereavement may benefit from social and recreational activities.

Over half of the respondents did not know where to obtain social services, indicating that social services are not accessible for the bereaved. Or the information given cannot be fully comprehended, probably because the respondents might be overwhelmed with grief and were still pre-occupied with the deceased. Two-thirds of the respondents did not receive or clearly remember whether they were given informational support in dealing with the remains, and where to obtain relevant aids.

This implies that informational support may be ineffectively rendered in many hospitals with hospice services. The situation might be even worse in hospitals without hospice services. Medical social workers should make their informational support more accessible to their clients, reassure them that help is available and evaluate how informational support was rendered.

Implications for Practice

The results of this study point the way to developing different service packages for bereaved spouses of different ages and gender. More professional efforts and time should be spent to help the younger bereaved spouses because of their greater need.

Based on the respondents' expressed service needs in different periods of bereavement and different types of stressors encountered, social workers should be time-specific in designing and developing their service programs. For instance, in the initial stage of bereavement, service programs should be therapeutic in nature, including individual counselling, group counselling, religious healing, network intervention, mobilisation of personal and community resources.

These service programs aim to alleviate the distress of the bereaved spouses, facilitate them to resolve their grief and prevent them from mental breakdown. In the later periods of bereavement, service programs should be social and recreational in nature, such as tea parties, picnics organised by churches, self-help groups or social clubs, with the aim of encouraging the bereaved spouses to expand their social circle, enjoy life and develop new meaningful personal relationships. Teamwork among different helping professionals is extremely important in the early stage of bereavement, while social workers in the community and volunteers should assume more active roles in the later stage of bereavement.

Our respondents value their family as their centre of living, suggesting that bereavement care service should be family-focused, rather than individual-focused. More family-based service programs such as multiple family groups (Cheng, 1996) and family therapy (Ma, 1996b) should be developed. A Family life education program should be introduced in helping the bereaved family live a happier life without the deceased.

Since informational support from the helping professionals is most desired by the respondents, and many respondents did not know where to obtain it, hospital social workers should improve their way of rendering informational support. Support for bereaved spouses should be more sensitive, and repetitive inquiries should be handled with patience. As contacts with friends related positively to higher perceived support, it is suggested that peer support or networking should be developed in hospice service. Social workers should assist the bereaved spouses to organise self-help groups or to encourage them to join social activities organised by social service agencies or churches.

Death and bereavement education, though a long-term work, should be promoted in society to educate the general public and prepare them for the death of the beloved or even themselves, and learn to offer appropriate help and support to the bereaved, if needed.

Conclusions

Empirical evidence gathered by this study has helped social workers in Hong Kong and elsewhere to plan and develop different service packages for surviving spouses at different periods of bereavement.

In view of the limitations of this study, a longitudinal study combined with a quantitative and a qualitative design is recommended for future study. The latter design would enable the investigator to examine the bereavement process in an in-depth manner. The impact of sudden death, such as suicide and car accidents, on families had been conducted in the West (Seguin, Lesage and Kiely, 1995) but had not been investigated in Chinese societies. The families with sudden death would be more difficult to adjust to bereavement than families experiencing the prolonged death of their beloved. Future investigators may examine how the manner of death and the attachment of the survivors with the deceased may affect bereavement (Reed and Greenwald, 1991; Reed, 1993).

Acknowledgments

Madam Tan Jen Chiu Endowment Fund financially supported this study. Gratitude is due to Dr Simon Au, Assistant Professor, the Department of Social

Work, Chinese University of Hong Kong, who has enlightened us on methods of statistical analysis. Special thanks are given to all the health care professionals who helped to recruit the respondents of this study. Without their consent and enthusiastic support, this research project could not have been completed. Thanks are also due to Dr Ho Wan Man who has authorised us to adopt her quality of life scale, and to Ms Hsu Suet-ming, the senior technician, Department of Social Work, Chinese University of Hong Kong, who helped in data-processing.

References

Baker, F., Jodrey, D. and Intagliata, J. (1992). Social support and quality of life of community support clients. *Community Mental Health Journal*, 28, 397–410.

Bankoff, E.A. (1983). Social support and adaptation to bereavement. *Journal of Marriage and the Family*, 45, 827–39.

Caplan, G. (1974). *Support Systems and Community Mental Health*. New York: Basic Books.

Caserta, M.S., Van Pelt, J. and Lund, D.A. (1989). Advice on the adjustment to loss from bereaved older adults: An examination of resources and outcomes. In D.A. Lund (ed.), *Older Bereaved Spouses: Research with Practical Application*. New York: Taylor and Francis/Hemisphere.

Cheng, B.Y. (1996). Bereavement program in multiple family group approach. In *Therapeutic Groups in Medical Settings*. Resource Paper No. 25, Department of Social Work and Social Administration, The University of Hong Kong.

Chow, Y.M., Koo, W.S., Koo, W.K. and Lam Y.Y. (2000). Turning grief into good separation: bereavement services in Hong Kong. In R. Fielding and C.LW. Chan (eds), *Psychosocial Oncology and Palliative Care in Hong Kong – The First Decade* (pp. 233–54). Hong Kong: Hong Kong University Press.

Clayton, P.J. (1974). Mortality and morbidity in the first year of bereavement. *Archives of General Psychiatry*. 30, 747–50.

Cohen, S. and Wills, T.A. (1985). Stress, social support and the buffering hypothesis. *Psychological Bulletin*, 98, 310–57.

Dimond, M.F., Lund, D.A. and Caserta, M.S. (1987). The role of social support in the first two years of bereavement in an elderly sample. *The Gerontologist*, 27, 599–604.

Elliott, G.R. and Eisdorfer, C. (1982). *Stress and Mental Health*. New York: Springer Publishing Co.

Fallowfield, L. (1990). *The Quality of Life: The Missing Measurement in Health Care*. Souvenir Press.

Glick, I.O., Parkes, C.M. and Weiss, R.S. (1975). *The First Year of Bereavement*. New York: Wiley.

Gottlieb, B.H. (1983). *Social Support Strategies: Guidelines for Mental Health Practice*. Newbury Park: CA. Sage.

Ho, M.W. (1991). *The Development of a Quality of Life Scale for Patients with Life Threatening Illnesses in a Chinese Context*. Unpublished PhD dissertation. The Chinese University of Hong Kong.

Hong Kong Government (1996). *1996 Population census – Summary reports*. Hong Kong: Hong Kong Government.

Horowitz, M., Wilner, N., Marmar, C. and Krupnick, J. (1980). Pathological grief and the activation of latent self-images. *American Journal of Psychiatry*, 137, 1157–62.

House, J.S. and Kahn, R.L. (1985). Measures and concepts of social support. In S. Cohen and S.L. Syme (eds), *Social Support and Health* (pp. 83–108). Orlando FL: Academic Press.

Jacobs, S. and Kim, K. (1990). Psychiatric complications of bereavement. *Psychiatric Annals*, 20, 314–17.

Kessler, R.C. and McLeod, J.D. (1985). Social support and mental health in community samples. In S. Cohen and S.L. Syme (eds), *Social Support and Health* (pp 219–40). San Diego, CA: Academic Press.

Lazarus, R.S. and Folkman, S. (1984). *Stress, Appraisal, and Coping*. New York: Springer Publishing Co.

Lehman, D.R., Ellard, J.H. and Wortman, C.B. (1986). Social support for the bereaved: Recipients and providers' perspectives on what is helpful. *Journal of Consulting and Clinical Psychology*, 54, 438–46.

Littlewood, J. (1983). *Loss and Change: A Consideration of Death-related Issues*. Unpublished PhD thesis. University of Leicester.

Lopata, H.Z. (1979). *Women as Widows: Support Systems*. New York: Elsevier.

Ma, L.C. (1996a). Patients' perceived and desired social support from family, friends and health professionals – A panel study of patients in Hong Kong suffering from Nasophargneal Carcinoma. *Journal of Psychosocial Oncology*, 14, 47–68.

Ma, L.C. (1996b). Family-centred social work intervention for the families of the chronically and the bereaved. In *Therapeutic groups in medical settings*. Resource Paper No. 25, Department of Social Work and Social Administration, the University of Hong Kong.

McGoldrick, M. and Giordano, J. (1996). Overview: Ethnicity and family therapy. In M. McGoldrick, J. Giordano and J.K. Pearce (eds), *Ethnicity and family therapy* (pp. 1–31). 2nd edin. New York: The Guilford Press.

Osterweis, M., Solomon, F. and Green, M. (eds) (1984). *Bereavement: Reactions, Consequences and Care*. Washington: National Academy Press.

Rando, T.A. (1988). *Grieving: How to Go On Living When Someone You Love Dies*. New York: Lexington Books.

Reed, M.D. and Greenwald, J.Y. (1991). Survivor-victim status, attachment, and sudden death bereavement. *Suicide and Life-Threatening Behavior*, 21, 385–401.

Reed, M.D. (1993). Sudden death and bereavement outcomes: the impact of resources on grief symptomatology and detachment. *Suicide and Life-Threatening Behavior*, 23, 204–20.

Seguin, M., Lesage, A. and Kiely, M.C. (1995). Parental bereavement after suicide and accident: a comparative study. *Suicide and Life-Threatening Behavior*, 25, 489–98.

Shinn, M., Lehmann, S. and Wong, N.W. (1984). Social support: an introduction to a comply phenomenon. *Journal of Social Issues*, 40, 1–9.

Stroebe, M.S. and Hansson, R.O. (1988). Bereavement research: a historical introduction. *Journal of Social Issues*, 44, 1–18.

Vachon, M., Scheldon, A.R., Lancee, W.J., Lyall, S.A., Rogers, J. and Freeman, S. (1982). Correlates of enduring stress patterns following bereavement: Social network, life situation and personality. *Psychological Medicine*, 12, 783–8.

Wellman, B. (1981). Applying network analysis to the study of support. In B.H. Gottlieh (ed.), *Social Networks and Social Support*. Beverly Hills: CA. Sage.

Wortman, C.B. and Dunkel-Schetter, C. (1987). Conceptual and methodological issues in the study of social support. In A. Baum and J.E. Singer (eds), *Handbook of Psychology and Health* (pp. 63–108). Hillsdale: Lewrence Erlbaum Associates, Publishers.

8 Death Education: A Tool of Child and Adolescent Suicide Prevention

JOHN W.L. TSE

Summary

The experience of death is a more common one for children and adolescents than popular culture would have us believe. This 'denial' and avoidance of death has implications for how Chinese cultures value life, and life-affirming values. Evidence is reviewed to show that involving children in a better understanding of the meaning of death through curriculum and classroom involvement is an essentially healthy activity. Knowing and understanding the full meaning of death also gives the young person a better understanding of the meaning of life, and should be an essential part of educational programmes for suicide prevention, which aim to counter the idea that death is an alternative to healthy and positive living.

Introduction

In Hong Kong, as in many Chinese societies, it is a widely accepted view that death is a very remote event for children and adolescents. This is incorrect. In the year 2000, some 33,000 persons died in Hong Kong (Census and Statistics Department, 2001). If one estimates that every death intimately affects at least six individuals (National Center for Health Statistics, 2000), at least 198,000 people, young and old, suffered the loss of a loved one in a single year alone. In a survey of over 1,000 adolescents, Ewalt and Perkins (1979) reported that 90 per cent had experienced the death of someone whom they loved.

Such figures show that children and adolescents do often encounter deaths. The loss of a parent or a close friend is particularly traumatic and increases the risk of complicated grief reaction. Research indicates that parentally bereaved children report significantly more post-traumatic stress disorder symptoms than children who have experienced natural disaster (Stoppelbein and Greening, 2000). One mode of preventive intervention is to educate children and adolescents about death so as to ensure that they are better prepared to accept death in loved ones and acquaintances, rather than being severely and adversely affected by loss (Aspinall, 1996; Edgar and Howard-Hamilton, 1994).

The purpose of this chapter is to address the following questions: Why should death education be provided? What should the curriculum consist of and how should one teach death education? In what capacity should parents be involved in providing death education? Should children be allowed to attend funerals?

These are just some of the questions readers may have concerning the role of death education as a tool of suicide prevention. In reality, Chinese societies can be described as a death-denying culture where death is treated as a taboo. Death has been an evaded and ignored issue. Many parents think that death should neither be discussed openly at home nor taught formally in schools. Death and dying has replaced sex as the unspeakable subject in modern societies (Gorer, 1965), east or west. Writing about, depicting and discussing death can even be considered to be a new form of pornography. As a consequence, most, if not all, schools do not teach death as a curriculum unit.

Aims of Death Education

'Death education' refers to the use of formal and informal methods of teaching issues related to death and loss (Corr, 1992). Death education teaches death, loss, grief and how these affect human beings. The goal of 'death education' is to encourage students to understand the facts, acquire the skills and develop correct attitudes needed to deal adequately with the meaning of death and with death anxieties (Gordon and Klass, 1979). Therefore, an important component of death education is for students to come to terms with death and the idea that death is a normal part of life, and should not be feared. The aims of death education are to enable students (Brinkman and Quarles, 1988; Gatliffe, 1988):

- *To understand the facts* and develop healthy attitudes towards death and dying;

- *To demonstrate understanding* of the social issues related to death and dying;
- *To understand the beliefs and practices* concerning death and after death; and
- *To accept death* as the inevitable end to life.

A research study in the United States revealed that out of 423 public schools, 11 per cent offered death education as part of a health education course (Wass, Miller, and Thornton, 1990). On the other hand, in a survey carried out in Ireland, over 70 per cent of parents and teachers supported the view that death should be discussed with children before they encounter it (McGovern and Barry, 2000). Interestingly, even though death education in schools is justified, it is not included in the traditional Irish school curricula.

Schools in Hong Kong do not provide death education and death education is not a component in the school curriculum. This may be due to the reluctance of teachers and parents who consider it unnecessary to provide death education to children and adolescents. Some are afraid that it may bring unforeseen negative effects, such as instilling fear and glorifying death. According to the Chinese folk tradition, death should not even be mentioned in school or at home. In a survey of attitudes towards death in Hong Kong, out of 500 adults, 19.3 per cent reported that death was an avoided topic in family discussion in childhood, while another 32.7 per cent indicated that death was 'never mentioned' (Cheng and Chen, 1999).

Children may have very limited knowledge of death, and their direct contact with death is minimal even though people near to them may have died. Their understanding of death comes mainly from how death is portrayed in television and movies. Very often death is depicted in a grossly distorted manner in the mass media (Lamers, 1995). It is not uncommon to find a person who died in one scene to be resurrected or become another character later in the movie, or in another movie. Given the high proportions of violent death on television programmes (Wass, Raup, and Sisler, 1989), it is not difficult to comprehend that many children do not understand the meaning of death and of living.

The situation is further aggravated in Chinese communities, where violence and death are presented frequently and in a much distorted, aggressive form, such as in video games, Kung-fu movies, television programmes, and even comic books. When young children are repeatedly exposed to these messages, this could only add to their confusion and further complicate the concept of death.

The knowledge and attitudes that children have concerning death could directly or indirectly affect their feelings about suicidal behaviour. Though many schools continue to tackle the problem of suicide by adopting a crisis intervention model, increasingly more educators see death education as a viable starting point to enable students to develop a better understanding of death and be more equipped in coping with loss (Aspinall, 1996).

The lesser the opportunity to discuss openly about death, the more mysterious it becomes, and the more ignorant are the children and adolescents. There is an urgent need for teachers to provide formal death education as a means of ensuring that children and adolescents may have facts, skills and attitudes about death and suicide.

Concept of Death

In a survey of 500 adults in Hong Kong, 49.2 per cent either agreed or strongly agreed with the notion that there is life after death (Cheng and Chen, 1999). When the respondents were asked whether death is eternal, 43.6 per cent either disagreed or strongly disagreed. Perhaps, more importantly 190 adults declined the interview once they knew the purpose was to investigate their attitudes towards death. Chinese folklore and horrible ghost stories, which stress pain and misery in the afterlife, can at least partially account for the fear of death among Chinese people (Chan and Mak, 2000). It is, therefore, quite conservative to say that a majority of the adults have inaccurate and, perhaps, negative views towards death. It is against this background of values and attitudes that Chinese children grow in Hong Kong society.

It is not uncommon for children to ask their parents, 'Why do people die?' 'Why do I die?' Adults often have a misconception: children are ignorant and, therefore they do not understand the concept of death. Adults may believe that children under say ten years old are incapable of comprehending that death is final. In research with young children in Hungary, Nagy (1948) found that children up to age five were unable to understand that death is final. Children ranged from five to nine years old realised that death is final but an element of personification affects the outcome. In other words, death can be escaped by hiding or by saying a few magical words.

Researchers (e.g., Speece and Brent, 1992), on the other hand, pointed out that children's understanding of the concept of death can be further subdivided into four categories: universality, irreversibility, non-functionality and causality:

- *Universality* refers to the knowledge that all living things must ultimately die which implies the logic that death is inevitable and unpredictable.
- *Irreversibility* refers to the state that death is permanent. Once the human body is dead, it cannot be resurrected.
- *Non-functionality* refers to the knowledge that after death, all functions (e.g., walking, drinking and thinking) stopped.
- *Causality* refers to the understanding that people die for different reasons. In this state, children began to have a mature conception of death. They may realise that the reason for death can be abstract and that different living organisms may die of different causes.

A key question is: When will children develop a clear understanding of death? There is considerable disagreement as to the age at which children develop adequate and mature understanding about these concepts of death. According to some scholars (Gothelf, Apter, Brand-Gothelf, Offer, Ofek, Tyano and Pfeffer, 1998), children between age five to seven years develop this conceptual maturity, while others (Speece and Brent, 1984) believed a more realistic age is seven years old, and still others (e.g., Zhang, 1996) propose the age of nine years. Nonetheless, it is generally accepted that if children fail to grasp the idea of death, they may have severe adjustment problems when a close friend or relative dies. The consequences of such misunderstandings are outlined in Table 8.1.

Children learn at different rates. Because of direct exposure of death in the family, and differences in age and intelligence, some children may understand death more readily than others. Children whose understanding comes slowly can be described as 'unstable' as far as the concept of death is concerned (Pfeffer, 1986). For instance, a 6-year-old child may realise that when a dog is dead, it will not be alive again. But the child may not understand that if she herself dies, it is final. In other words, there may be a discrepancy in evaluating one's death and other's death.

In reality, research studies have repeatedly shown that many children and adolescents, who had committed suicide, or made attempts or threats to kill themselves, had fantasies and distorted image about death (Tse, 2000). Orbach and Glaubman (1978) reported that children with suicidal behaviour attributed living qualities to the state of death. Compared with normal children, they were more likely to agree that there is resurrection and life after death. Children with suicidal behaviour may not understand that death is final. Some might even consider death as a pleasant state (Carlson, Asarnow and Orbach, 1994;

Table 8.1 Effects of children's misunderstanding of the concept of death

Universality
Inadequate understanding: When a child does not fully understand that death is universal, he or she may ask the following question. 'Is it true that all human beings will die?' These children may wrongly think that others would die, but not their parents, teachers and themselves. *Effects*: The concept of universality is a double-edged sword. For those who do not understand it, death may be considered a penalty for the dead. On the other hand, some of the children, who 'understand' it, may wrongly think that death is inevitable. There is no escape. Therefore, one might as well die early by committing suicide.
Irreversibility
Inadequate understanding: The child may ask: 'If we give medicine to the dead person, will he resurrect? 'After a person dies, will she live again?' *Effects*: Some Chinese children and adolescents, who believed in reincarnation, may have more positive attitudes towards death and suicide (Zhang, 1966). The concept of irreversibility is particularly important for such individuals are likely to resort to suicide as a means of starting a cycle.
Non-functionality
Inadequate understanding: 'After my relatives die, would they still recognise me?' *Effects*: Children, who do not know that being dead is a permanent loss of functions may show exaggerated concerns of the physical suffering of the deceased. This tends to create adjustment problems for the child.
Causality
Inadequate understanding: 'Why would a person die?' 'If I treat others badly, what would happen to me after I'm dead?' *Effects*: Chinese children and adolescents may be particularly confused by the concept of causality. Some may think that doers of good works would be rewarded. Hence, if people treat others kindly, they would be rewarded by longevity.

Gothelf et al., 1998). Such children and adolescents tend to glorify death and consider death as reversible – a peaceful and quiet condition.

Research has shown that adolescents with suicidal behaviour and adolescents without suicidal behaviour hold different views towards life and death. For instance, Orbach (1988) postulated that there are four important attitudes affecting one's suicidal behaviour:

- *Attraction to life* refers to the level of satisfaction one gets from life. When the level of perceived support and encouragement is high, the more the adolescent is attracted to life. Attraction to life can be considered as protective factor against self-destructive, suicidal behaviour.
- *Repulsion by life* is the level of psychological pain the adolescent is suffering. When the adolescent is facing an insurmountable distress, a profound rejection or alienation, he or she may not have any interest in living. Repulsion by life is an important force in causing self-destructive behaviour.
- *Attraction to death* refers to the belief that death is preferred to life, therefore one chooses to die rather than to survive. Attraction to death is affected by cultural and/or religious factors. For instance, if a child thinks that death can complete his or her wishes, and that death is reversible, then death can become more attractive. Some adolescents may, in the process of searching for existential meaning in life, have fantasies and distortions about death. To these youngsters, death can be a form of tranquillity and a peaceful state. Holders of such beliefs may ponder about death and see its attractions.
- *Repulsion concerning death* means that one is having a realistic knowledge about death and holds a fearful attitude towards death. Children with such beliefs tend to consider death as a lonely and frightened state. Repulsion by death can be regarded as a means of protection against self-destructive behaviour.

From a suicide prevention perspective, it is important to help children and adolescents see that life has its own attractions and death is repellent. The more reasons for living and fewer reasons for dying, the more likely they would develop negative attitudes towards death. As a likely consequence, the lesser the chance of considering suicide as an option in the face of stress.

Research shows that among these four factors, repulsion by life has the great impact on suicidal behaviour (Payne and Range, 1995). Children and adolescents with suicidal behaviour have low or moderate attraction to life, high repulsion by life, high attraction to death and low repulsion by death.

People who hold these attitudes are more likely to consider death as a solution to a distress. On the other hand, children and adolescents without suicidal behaviour have high attraction to life, low repulsion by life, low attraction to death and high repulsion by death.

Curriculum Contents

Every year, it is a Chinese custom to worship the ancestor's grave in Ching Ming and Chung Yeung Festivals. In Yu Lan Festival (Festival of the Ghost), it is a ritual for community organisations to celebrate by giving out rice to the poor and hosting free Chinese opera, while people make offerings to ghosts by burning incense. It would be particularly relevant if teachers could make use of these occasions to teach about death and Chinese customs. In the traditional Chinese culture, there are four most significant life events: birth, aging, illness and death (Chow, Koo, Koo and Lam, 2000). Teachers may teach these topics formally.

Before teachers begin to teach or set the curriculum contents of death education, teachers should, in so far as possible, seek the endorsement and support of parents. In order to ensure parental support, death education should meet the divergent needs of children and adolescents.

Parents should be convinced that when students have an adequate understanding of death and dying and the grieving process, this might also help to prevent the emotional scarring and permanent damage that a death can cause them. The following topics may be considered in the death education curriculum (Stevenson and Stevenson, 1996; Tse, 2000; Weeks and Johnson, 1992):

- AIDS and HIV;
- aging;
- ancestor worship and Chinese customs;
- bad luck, karma and death;
- bereavement and grieving process;
- cemeteries and cremation;
- children's understanding of death;
- chronic and terminal illnesses;
- cryonics (freezing bodies);
- death and the law;
- death customs and birth rituals;

- euthanasia and good death;
- family support;
- is there life after death?;
- language and death;
- organ donations and Chinese folk beliefs;
- peace and holocaust;
- quality of life;
- reasons to die vs. reasons to live;
- religious and philosophical explanations of death;
- right to life;
- stages of life changes;
- suicide and self-destructive behaviour;
- temporary loss and permanent death;
- terrorism;
- warfare and destruction; and
- wills and living wills.

Teachers and parents may ask: When is the most appropriate time to provide death education? There is no definite period.

No death education programme is perfect and teachers may have to tailor-make the contents according to the educational needs of different age groups. The content areas suggested may be taught as a topical unit or be included as an integrated part of other curriculum areas, for instance, social studies and mathematics. The key to designing a curriculum on death education is age appropriateness. The contents and methods of instruction should be relevant and one way of ensuring it is to put more emphasis on age-related matters.

Another way is to adopt an incidental learning approach, that is, make use of teachable moments as the occasion arises (Good and Brophy, 1995). For instance, the death of a teacher or a movie star may be the basis for a class discussion. This will not only stimulate intellectual growth but also present death in a natural, non-threatening manner (Corr, 1982).

When teachers adopt an incidental learning approach, death education may be particularly meaningful to the students. Any moment, when death occurs, is an appropriate opportunity for death education. For instance, if death is mentioned in a poem or a passage, or when someone in school died, a teacher can make use of this occasion to talk about death. Needless to say, in the course of instruction, teachers should pay special attention to the students' background. Deep religious conviction and recent death in the family must be taken into consideration.

Mass lectures may not be the most effective method of instruction in death education. An activity approach is recommended. In Hong Kong, there had been a number of widely reported incidents with many deaths and casualties – the hill fire at Pa Sin Plateau (where teachers and school children were killed), at Lan Kwai Fong (where in a stampede many people suffocated to death), and the fires at Ka Li Mansion and Top One Karaoke (where many people were burnt to death).

Teachers can also formally teach grief, burial rites, children and death, and other death-related topics (Brookshire and Noland, 1992; Weeks and Johnson, 1992). Death education can be delivered in the form of an activity approach, for instance, a one-day trip to visit a delivery room, an institution for elderly people, and a graveyard. Students may be asked to submit a report of the visits and to reflect on the experience they encountered. The method of instruction on death education should be open and free discussion should be encouraged.

In primary school, teachers may adopt a story telling approach. Students are more likely to be influenced by a personal approach, if the teacher chooses to present the way he or she copes with loss and grief. Teachers may use puppets, which are appropriate for young children, as a means of instructions. On the other hand, in order to provide death education to adolescents, 'experts' such as a priest, a monk, a doctor or nurse may be invited as guest speakers and discuss about death-related topics.

Guidelines on Death Education

Death education, as an area of instruction, is a rather controversial subject. Prior to offering death education, parents must be notified and given a choice to allow or not to allow the student to participate. Teachers may also solicit the students' personal opinions, whether they would like to pursue this topic. Alternative curriculum options should be offered for those who choose not to participate. Generally most students are ready and, in fact, eager to participate.

Instruction on death education must be carefully planned, executed and evaluated. The following guidelines on death education are recommended (Brookshire and Noland, 1992; Rees, 1997; Tse, 2000).

Allow Children and Adolescents to Express Freely Personal Feelings, Opinions and Anxieties

One of the major characteristics of students in Hong Kong is that they are generally more reserved than their counterparts in the West and seldom ask questions in class. Students are more used to a highly structured class environment, which is often teacher-centered. Death education may pose additional difficulties for students as well as teachers. At the initial stage of death education, teachers are recommended to provide guided instructions. Later on as students become more competent and mature, they may gradually take up more responsibilities and come up with more initiatives. For instance, teachers may have to list out concrete objectives and present students with worksheets before visiting a cemetery. It is desirable to arrange class discussion at a later stage.

One of the important first steps in understanding the concept of death and coping with bereavement is to be aware of personal feelings and emotions. By having a chance to express one's thoughts, the child may develop a better grasp of his or her feelings and emotions. Many teachers do not like to see students experiencing grief, or suffering from misery. There is a Chinese proverb saying that 'A man may breed, but he does not cry.' Such statements are inappropriate. At times of bereavement, mourning is normal. Suppressing one's grief can have negative impacts on one's mental health.

Proceed with Caution and be Honest

When answering questions on death and loss, teachers must be sincere and careful. When teachers give instructions to primary school pupils, teachers are advised not to provide all materials and information within one lesson. This tends to over-load the students.

Avoid Euphemisms and Use Accurate Terms

Sometimes teachers may unknowingly perpetuate misconceptions about death. A common example is that very often Chinese teachers tend to refrain from using the term 'death' and substitute it by using phrases such as the Chinese equivalents of 'passed away', 'gone to heaven', 'taking a long sleep', 'gone for a long vacation', 'return to the West' (place of eternal happiness) and 'left us'. Such terminology may create confusion and are often negative in impact or portent. Why would anyone taking a long sleep refuse to wake up? Young children may be particularly anxious, thinking that they may not wake up in their sleep. On the other hand, some children may wrongly perceive that the relative who had committed suicide 'has now gone to heaven, sitting next to God'. Such children tend to consider suicide more favourably and may see it is a viable problem-solving method.

When a body ceases to function, in physical terms it is dead. Teachers should describe this condition more accurately by using the expression 'dead'. When simple, concrete and direct terms are used, children are more likely to understand. This would prevent any unambiguity and complexity, which might affect the children and create unnecessary confusion.

Be Aware of Negative Emotions

Students may reaction in a different way when they are confronted with death issues. When death education is being taught in class, teachers should be particularly sensitive to the possibly depressing responses from the students. Some students may be pre-occupied with death anxiety. Still some others may have nightmares or suffer from insomnia, while occasionally a few may feel distressed by the concept of death. When these responses occur, it does not automatically mean that death education has to be terminated.

Teachers should make use of their sound judgement and make the necessary referral, if it is so required. As a way of not arousing negative emotional responses, teachers are advised to take a cautious stance in the beginning, using mild teaching materials such as dried flowers, and then slowly proceed to more arousal provoking topics. This gradual approach can facilitate students to be able to discuss death in the open, rather than subjecting them to the sudden impacts of death.

Clarify the Meaning of Death

One of the main duties of a teacher is to enable children to understand that it is not their fault that someone close to them has died. Young children often regard death as mystic and magical. If they put a spell on someone, he or she may actually die. Teachers have the obligation to clarify this glaring misconception, let children know the fact and put them at ease.

Provide Systematic and Comprehensive Explanations

Avoid giving over-simplified explanations of the cause of death. Sometimes providing a more comprehensive picture may help to ease anxiety. For instance, if teachers say illness causes death, children may be very worried about occasional sickness. Teachers may explain that though people get sick, we recover from illness. Only severe illness causes death. If teachers fail to provide a more detailed explanation, some young children may think that being ill is equivalent to death. As a consequence, even a common cold may create much anxiety.

Avoid Moralisation

Even though a mass lecture is an effective means of delivering knowledge, teachers should avoid it when giving instruction in death education. Mass lectures encourage one-way communication and ignore individual needs. A small group discussion format is preferred (Thornton, 1991). Teachers should, in so far as possible, avoid using a religious stance to explain death. The religious perspective may at the same time help or hinder children's understanding of life after death. Therefore teachers are recommended to adopt an open-minded approach. While respecting the child's religion, teachers can encourage children to go to a church or temple and seek help from priests or monks.

Help a Child Pass through the Mourning Process

Children, especially older ones, may need a more detailed explanation, which is age-appropriate, to deal with mourning. This may enable them to accept death as a reality and believe death is irreversible and final. Very often language communication has its own limitations and may not make it possible for children to fully comprehend. Teachers may advise the children to attend the funeral, observe and participate in the burial rites. When children physically participate in a funeral and acquire a first-hand experience, and when they have a chance to say goodbye and witness the cremation ceremony, it may help them pass through the normal mourning process. At least, it is a public recognition of their status in the family, which should be an enhancement of their self-concept.

Do not Pretend you Know it All

Teachers should not give children a wrong impression that he or she knows everything about death. It is useful for children to realise that in reality people do not fully understand death.

Possible Pitfalls?

A few years ago, a book entitled *Complete Handbook on Suicide* was published in Japanese and translated into Chinese – complete with instructions on the various ways of committing suicide. Even though this book was eventually banned in Hong Kong, it is a strong reminder that when death and suicide are not presented in a proper manner, there might be some 'unforeseeable and unwelcome components' in this form of so-called 'instruction' (Gordon and Klass, 1979).

A word of caution is needed here. Death education does not require children and adolescents to think of death frequently. Nor does it require them to be fearful of death. Experienced death educators would most likely support this assertion: death education is positive. This is contrary to the common belief that 'death education may arouse negative feelings such as suicide and therefore should best be avoided'.

All affective curricula, which relate to emotion, may inevitably involve certain risk. Death education is certainly no exception. It is not absolutely risk free. But an important part of good teaching is to anticipate these calculated risks at an early stage and try to do the best to minimise any negative impacts. As a way of justifying death education, Gatliffe (1988) stated:

> The child who is presented with the facts (about death education) and different ways of looking at a particular life problem will probably have more flexibility with which to solve the problem. It would be unwise to ignore the dangers attached to teaching such a sensitive topic; however, to avoid the topic would be unreal. It would certainly require great sensitivity on the part of the teacher, but it would be wrong to believe that we have to be 'psychological wizards' to teach about death and dying.

Gordon and Klass (1979) also reiterated:

> As adults, we have given up the notion that ignorance is bliss. If we try to promote this notion for our children and try to insulate them from reality, we only make them more vulnerable and less able to cope with that reality.

Readers may ask. 'Can death education reduce suicidal crises?' Research findings indicate that after 53 American college students between the ages of 19 to 51 years had completed a course on death education, suicide potentiality had not increased (Rosenthal, 1983). Since this research focused on primarily adult college students, the results may not be readily applicable to children and adolescents. Readers must interpret this research with caution and question its generalizability.

Edgar and Howard-Hamilton (1994), after offering death education to elementary school children over a 10-year period, reminded us:

> It should not be assumed that a child who attends the class can later face death rationally or calmly. That, of course, is neither true nor necessarily desirable. What is true is that by calmly presenting reality rather than imagination, by helping children learn the words that elucidate their experiences, and by helping them find supportive and dependable networks, children are able to deal with the reality of death.

When death education is offered in a systematic and professional manner, the potential benefits are clear. But teachers and parents must remain vigilant of the possible negative impacts of death education. Now, the question is not whether death education should be provided, but rather how best to provide it.

Suicide Prevention Programmes

There is at least one functional distinction between death education and suicide prevention programme. Most suicide prevention programmes stress the recognition of suicide warning signs such as depression, drastic behavioural change, and suicidal threats. The primary objective is to increase the level of awareness of people surrounding a child or adolescent, so that they are able to identify the warning signs prior to a suicidal act, and be able to make immediate referral to defuse the crisis. The focus of attention is, therefore, the accurate and prompt reactions of people around the person.

On the other hand, the purpose of death education is to educate children and adolescents to understand the concept of death and to cope with grief. Some children and adolescents with suicidal feelings may have a distorted image of death. When they have a proper understanding of the concept of death, they may be more effective in coping with loss and grief. They may view suicide as less attractive during times of depression (Bernhardt and Praeger, 1985). Hence the focus of death education is on the pro-active responses of the children and adolescents.

Even though suicide prevention programmes and death education have a different focus, the aim can be similar: to reduce suicidal ideas and behaviour. Suicide prevention programming and death education are like the two sides of a coin. Both should be implemented if people are serious in identifying high-risk children and adolescents and helping them to cope more successfully.

It is, indeed, fashionable for teachers to give a lesson on 'The Values of Life' as a way of preventing suicide. But, are these lessons effective? If we were to ask children: 'Is suicide a correct behaviour?' Most, if not all, would say that suicide is a mistake. In fact, 'The Values of Life' lessons are just repetition of what had already been known for a long time – life is precious. If we ask children and adolescents: 'Do you think that cigarette smoking is harmful?' most would agree and yet they continue to smoke.

At times, there are apparent differences in attitudes and behaviour. Such discrepancy implies that suicide prevention strategies must focus directly on the behaviour, and not merely on attitudes. One of the major weaknesses of value education is that it is a circumvention that altogether ignores the central focus - suicidal behaviour (Tse, 2000).

The strengths of death education and suicide prevention programmes lie in directly addressing the problematic behaviour.

The former creates a possible change of distorted cognition while the latter focuses on the identification of high-risk individuals and increasing their abilities to cope with distress. Depressed children and adolescents, who may have a grossly distorted view of reality, are not able to think rationally. When mood and emotions prevail, they are less likely to make sound judgement and evaluate the reasons for living. All in all, the more chances for students to learn about thinking skills and problem-solving abilities, the more effective it is to prevent the occurrence of suicidal behaviour.

Involvement of Parents

In Hong Kong, just as in many other places, parents are reluctant to talk about death. Even if the topic were discussed, the information given might not be accurate. Apparently, many parents are anxious and try to avoid mentioning the term death. Most parents, even the more westernised ones, may consider funeral parlour a dreadful place, which is totally unsuitable for children (Cheng and Chen, 1999). Some may think that buying an insurance policy is a sign of misfortune and it will bring bad luck to the family (Chan and Mak, 2000).

Getting rid of these superstitious behaviours is an important first step in creating correct attitudes and positive changes towards death. There is a need for parents to be open, be more aware and willing to discuss matters relating to life and death with their children.

During the course of development, children ask parents questions on sex, life, and death, and parents should not ignore these questions. It is, therefore, important not to be evasive, but to grasp the opportunity and put forward clear and rational explanations. If parents shrink their responsibilities and treat death as a taboo at home, this would only increase the level of misunderstanding.

The least that parents should do is to put a stop to this superstitious cycle from perpetuating. Ignorance is certain not a problem-solving technique and parents have to take up this responsibility, even more so when teachers have not been actively teaching death education. Research in the West has shown that parents, who are more knowledgeable about death, suicide, and bereavement, are more likely to support death education programmes in schools (Jones, Hodges, and Slate, 1995).

When confronted with death education, many parents and teachers may take the 'let sleeping dog lie' approach. They are afraid of death education, which they think might arouse negative emotions and cause children and adolescents to view death as an option! Unfortunately, this myth widely exists. Scholars have, on the other hand, repeatedly urged parents to take a more positive approach and discuss death at home (McNeil, 1986):

- *Increase the level of awareness* and talk about death and other interested topics with children and adolescents.
- *Actively listen to their fears and anxieties.*
- *Acknowledge the children's emotions* and make them realise that such feelings are important and normal.
- *Empathise with the children.*
- *Parents are advised* not to solve the problems for the children. In fact, tell the children that you would not mind looking for the answers together.
- *Even though parents may be busy*, it is important to find time to talk to the children on a regular basis.

Death is such an important topic that schools should not be the institution having the monopoly over death education. Parents and teachers, who find it difficult to discuss or teach about death and dying, may find Turner's (1998) workbook and Brinkman and Quarles (1988) resource book informative. In Hong Kong, the Civil Disaster Management Committee of the Hospital Authority and non-government organisations such as Society for the Promotion of Hospice Care and Comfort Care Concern Group can provide useful information as well as direct service in enabling people to deal with death and dying. The concept of 'good separation' which stresses the importance of having desirable outcome of bereavement is particularly worth mentioning (Chow et al., 2000).

Children and Funeral Attendance

It is a custom in the Chinese culture to give out a 'white pocket', which contains a handkerchief, a sweet and some money, to each individual who attends a funeral. The view that death may invite evil spirits into the family widely exists, and these gifts surround the rituals for warding off these spirits. Thus the money should be spent on travelling away from the place of burial, the sweet should be eaten and the handkerchief is to be discarded before going home (Chan, 2000). It is easy to understand the attitudes of Chinese toward funerals. Chinese culture does not encourage children to attend funerals. Indeed, children are often segregated from the rituals surrounding death or cremation.

It is interesting to observe that adults may have two common myths about children and loss. These range from the view that 'children should not go to funerals' to another extreme 'children must go to funerals'. Attending a funeral and participating in the mourning rituals are generally important to children, adolescents and adults. Such activities may enable children to understand more about death and help them through the normal course of loss and grief.

Just as some children have a fear of hospital, they may unlearn and reduce death anxiety. One way of decreasing this phobia is to have a guided tour of the hospital under the close supervision of supporting adults. Children may also play with dolls (dressed as doctors, nurses and patients) and pretend to have injections.

Such activities tend to lower the level of anxiety and make hospitals more acceptable. The same token applies to attending a funeral or understanding death: the child should be prepared. If a close relative is dying, and if the child is permitted to pay a visit, together with the help of a sympathetic adult, it would enable the child to know more about death and dying. When the child is supplied with the information, and is allowed to express his or her emotions freely, the child would benefit. After the death of the relative, the child should be more ready to accept death. Thus adults have an active role to play in helping the child to cherish the memory of the deceased.

Should children be allowed to attend funerals? Research scholars (Weller, Weller, Fristand, Cain and Bowes, 1988) recommend that children from about age seven should be encouraged to attend a funeral ceremony. But it does not mean that it is absolutely inappropriate that children under seven be allowed to attend.

In the United States, researchers (Weller et al., 1988) studied the impact of attending a funeral on 38 children between five to 12 years of age who had lost a father or mother. Results indicate that 79 per cent considered themselves able to control in the funeral ceremony. This reflects the fact that there was little crying.

On the other hand, 21 per cent indicated they had rather unusual behaviour during the ceremony, such as withdrawal and passivity, or felt extremely distressed. Results showed that when children were forced to participate or when they did not have an adequate understanding of death, they were more likely to act in an unusual manner. The researchers again interviewed these children two months after the death. In terms of mental health, the findings indicate that children's attendance at the funeral had no relationship either with depression or anxiety.

Taking these results altogether, even if there is negative impact when children attend a funeral, the impact is temporary. In the long run, attending funerals would be beneficial to the children.

Funerals are meaningful family, religious and cultural events. If children are allowed to participate and assist in the funeral ceremony, this may enable them to go through the mourning stage more smoothly. Children may be asked to assist in burning incense, ushering and distributing 'white pockets'. Such participation helps children say goodbye to the deceased. A funeral can facilitate mourners to comfort loss, grieve normally and offer support to each other. In fact, years after the funeral they could still consider their attendance significant and meaningful, while those who were not allowed to attend felt regretful and somewhat shamed (Silverman and Worden, 1992).

In fact, funeral ceremony is a separation ritual – a formal way of saying farewell. Children who chose to attend might come to an understanding that death is final and this would also put an end to the distortions the children might have prior to the funeral.

These various research studies all indicated that not only should children be allowed to attend a funeral, they should also participate in the ceremony. But it is important to make sure that a supporting adult should accompany the child at the critical moments. Let the child take his or her turn viewing or even touching the deceased and appropriately bid a final farewell.

The basic principle is to never force a child to attend a funeral (Grollman, 1995). Children should be helped to make informed choice whether to attend a funeral or not. Parents and teachers could begin by explaining what the funeral is and what events are likely to occur. Mourning is a normal emotional response, which should not be suppressed. On the contrary, adults may have to assist children to express their sadness, and not to end grieving absurdly. During the course of the funeral ceremony, adults may pay special attention to culturally relevant concepts and take the following steps in order to facilitate mourning:

- *Prepare in advance*: Adults may inform the child of the customs and procedures involved in the funeral prior to the burial ceremony. The child should be given the opportunity to choose whether to participate or not. On the other hand, the adult should explain the reasons for the activities.
- *Look after the child*: In the course of the ceremony, an adult, whose main responsibility is looking after the needs of the child, should accompany the child. An adult, who is too grief stricken, may neglect the child and therefore is not an appropriate person to take up that role.
- *Allow time for discussion*: Permit the child to view the decreased and attend the cremation ceremony. After the ceremony, the child should be given the opportunity to discuss freely with the adult about his or her emotional feelings. The adult may have to answer questions, reflect on the reactions, share the sentiment and support the child.

Forced compliance may often have negative consequences. Even adults would be apprehensive, when attending an unfamiliar event, this is understandable. For children who are reluctant to attend a funeral, parents should neither use force nor negative remarks. Parents could suggest making a family visit to the grave later on. Particularly for the children who choose not to attend, parents and teachers may invite them to write letters, draw pictures or offer objects that can be placed in the casket.

Conclusions

It is unrealistic for adults to segregate and insulate children from knowing more about death and dying. Ignorance is certainly not a problem-solving strategy. Death is an important curriculum area, which requires the collaborative efforts of parents and teachers to get rid of the fears and misconceptions that children and adolescents may have.

One of the most effective ways is to provide systematic death education, which may also serve as an agent of suicide prevention. Death education should help children and adolescents to realise that they are not alone in wondering about death. In fact, death has puzzled the human race since the beginning of time.

All in all, if people are seriously thinking of promoting death education, the following points have to be understood and implemented:

- *All living things die*. In fact, death is a common event, which should not be treated as a taboo.
- *Death education should be provided in schools*. This would enable children and adolescents to develop positive attitudes towards death, loss and bereavement.
- *Prior to offering death education*, parents' approval and support must be sought.
- *Teachers should encourage parents* to grasp every available opportunity to discuss death freely with their children.
- *Establish clear and concise guidelines on death education*. The more systematic training the teachers have on death education, the less likely the chance of making mistakes.
- *Identify the curriculum content of death education*. Special attention must be given to the divergent needs of children and adolescents at different age groups. Periodic evaluation and review of content and methods of teaching is required.
- *Parents and teachers should encourage children and adolescents* to attend and participate in funeral rituals. This may enable them to understand more about death and pass through the mourning stage smoothing. But children must not be forced to participate.

References

Aspinall, S.Y. (1996). Educating children to cope with death: a preventive model. *Psychology in the Schools*, 33(4), 341–9.

Bernhardt, G.R. and Praeger, S.G. (1985). Preventing child suicide: the elementary school death education puppet show. *Journal of Counseling and Development*, 63(5), 311–12.

Brinkman, J.M. and Quarles, T.F. (1988). *Death Education Resource Book*. Portland, Maine: J. Weston Walch.

Brookshire, M. and Noland, M. (1992). Teaching children about death. In G. Walz and J. Bleuer (eds), *Help Students Cope with Fears and Crises*. Washington, DC: Office of Educational Research and Improvement.

Carlson, G.A., Asarnow, J.R. and Orbach, I. (1994). Developmental aspects of suicidal behavior in children and developmentally delayed adolescents. In G.G. Noam and S. Borst (eds), *Children, Youth, and Suicide: Developmental Perspectives*. San Francisco: Jossey-Bass.

Census and Statistics Department. (2001). *Components of Population Growth, 1996–2000*. Hong Kong: HK Government.

Chan, C.L.W. (2000). Death awareness and palliative care. In R. Fielding and C.L. W. Chan (eds), *Psychosocial Oncology and Palliative Care in Hong Kong: The First Decade*. Hong Kong: Hong Kong University Press.

Chan, C.L.W. and Mak, J.M.H. (2000). Benefits and drawbacks of Chinese rituals surrounding care for the dying. In R. Fielding and C.L.W. Chan (eds), *Psychosocial Oncology and Palliative Care in Hong Kong: The First Decade*. Hong Kong: Hong Kong University Press.

Cheng, B. and Chen, L. (1999). *Attitude of Hong Kong People towards Death and Bereavement*. Hong Kong: Comfort Care Concern Group.

Chow, A.Y.M., Koo, B.W.S., Koo, E.W.K. and Lam, A.Y.Y. (2000). Turning grief into good separation: bereavement services in Hong Kong. In R. Fielding and C.L.W. Chan (eds), *Psychosocial Oncology and Palliative Care in Hong Kong: The First Decade*. Hong Kong: Hong Kong University Press.

Civil Disaster Management Committee, Hospital Authority (undated). *In Distress for You in Bereavement*. Hong Kong: The author (free pamphlet).

Civil Disaster Management Committee, *Smiles Again*. Hong Kong: The author (free pamphlet).

Civil Disaster Management Committee, *The Anguish of Children*. Hong Kong: The author (free pamphlet).

Civil Disaster Management Committee, *'You can never tell.'* Hong Kong: The author (free pamphlet).

Corr, C.A. (1982). Helping with death education. In H. Wass and C. Corr (eds), *Helping Children with Death*. New York: Hemisphere Publishing Corporation.

Corr, C.A. (1992). *Someone You Love is Dying: How Do You Cope?* Houston, TX: Service Corporation International.

Edgar, L.V. and Howard-Hamilton, M. (1994). Noncrisis death education in the elementary school. *Elementary School Guidance and Counseling*, 29(1), 38–47.

Ewalt, P.L. and Perkins, L. (1979). The real experience of death among adolescents: an empirical study. *Social Casework*, 60, 547–51.

Gatliffe, E.D. (1988). *Death in the Classroom*. London: Epworth Press.

Good, T.L. and Brophy, J. (1995). *Contemporary Educational Psychology*. (5th edn). New York: Longman.

Gordon, A.K. and Klass, D. (1979). *They Need to Know: How to Teach Children about Death*. NJ: Prentice-Hall.

Gorer, G. (1965). *Death, Grief and Mourning in Contemporary Britain*. London: Cresset Press.

Gothelf, D., Apter, A., Brand-Gothelf, A., Offer, N., Ofek, H., Tyano, S. and Pfeffer, C. (1998). Death concepts in suicidal adolescents. *Journal of the American Academy of Child and Adolescent Psychiatry*, 37(12), 1279–86.

Hwang, M.T.C. (1991). *An Introduction to Death Education*. Taipei: Longwind Publications.

Jones, C.H., Hodges, M. and Slate, J.R. (1995). Parental support for death education programs in the schools. *School Counselor*, 42(5), 370–76.

Lamers, E.P. (1995). Children, death, and fairy tales. *Omega*, 31(2), 151–67.

McGovern, M. and Barry, M.M. (2000). Death education: knowledge, attitudes, and perspectives of Irish parents and teachers. *Death Studies*, 24(4), 325–33.

McNeil, J. (1986). Talking about death: adolescents, parents, and peers. In C.C. Corr. and J.N. McNeil (eds), *Adolescence and Death*. New York: Springer.

Nagy, M. (1948). The child's theories concerning death. *Journal of Genetic Psychology*, 73, 3–27.

National Center for Health Statistics (2000). *U.S.A. Suicide: 1996 Official Final Data*. Washington, DC: The Author.

Orbach, I. (1988). *Children Who Don't Want to Live*. San Francisco: Jossey-Bass.

Orbach, I. and Glaubman, H. (1978). Suicidal, aggressive, and normal children's perception of personal and impersonal death. *Journal of Clinical Psychology*, 34, 850–56.

Payne, B. and Range, L. (1995). Attitudes toward life and death and suicidality in young adults. *Death Studies*, 19, 559–69.

Pfeffer, C.R. (1986). *The Suicidal Child*. New York: Guilford.

Rees, D. (1997). *Death and Bereavement: The Psychological, Religious and Cultural Interfaces*. London: Whurr.

Rosenthal, N. (1983). Death education and suicide potentiality. *Death Education*, 7, 39–51.

Silverman, P.R. and Worden, J.W. (1992). Children's understanding of funeral ritual. *Omega*, 25, 319–331.

Speece, M. and Brent, S. (1984). Children's understanding of death: a review of three components of a death concept. *Child Development*, 55, 1671–86.

Speece, M. and Brent, S. (1992). The acquisition of a mature understanding of three components of the concept of death. *Death Studies*, 16, 211–29.

Stevenson, R. and Stevenson, E. (1996). Adolescents and education about death, dying, and bereavement. In C. Corr. and D. Balk (eds), *Handbook of Adolescent Death and Bereavement*. New York: Springer Publishing Co.

Thornton, G. (1991). Assessment of small group discussions in a death-and-dying course. *Death Studies*, 15, 473–80.

Tse, J.W.L. (2000). *Youth Suicide: Facts, Prevention and Crisis Management*. Hong Kong: Chinese University Press. (in Chinese)

Turner, M. (1998). *Talking with Children and Young People about Death and Dying: A Workbook*. London: Jessica Kingsley.

Wass, H., Mill, M. and Thornton, G. (1990). Death education and grief/suicide intervention in the public schools. *Death Studies*, 14, 253–68.

Wass, H., Raup, J.L. and Sisler, H.H. (1989). Adolescents and death on television: a follow-up study. *Death Studies*, 13(2), 161–73.

Weeks, D. and Johnson, C. (1992). A second decade of high school death education. *Death Studies*, 16(3), 269–79.

Weller, E.B., Weller, R.A., Fristand, M.A., Cain, S.E. and Bowes, J.M. (1988). Should children attend their parent's funeral? *Journal of American Academic Child Adolescent Psychology*, 27, 559–67.

Zhang, S.M. (1996). *Thanatology and Death Education*. Kaohsiung: Kaohsiung Fu Mun Press (in Chinese).